# On Point
## Pre-Intermediate English

**Student's Book**
+ AUDIOS + VIDEOS ONLINE

Louis and Cathy Rogers

1st edition 1  3  2  1  | 2022 21 20

The last figure shown denotes the year of impression.

All rights reserved. No part of this publication may be reproduced, stored in a retrieval system, or transmitted, in any form or by any means, electronic, mechanical, photocopying, recording, or otherwise, without prior written permission from the publisher.

Delta Publishing, 2020
www.deltapublishing.co.uk
www.klett-sprachen.de/delta

© Ernst Klett Sprachen GmbH, Rotebühlstraße 77, 70178 Stuttgart, 2020

**Editor:** Sheila Dignen
**Advisers:** Sophie Bennett, Elaine Hodgson, Sarah Walker
**Layout and typesetting:** Wild Apple Design Ltd.
**Cover:** Andreas Drabarek, Wild Apple Design Ltd.
**Cover picture:** Getty Images (Martin Barraud), Munich
**Printing and binding:** DRUCKEREI PLENK GmbH & Co. KG, Berchtesgaden
Printed in Germany

ISBN 978-3-12-501263-9

This book contains audios, videos and flash cards available on the DELTA Augmented app.

 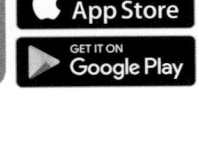  

| Download the free DELTA Augmented app onto your device | Start picture recognition and scan the pages with this symbol or audio/video icons | Download files and use them now or save them for later |

Apple and the Apple logo are trademarks of Apple Inc., registered in the US and other countries. App Store is a service mark of Apple Inc. | Google Play and the Google Play logo are trademarks of Google Inc.

# On Point

On Point is a modern course with new and innovative topics, but it is also traditional in its approach. With a clear structure and careful progression, we're sure you will sense your progress as you enjoy working through the course.

## Lessons A and B
Lessons A and B are the main lessons for grammar. Presented via listening or reading texts, all of the grammar is then analysed and practised before you produce it in an authentic situation. Lessons A and B also present relevant vocabulary for each topic and practise any necessary pronunciation points.

## Lesson C
Lesson C is a chance to practise your reading skills with a longer text. Many of the texts are from real-world sources or based on things happening in the world. The grammar from the previous lessons is recycled and a new set of vocabulary is presented. The Workbook Lesson C focuses on extended listening to further practise this skill.

## Lesson D
The last lesson in each unit is divided into two halves. The first page presents a set of phrases or a language point that is useful for a particular speaking context. The second page follows a guided approach to help improve your writing skills.

## Video Pages
After every two units there is a two-page video lesson related to one of the themes from the previous lessons. The structure of these lessons allows further listening and reading practice. There is also a short review of the main language points covered in the previous two units.

## The app
DELTA Augmented lets you play all the audio files, videos and flash cards via the app for free. Simply download the app onto your device and scan the pages with the audio ( ), video ( ) or flash cards icon ( ). Save the files onto your device to use them wherever and whenever you want.

## Appendix
The back of the book contains an extended Grammar Reference for you to learn further details of each grammar point. There is also an Irregular Verb list to help you remember these tricky forms as well as pair work speaking files for some of the lessons.

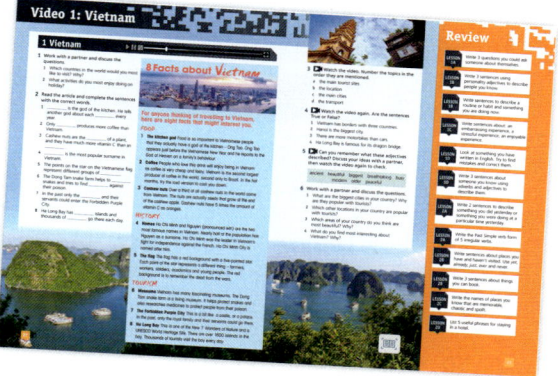

# Contents

| | Grammar | Vocabulary | Reading / Listening | Speaking / Writing |
|---|---|---|---|---|
| **1 People**<br>1A Introductions p6<br>1B What are they like? p8<br>1C The good and the bad p10<br>1D New people p12 | Questions<br>Present Simple and Present Continuous<br>**Pronunciation:** Questions | Personality adjectives<br>Adjectives to describe experiences | Introductions<br>What kind of friend are you?<br>Life as an au pair | Small talk<br>An informal email<br>Correcting mistakes<br>Describing people |
| **2 Travel**<br>2A When holidays go wrong p14<br>2B Holiday romance p16<br>2C Family backpacking in Vietnam p18<br>2D Holiday experiences p20 | Past Simple and Past Continuous<br>Present Perfect Simple + *yet, already, just, ever, never*<br>**Pronunciation:** Past Simple verb endings; Weak forms *was / were* | Verb + noun collocations<br>Adjectives for holiday experiences | A safari story<br>A nightmare flight<br>A holiday romance<br>A backpacking holiday | Staying in a hotel<br>**Pronunciation:** Intonation in polite questions<br>A travel blog post<br>Time sequencers |
| **Video:** Vietnam  p22 | | | | |
| **3 Work**<br>3A Stress p24<br>3B Is that really true? p26<br>3C Getting rich on Instagram p28<br>3D Skills and interests p30 | Quantity: *much, many, some, any,* etc.<br>**Pronunciation:** Stress on quantity words<br>*Something, anything, nothing,* etc. | Work – Benefits and tasks<br>Work – Experience<br>Work and social media | Stress at work<br>Liar!<br>Making money from Instagram | Likes and dislikes<br>A formal email<br>Starting and closing an email |
| **4 Childhood**<br>4A How we lived p32<br>4B School days p34<br>4C Childhood then and now p36<br>4D Life decisions p38 | Used to<br>**Pronunciation:** *Used to*<br>Modals: *can, have to, must*<br>**Pronunciation:** *Have to* | Kitchen equipment<br>School / studying collocations<br>Synonyms | Childhood memories<br>School rules<br>Why childhood is better now<br>Kids in the UK | Giving and responding to advice<br>A paragraph about a big decision<br>Structuring a paragraph<br>Reasons and results |
| **Video:** The good old days  p40 | | | | |
| **5 Health**<br>5A Fit and healthy p42<br>5B Food in the future p44<br>5C Are we healthier or unhealthier now? p46<br>5D Getting better. p48 | *Will* for decisions, offers and promises<br>Future forms: *will, be going to,* Present Continuous<br>**Pronunciation:** Word stress | Health and fitness<br>Word families<br>Nouns for diet and illness | Three health plans<br>Healthy habits<br>Can we feed the world?<br>Modern health problems | Talking about health and illness<br>**Pronunciation:** Difficult words<br>A new year plan<br>Connecting contrasting ideas |
| **6 City Life**<br>6A Calm or crowded? p50<br>6B The best city in the world p52<br>6C Changing cities p54<br>6D Places p56 | Comparatives<br>Superlatives | Describing towns and cities<br>Recommending places<br>Adjectives to describe cities | Comparing places<br>Vienna<br>Changing cities | Asking for and giving directions<br>A description of your hometown<br>Describing and recommending places |
| **Video:** Parkrun  p58 | | | | |

# Contents

| | Grammar | Vocabulary | Reading / Listening | Speaking / Writing |
|---|---|---|---|---|
| **7 Connections**<br>7A Time p60<br>7B Relationships p62<br>7C The story behind the place p64<br>7D Events p66 | Tense review<br>Present Perfect: *for* and *since* | Relationships<br>Society | Thinking about the past, present and future<br>Childhood sweethearts<br>A historic building and the people who lived there | Reacting to news<br>**Pronunciation:** Sounding enthusiastic and sympathetic<br>An invitation |
| **8 Stories**<br>8A A famous writer p68<br>8B Fact is stranger than fiction p70<br>8C A Sherlock Holmes story p72<br>8D Feelings and events p74 | Past Perfect<br>**Pronunciation:** Contractions<br>Narrative tenses | Types of books<br>Connecting words<br>Adjectives<br>Adjectives ending in *-ed* and *-ing* | Agatha Christie<br>Cave rescue<br>The problem of Thor Bridge | Talking about feelings<br>A short story<br>Adverbs<br>**Pronunciation:** Emphasizing feelings |
| **Video:** Film locations p76 | | | | |
| **9 Opportunities**<br>9A Luck p78<br>9B Happiness p80<br>9C Enjoying life p82<br>9D Opinions p84 | Infinitive with *to*<br>**Pronunciation:** Weak forms of *to*<br>Gerunds | Negative prefixes<br>Verbs + gerund or infinitive<br>Phrases for time | You make your own luck<br>Being happy<br>Things that make me happy<br>Getting more out of life | Agreeing and disagreeing<br>**Pronunciation:** Intonation in opinions<br>An opinion blog<br>Opinions and reasons |
| **10 Environment**<br>10A Going green p86<br>10B Looking to the future p88<br>10C Plastic life p90<br>10D Structuring ideas p92 | Modals of advice<br>*Will*, *may*, *might* | Environment<br>Geographical features<br>Change | Living a greener life<br>Environmental problems<br>Plastic pollution | Structuring a presentation<br>A summary of survey results<br>Connecting ideas |
| **Video:** Saving the planet p94 | | | | |
| **11 Life**<br>11A Optimist or pessimist? p96<br>11B The grass is always greener? p98<br>11C Thinking negatively p100<br>11D Making a complaint p102 | First conditional<br>**Pronunciation:** Contractions<br>Second conditional | Phrasal verbs<br>Adverbs<br>Collocations | Are you a pessimist or optimist<br>If I lived in London, …<br>The power of pessimism | Making and dealing with complaints<br>**Pronunciation:** Apologizing<br>An email of complaint |
| **12 Technology**<br>12A New designs, old ideas p104<br>12B Tech free p106<br>12C Social media p108<br>12D What did you hear? p110 | Passives<br>Reported speech | Word families<br>Verb + noun collocations<br>Compound nouns | Bicycles then and now<br>A digital detox<br>Social media | Talking about and reacting to news<br>**Pronunciation:** Emphasizing your feelings<br>A summary<br>Note-taking |
| **Video:** Are you addicted? p112 | | | | |

Grammar Reference **p114**  Communication bank **p126**  Irregular verbs **p131**  Audio Scripts **p132**

# 1 People

- **Grammar:** Questions
- **Listening:** Introductions
- **Pronunciation:** Intonation in questions

A

B

C

## 1A Introductions

1. ▶001 Listen to three conversations. Match the people to the places in the pictures.

2. ▶001 What do the people talk about? Listen again and match the topics to the conversations.
   a  hobbies and interests ............
   b  holidays ............
   c  home and family ............
   d  work and studies ............

3. ▶002 Complete the questions with the words in the box. Then listen and check.

   | are   do x 2   doing   have x 2   go   work |

   1  What do you ................?
   2  Who do you ................ for?
   3  What do you like ................ at the weekend?
   4  What do you ................ in your free time?
   5  Where ................ you from?
   6  Do you ................ any brothers or sisters?
   7  Where do you usually ................ on holiday?
   8  Do you ................ any holiday plans this summer?

4. Match the questions in exercise 3 to the topics in exercise 2.

5. Complete the questions with the correct form of the verb in brackets. Then match them to the topics in exercise 2.

   1  Do you ................ (have) any hobbies?
   2  What ................ (do) last weekend?
   3  Where ................ (go) on holiday last summer?
   4  Do you ................ (like / go) on city breaks?
   5  Where ................ (be) you born?
   6  Who do you ................ (live) with?
   7  Which company ................ (work) for?
   8  What subjects ................ (study) at the moment?

6. ▶003 Listen and notice the intonation in the questions. Listen again, repeat and practise.
   1  Do you have any hobbies?
   2  What did you do last weekend?
   3  Where did you go on holiday last summer?
   4  Do you like going on city breaks?

7. Work with a partner. Student A: ask your partner the questions in exercise 3. Student B: ask your partner the questions in exercise 5.

8. Work in groups of four. Tell your classmates something you found out about your partner.

People

**9** Read the questions and guess the answers. Then read the text to check.
1 Which age groups find it most difficult to meet new people and make friends? Why?
2 What modern ways are there to meet people and make friends?
3 Do you think more young people or old people feel lonely?

## LONELY?

When the BBC asked people to complete an online survey about being lonely, over 55,000 people answered the questions. So, which age group felt lonely? Nearly forty per cent of people aged 16 to 24 said they felt the most lonely. This is perhaps not surprising when you think about all of the changes that happen at this age. People leave school, start work, go to college or university and they often move out of their parents' home. Many of these changes can mean moving to new towns or cities and when you do this, it can be very hard to meet new friends. One way to look for new friends is to use an app such as Bumble BFF, Huggle, Hey Vina, Go Green Go or Peanut. Simply write a profile, add a picture and you're ready to search for a new friend. Swipe right on the people you like and simply start a conversation.

**10** Work with a partner. How would you feel about using an app like this? What questions would you ask someone when you first met them?

*What do you like doing at the weekend?*

*What kind of music do you like?*

*What's your favourite TV programme?*

**11** Notice the word order in the questions in exercise 10. Complete the rules in the grammar box with *before* or *after*.

> **GRAMMAR: Questions** ▶ PAGE 114
>
> In questions with *do/does/did*, we put these words
> 1 .................... the subject.
>
> In questions with *be*, we put *am/is/are/was/were*
> 2 .................... the subject

**12** Put the words in the correct order to make questions.
1 did / last / night / go / out / you?
2 this / weekend / what / you / doing / are?
3 sport or exercise / you / do / do / any?
4 how often / you / go / do / to the cinema?
5 TV programmes / what / do / you / watch?
6 at the weekend / do / ever / work / you?

**13** Complete each question with one missing word.
1 What you doing tonight?
2 What are you going do after the class?
3 When did you meet best friend?
4 How often you see your parents?
5 Where your best friend live?
6 What kind of music do you like listening?

**14** Work with a partner. Ask and answer the questions in exercises 12 and 13.

**15** Imagine you are meeting some new people. Think of four or five questions to ask them. Then walk around the class. Ask and answer your questions.

7

## 1B What are they like?

> **Grammar:** Present Simple and Continuous
> **Vocabulary:** Personality adjectives
> **Reading:** What kind of friend are you?

1 Write down the names of three friends. Work with a partner and tell them:
   1 the reason you like each person.
   2 the things you usually do together.
   3 something about their personality.

2 Read the article. Do your friends match these friend types?

# What kind of friend are you?

A survey by *Onepoll* and *HF Holidays* of 2,000 people in the UK found that the average person has 40 friends. It also found there are seven different personality types in every friendship group. So which type of friend are you?

**THE ORGANIZER** Constantly planning and organizing nights out and activities. They are very <u>efficient</u> and have everything planned to perfection.

**THE MOTIVATOR** The <u>curious</u> friend who always wants to try something new and exciting. They are <u>confident</u> in new situations and always encourage you to do new things.

**THE ORACLE** When you come up with a new idea for something to do, they have already done it. In fact, they are so <u>arrogant</u> they have probably done everything!

**THE ELEPHANT** Like an elephant, they never forget. They are <u>thoughtful</u> and always send birthday or anniversary cards. However, they also won't ever forget anything bad you have said or done.

**THE MAVERICK** The most <u>sociable</u> friend. They are always fun to be with, but just don't rely on them to be on time.

**THE SCROOGE** They are never <u>careless</u> with money and are perfect for dividing the bill at the end of a meal. Just don't expect them to pay for everyone's drinks.

**STEADY EDDIE / EDWINA** The most <u>reliable</u> friend you have. They are the first person you call when you have a problem.

3 ▶004 Look at the underlined adjectives in the article. Then choose the correct adjectives to complete the sentences below. Listen and check your answers.
   1 Mark is very *sociable / reliable*. If he promises to do something, he will do it.
   2 Their daughter is so *curious / arrogant*. She's always exploring everything.
   3 Harry is always really *confident / careless* with his work. It's full of mistakes!
   4 Thank you for the flowers! It was very *curious / thoughtful* of you.
   5 Lisa is so *efficient / confident*. She never seems nervous or shy.
   6 Tom really loves himself. I don't think I know anyone else who is so *sociable / arrogant*.
   7 Lucas is a really *sociable / careless* guy. Whenever there's a party, he's there.
   8 Ahmed is really *efficient / thoughtful*. He finishes everything really quickly and never wastes time.

People

**4** Work with a partner. Use personality adjectives from exercise 3 to describe some of your friends. Give examples to support the things you say.

> *Jenny is really arrogant. She's always right and never wrong!*

**5** ▶005 Listen to Hayley talking to five friends. Are the sentences True or False?

1 Matt wants to pay for the things he ate.
2 Mia likes to do the same things all the time.
3 Mohammed has forgotten Sam's birthday.
4 Hayley is breaking up with her boyfriend.
5 Emma has always done the things Hayley has done.

**6** ▶005 Complete the sentences with the verbs in the box. Then listen again and check.

| 'm breaking  'm buying  're spending |
| go   owe   says |

1 You ................ £32.50.
2 We always ................ there!
3 I ................ flowers for Sam.
4 I think I ................ up with Dave.
5 We ................ less and less time together and he never calls.
6 Everyone ................ Uganda is really beautiful.

**7** Match the sentences in exercise 6 to the rules in the grammar box.

---

**GRAMMAR: Present Simple and Continuous** ▶ PAGE 114

We use the Present Simple:
a to talk about things that are generally true. ............
b to talk about habits and routines. ............
c with state verbs and feelings. ........1....

We use the Present Continuous to talk about:
d actions happening right now. ............
e actions happening around now. ............
f changing situations. ............

---

**8** Complete the social media updates with the correct Present Simple or Present Continuous form of the verbs in brackets.

1 I ................ (hate) it when people are late! ✓✓
2 We ................ (sit) in the airport.
  We ................ (wait) to go on holiday 😊 ✓
3 I don't know, but I think people ................ (spend) more and more time on their phones.
4 The food here ................ (be) amazing! ✓✓
5 Normally, I ................ (get up) at 8 but today I ................ (stay) in bed! ✓✓

**9** Use the prompts to write questions.
1 why / you / study / English?
2 how often / you / meet / your best friend?
3 what / make / someone / a good friend?
4 how / you feel / when / you meet / new people?
5 you spend / more or less time / with your friends / at the moment?

**10** Work with a partner. Ask and answer the questions in exercise 9.

**11** Find photos of you and your friends on your phone and imagine posting them on social media. Write what is happening under each picture.

*We're travelling on the train to Milan together.*

*Susie is trying on another pair of sunglasses*

# 1C The good and the bad

▶ Reading: *Life as an au pair*
▶ Vocabulary: *Adjectives to describe experiences*

1  Do you enjoy going to new places? Complete the table with your own ideas. Share your answers with a partner.

| Things I enjoy about going to new places | Things I miss about home |
|---|---|
| trying new food | my family |

2  What is an au pair? Do you know anyone who has worked as an au pair?

3  Read the first paragraph of the article. What might someone enjoy about being an au pair?

4  Student A: read about Lina. Student B: read about Archie. When you have finished, close your books and tell your partner what you remember.

5  Read about the other person. Are the sentences True or False?
   1  The children go to school.
   2  The children laugh at the au pair.
   3  The children are not nice to the au pair.
   4  The au pair's language skills have improved a lot.
   5  The au pair enjoys the local food.
   6  The au pair is going out tonight.

6  Work with a partner. Compare the experiences of the two au pairs.

> *The children Lina looks after don't go to school, but the children Archie looks after do.*

# A NEW FAMILY

Young people often choose to become an au pair because they want to live somewhere warmer, learn another language, practise their skiing or simply because they love children. There are lots of different websites that match au pairs with families and these sites always talk about 'an <u>amazing</u> time', 'an <u>enjoyable</u> experience' or 'the time of your life'. Is this really always the experience of an au pair? We spoke to two au pairs about their experiences in two very different places.

## LINA, 21

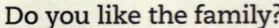

**What's your typical day like?**
I get up at six, have a shower and then make breakfast for the kids. They usually get up about 6:30 so my day starts early! In the morning, we just play games inside and I read them stories. Most afternoons, we go out in the snow to play. The parents are ski instructors and they usually get home around six in the evening.

**Do you like the family?**
The family are really friendly and sociable. I'm lucky as well because they are pretty generous. An au pair is normally paid around 300 euros, but I get 600 euros a month. The kids are only five and three years old, but they're very sensible and follow all my rules. It's a bit <u>embarrassing</u> though, because they're always correcting my French and laughing at my mistakes! Unfortunately, the parents are a bit careless and forgetful. They often forget to do the food shopping and then I have to make dinner from just tins and packets! Once they also forgot to pay the gas bill. I had to have a shower in freezing water and it was minus 10 degrees outside! The family seem to find it all very <u>amusing</u>, but I don't!

**What do you like about living in the Alps?**
It's an incredible location to look at, but seriously <u>dull</u> after a couple of weeks living here with nothing much to do. My French has improved a lot because I only have two English friends and they live in the next village!

**What do you miss most about home?**
I miss the food from home. The Alpine food has too much cheese and the meat is hardly cooked! It can be quite hard being a woman here, too. Women are expected to look amazing all the time and the mum often criticizes my choice of clothes!

**What are you doing now?**
I'm making lunch while the kids are watching TV. I'm also packing my suitcase because I'm going away for the weekend. I can't wait!

# People

### ARCHIE, 22

**What's your typical day like?**
It's quite tiring really. After getting the kids to school, I have to do the shopping, the cleaning, the ironing and prepare lunch. In the afternoon, I seem to spend most of my time trying to stop the children using their phones when they need to do homework. It's really <u>stressful</u>!

**Do you like the family?**
When I first got here, they gave me a tour of the house and they were very friendly. However, the kids are really <u>annoying</u>! They don't listen to me or respect me. They have told me to go back to England several times! They are clever, though. In front of their parents they are always very polite towards me and helpful around the house. It can be really <u>challenging</u> at times.

**What do you like about living in Madrid?**
Madrid is the best thing about this experience. It's a really international city and I have friends here from all around the world. Unfortunately, my Spanish hasn't got much better because we all speak in English!

**What do you miss most about home?**
I actually really miss green vegetables and salad! They don't serve many vegetables with the food here, and a lot of the food is fried.

**What are you doing now?**
Marta, the mum, has just got home, so I'm getting ready to go out. We're going to a concert tonight so I might feel a bit tired in the morning. That always makes the next day go more slowly.

**7** Look at the underlined adjectives in the article and check the meaning. Then choose the correct adjectives to complete the sentences.
 1 It's really .................... watching football with Carlos. He always shouts and I can't hear anything!
   a annoying     b dull     c enjoyable
 2 The film was so .................... I turned it off after half an hour.
   a dull     b amazing     c enjoyable
 3 Jessica is so loud when we go out. It's a bit ...................., but funny as well.
   a challenging     b stressful     c embarrassing
 4 It's a really .................... job. One of the most difficult I've ever had.
   a challenging     b dull     c amusing
 5 The film was quite ...................., but I didn't laugh that much.
   a stressful     b amusing     c amazing
 6 I had an .................... time staying with the family. It really was a wonderful experience.
   a annoying     b stressful     c amazing
 7 It was an .................... holiday. We had lots of fun!
   a enjoyable     b embarrassing     c annoying
 8 The course is so .................... because of all the work and exams! I have no time to relax.
   a stressful     b dull     c enjoyable

**8** Work with a partner. Which person do you think had the better experience, Lina or Archie? Why? Use adjectives from exercise 7 in your answers.

**9** Work with a partner. Both of you are au pairs. Student A: you are having a terrible time. Student B: you are having an amazing time. Make notes on:

> your usual day   the family   the place where you live
> what you miss about home   what you are doing now

**10** Work with a partner. Use your notes to tell your partner about your experience.

# 1D New people

▸ Speaking: *Small talk*
▸ Writing: *An informal email; Correcting mistakes; Describing people*

## Speaking

1 Work with a partner. Look at the conversation topics in the box. Imagine you are speaking to someone new. Which topics would you talk about? Which would you avoid? Why?

> books  cars  family  films  your age
> food and drink  music  politics  your job
> people you both know  religion  your last holiday
> your health problems  the news  the weather

*I wouldn't talk about my health problems. They're too personal!*

2 Work in groups of four. Compare your ideas from exercise 1.

3 ▶007 Listen to four short conversations. What topic(s) do the people talk about?

|   | Topic(s) |
|---|---|
| 1 |  |
| 2 |  |
| 3 |  |
| 4 |  |

4 ▶007 Complete the phrases in the *Key Language* box with the words in the box. Listen again and check.

> drink  enjoying  just  know x 2
> 'll  time  was  way

### KEY LANGUAGE Small talk

1 Do you ................ many people here?
2 Can I get you a ................?
3 Do I ................ you from somewhere?
4 Are you ................ the party?
5 Sorry, one moment. I've ................ seen Michael.
6 Is this your first ................ in London?
7 It ................ great to meet you.
8 What do you do, by the ................?
9 Will you excuse me a moment?
  I ................ be right back.

5 Match the phrases in the *Key Language* box to the categories below.
   a  Opening a conversation ................
   b  Keeping a conversation going ................
   c  Ending a conversation ................

6 ▶008 Listen and repeat the questions and sentences. Try to sound natural and relaxed.
   1  Did you have a good weekend?
   2  This is my friend Tara.
   3  Would you like a drink?
   4  I'd love a cola!
   5  How was your holiday?
   6  It was amazing!

## ⚡ YOUR TURN

7 Imagine you are going to a party. You will know hardly anyone there. Prepare five or six questions to ask other people.

*What do you do in your free time?*
*Where are you from?*

8 Imagine you are at the party. Half the class are Student A and half the class are Student B. Move around the class.

Student A:
introduce yourself
ask a question

Student B:
keep the conversation going
end the conversation

9 Swap roles and repeat the task in exercise 8.

12

# People

## Writing

**1** Read Ella's email and answer the questions.
  1 What does Mia want?
  2 Why does Ella recommend Sophie?

**2** Work with a partner. Correct the highlighted mistakes in the email.

---

Hi Mia,

How are you? I hear ¹ <mark>you looking</mark> for a new flatmate. I have a really good friend, Sophie, and she is looking for a new flat. I think you two would have ² <mark>much</mark> fun together. When you first ³ <mark>met</mark> her she's <u>a bit nervous</u> but when you get to know her she's <u>really easygoing</u>. She's <u>reasonably neat and tidy</u> and she's ⁴ <mark>reliable extremely</mark>. She can be <u>a bit noisy</u> at times but when we lived together I ⁵ <mark>am</mark> terribly busy and she was always <u>very considerate</u>. She ⁶ <mark>doesnt</mark> know that many people ⁷ <mark>on</mark> the city because she ⁸ <mark>hasnt</mark> lived there for that long. However, she's <u>incredibly sociable</u> and I'm sure you'll love living with her. And she's also <u>amazingly creative</u>! Our flat ⁹ <mark>at</mark> Munich was beautiful and really cool because of the changes she ¹⁰ <mark>make</mark>! One <u>slightly annoying</u> thing is that she ¹¹ <mark>spend</mark> ages in the bathroom, but ¹² <mark>their</mark> are two bathrooms in your flat so it shouldn't be a problem 😊

Would you like to meet her? Let me know and I can give you her number.

Love
Ella

---

**3** Match the mistakes in the email to the types of mistake in the box.

> sp = spelling    ww = wrong word
> wo = word order    gr = grammar    t = tense
> p = punctuation    ↑ = missing word

**4** Use the symbols to help you correct the mistakes in the sentences.
  1 <u>Hell</u> make a really great flatmate. (p)
  2 I <u>meet</u> him at work. (t)
  3 <u>His</u> a great cook. (gr)
  4 Harry is one of the <u>friendlyest</u> people I know. (sp)
  5 I lived with him for a while <u>at</u> Munich. (ww)
  6 He drives a <u>car blue</u>. (wo)
  7 He very funny and great to hang out with. (↑)

**5** Add the underlined adverb + adjective phrases in the email to the *Key Language* box.

> **KEY LANGUAGE** Describing people
>
> 1 Positive – really good, ............., .............,
>    ............., ............., .............
>
> 2 Negative – a bit lazy, ............., .............,
>    .............
>
> Tip! *A bit* and *slightly* are always used with negative adjectives

**6** Choose the correct adverbs to complete the sentences.
  1 He's *reasonably / incredibly* sociable, but he doesn't go out that much.
  2 Mary can be *extremely / fairly* noisy sometimes but she's never that loud.
  3 Carl is *incredibly / a bit* busy at work, so you'll hardly ever see him.
  4 You'll love it when Daniel cooks. He's a *really / reasonably* good cook.
  5 Ana is *extremely / quite* thoughtful. She always leaves lovely notes and presents around the flat to cheer me up.
  6 She's *a bit / extremely* lazy but when you remind her about something, she does it.

## YOUR TURN

**7** Think about your best friend. Write an email to someone recommending them for a flat share. Use adverb and adjective phrases to describe them.

**8** Swap your email with a partner. Use the correction code in exercise 3 to mark any mistakes you think they have made.

**9** Swap back and correct the mistakes that your partner has marked.

13

# 2 Travel

- **Grammar:** Past Simple and Past Continuous
- **Pronunciation:** Past Simple verb endings; Weak forms of 'was' and 'were'
- **Reading:** A scary safari
- **Listening:** A nightmare flight

## 2A When holidays go wrong

### A scary safari – DAN'S STORY

I was on holiday in Zambia with my wife and we were having a great time. First, we ¹ _visited_ Victoria Falls – the largest waterfall in the world. It ² _____ absolutely amazing and we ³ _____ hundreds of photos! After that, we ⁴ _____ to one of the National Parks, where we ⁵ _____ in a small lodge in a bushcamp.

Our guide ⁶ _____ us that evenings are the best times to see the animals, so one night, we ⁷ _____ to go on a 'dusk' safari. We ⁸ _____ into the jeep. As we were driving along, we ⁹ _____ a large group of elephants – it was an amazing sight! We ¹⁰ _____ closer and suddenly ¹¹ _____ that it was a group of mothers with their babies. They ¹² _____ to cross the road in front of us, but then they stopped. One of the babies was left on the wrong side of the road. Now we ¹³ _____ we were in danger! One elephant ¹⁴ _____ very angry and started to run towards our jeep. Our guide drove faster and faster, but the elephant was still following us, even though we were driving at 30km/h. I was terrified – the elephant's angry face was so close to ours. It was like being in Jurassic Park! Luckily, after a few minutes, the elephant became tired and ¹⁵ _____ and we drove back to camp. We all ¹⁶ _____ lucky to be alive!

1 Work with a partner. Discuss the questions.
1 Where was your last holiday?
2 Did you enjoy it? Why? / Why not?
3 What do you remember most about it?

2 What is the Past Simple form of the verbs in the box?

| be become climb decide drive feel know realize see start stay stop take tell travel ~~visit~~ |

3 ▶010 Listen and check. Which verbs are irregular?

4 ▶010 Listen again and think about the pronunciation of the Past Simple forms. Then listen, repeat and practise.
1 Which ones end in /ɪd/?
2 Which end in /d/?
3 Which end in /t/?

5 Look at the photos of Dan's scary safari. Where do you think Dan went on holiday?

6 ▶011 Complete Dan's story with the Past Simple form of the verbs in exercise 2. Then read and listen to the story and check your answers.

Travel

**7** Work with a partner. Write the questions for the answers.
1 He went to Zambia. **Where did Dan go on holiday?**
2 They stayed in a lodge in a bushcamp.
3 Because her baby was left on the wrong side of the road.
4 Because she became tired.
5 They all felt lucky to be alive.

**8** ▶012 Listen to Jenny talking about her holiday. Answer the questions.
1 Who was she with and where were they going?
2 Why did the plane drop and was it dangerous?
3 Why was it the best holiday of her life?

**9** ▶012 Complete the sentences with the verbs in the box. Listen again and check. What tense are the verbs?

| were lying | was reading | were feeling |
| were having | were flying | was panicking |
| were looking forward to | was watching | |

1 We ............... to Las Vegas for a two-week holiday.
2 We ............... a break, because we both had really stressful jobs …
3 I ............... my book and Neil ............... a film, when suddenly the plane dropped …
4 … the air stewards who weren't in their seats ............... on the floor …
5 … most of the passengers ............... really sick.
6 I ..............., but Neil stayed calm.
7 As we ............... dinner on our last night, Neil asked me to marry him!

**10** Choose the correct words to complete the grammar box.

### GRAMMAR: Past Simple and Past Continuous ▶ PAGE 115

We use the Past Simple to talk about ¹ *actions in progress in the past / finished past actions*: *We stayed in a small lodge.*

To make questions and negatives in the Past Simple, we use the auxiliary ² *had / did*.

To make the Past Continuous, we use *was* or *were* verb + *-ing*: *We were flying to Las Vegas.*

We use the Past Continuous to talk about ³ *actions in progress in the past / finished past actions*.

When we use the tenses together, we use the ⁴ *Past Simple / Past Continuous* for short actions that interrupt a longer past action.

**11** ▶013 Choose the correct verbs to complete the sentences. Listen and check.
1 I *was walking / walked* to work when my phone was *ringing / rang*.
2 *Did you have / Were you having* a nice weekend?
3 It *was starting / started* to rain while the children *were playing / played* football.
4 '*Did you see / Were you seeing* the sun go down? It was so fast!' 'Sorry, I *wasn't watching / didn't watch*!'
5 I *was running / ran* the London marathon in 2017.
6 He *cooked / was cooking* the dinner, when suddenly he *had / was having* an amazing idea!

**12** ▶014 Listen. Do you hear *is*, *was*, *are* or *were*? Listen again, check and repeat.
1 ............... 2 ...............
3 ............... 4 ...............

**13** Work with a partner. Ask and answer the questions.
1 What were you doing at 7.00 p.m. yesterday?
2 Where did you go on your last holiday?
3 Where were you living in 2012?
4 What did you do last weekend?

**14** Work in small groups. Discuss the questions.
1 Whose holiday was more frightening – Dan's or Jenny's? Why?
2 Do you like flying? Why? / Why not?
3 Think of a frightening holiday experience.
   • Write the verbs you need to tell the story.
   • Share your list of verbs with the group. Can they guess what happened?
   • Tell your story.

## 2B Holiday romance

> **Grammar:** Present Perfect Simple + yet, already, just, ever and never
> **Vocabulary:** Verb + noun collocations
> **Listening:** A holiday romance

1 Work with a partner. Look at the photos and discuss the questions.
  1 Can you name the countries in the photos.
  2 Have you visited any of them?
  3 Which would you like to visit? Why?

2 ▶015 Complete the verb + noun collocations in the sentences with the verbs in the box. Listen to the conversations and check.

| arrive   book (x2)   experience   fall   get (X2)   go |
| --- |

  1 I really want to ............... **a holiday** to Florida for next summer!
  2 What time does your train ............... **in** London?
  3 We stayed with a local family in Jamaica and it was a chance to really ............... **the culture**!
  4 We like to plan every detail before we go. We ............... **restaurants, trips, tickets** – everything we want to do!
  5 She wants to ............... **a job** in Chile for a year so that she can learn Spanish.
  6 My brother wants to ............... **travelling** in India next year.
  7 I don't think it's possible to ............... **in love** with someone you meet on holiday.
  8 We want to ............... **married** in Norway in winter so we can see the northern lights!

3 Work with a partner. Ask and answer the questions.
  1 Have you booked a holiday recently? Where to?
  2 Imagine you have a whole year free – where would you go travelling? Why?
  3 Have you ever fallen in love, got married or got a job in another country?

4 Read about Kate's Greek adventure. Where did she go? Who did she fall in love with?

### MY GREEK ADVENTURE

I didn't expect to find love on a girls' trip to Greece, but when we arrived on the island of Santorini, romance was definitely in the air – it was so beautiful! The barman in our hotel was a Greek man called Nicos. He was really friendly and we spent a lot of time talking. We fell in love quickly! My friends went back to the UK after two weeks, but I didn't go with them!

That was nearly three months ago and we're still completely in love. I've already met Nicos' family and I've started to learn Greek. We've just moved into a flat together and I've found a job as a hotel receptionist. I've never felt this way about anyone before, and Nicos feels the same. We plan to get married soon, but I haven't told my parents yet. They're still upset that I didn't come home with my friends!

Nicos   Kate

# Travel

**5** Work with a partner. Underline all the verb forms in the text. Then answer the questions.
1. What tenses did you find in the 1st paragraph?
2. What tenses did you find in the 2nd paragraph?
3. Which paragraph talks about the past? Which talks more about the present?

**6** Work with a partner. Ask and answer the questions.
1. Has Kate met Nicos' family?
2. Has she started to learn Greek?
3. Has she ever felt this way about anyone before?
4. What hasn't she told her parents?

**7** Complete the rules in the grammar box with the words in the box.

past   has   never   present

### GRAMMAR: Present Perfect Simple ▶ PAGE 116

We form the Present Perfect Simple with *have* or
¹ .................... + past participle.

The Present Perfect Simple connects the past with the
² .................... .

We use the Present Perfect Simple for:
- recent ³ .................... actions that have a present effect: *We've just moved into a flat together* ... (present effect = we now live together).
  We often use *just*, *already*, and *yet* with this use.
- experiences in our life up to now: *I've never felt this way about anyone before*.
  We often use *ever* or ⁴ .................... with this use.

**8** Use the ideas below to write questions with *Have you ever ...?*

**Have you ever ...?**
... (fall) in love on holiday
... (work) abroad
... (eat) shark
... (lose) your passport
... (meet) a famous person
... (swim) in a river

**9** Work with a partner. Ask and answer the questions in exercise 8. Give more information where possible.

*Have you ever fallen in love on holiday?*

*Really? What happened?*   *Yes, I have.*

**10** Find and underline *already*, *just* and *yet* in the text in exercise 4. Which word ...
1. means *very recently*?
2. means *before this*?
3. is only used in questions or negatives?

**11** ▶016 Listen to a radio interview with Will. Where did he go to work and who did he fall in love with?

**12** Use the prompts to write questions in the Present Perfect Simple.
1. Where / Will and Yuki / decide / to live?
2. What difficulties / Will / have / in Japan?
3. What / he / just / book?
4. Who / Yuki / not meet / yet?
5. What / they / already / book / tickets for?

**13** ▶016 Work with a partner. Ask and answer the questions in exercise 12. Listen again to check your answers.

**14** Correct the mistakes in the sentences.
1. Have you did your homework yet?
2. I have decided where to go on holiday yet. It's so hard to choose!
3. 'Have you seen James this morning?' 'Yes, I've.'
4. I've emailed the report to my boss just.
5. I never been to South America.
6. I'm not hungry – I've already ate dinner.

**15** Work with a partner. Ask and answer questions in the Present Perfect Simple about the topics below. Try to use *already*, *yet* or *just*. Give more information if possible.
- book a summer holiday
- do your homework
- do your Christmas shopping
- take your driving test

*Have you booked your summer holiday yet?*

*Yes, I've just booked it! We're going to Marrakech in Morocco!*

17

# 2C Family backpacking in Vietnam

> **Reading:** A backpacking holiday
> **Vocabulary:** Adjectives for holiday experiences

## Family backpacking – a Vietnamese adventure

In the summer of 2018, Nina and her husband, Paul, took their children, Luke (11) and Sophie (8) on a backpacking holiday to Vietnam. We asked Nina to tell us all about it.

**Why did you choose Vietnam for your family holiday?**

In 2017, we went to Thailand for our first family backpacking trip. We met a lot of international travellers there, and so many of them recommended Vietnam for our next trip. They said it was less <u>spoilt</u> than Thailand. So as soon as we returned home, we booked flights to Vietnam for the summer of 2018!

**What was your plan for the trip?**

We had just over 3 weeks and we knew we had to focus on one area as Vietnam is so <u>huge</u>. The coastline is 5,283 kilometres long, but in some places the country is only 48 kilometres wide!

In Thailand, we loved the jungle more than the beaches because there were more opportunities to meet local families, so we decided to go as far north in Vietnam as possible. The plan was to travel from Hanoi to Halong Bay, Halong to Sapa, and then Sapa to Hoi An and fly back to Hanoi.

**What was your homestay experience like?**

We found our homestay on Airbnb. We searched in the area where we wanted to stay and looked at the reviews. We decided on the village Ta Van, about 10km from Sapa, and found a home called the Lazy Crazy Homestay, hosted by John (a translation of his name) and his girlfriend.

The home was on a hill overlooking the Ta Van valley and had six <u>separate</u> rooms. When we arrived, John showed us our room and introduced us to the other people staying there. We met couples from Spain, France, Germany and Vietnam – a lot of them were doing charity work there or teaching.

One of the local girls from the village cooked for us every day, but we all helped to serve the meals and wash up. The kitchen area was clean but very <u>basic</u>, with a clay oven. There was a <u>shared</u> toilet and shower and we cleaned our teeth using rain water or water from the river next to the house!

**What are the advantages of a homestay over a hotel?**

You really experience the people, the culture and how they live on a <u>daily</u> basis. We got to know John and his family really well. We also became very friendly with two little girls in the village (four and five years old). My kids fell in love with these girls and we're putting a Christmas package together for them to send out to Vietnam! We still talk to John on Instagram and he often posts to say he's missing us!

# Travel

**What are your favourite memories from the holiday?**

Vietnam is so beautiful, but actually the most <u>memorable</u> moments came from connecting with people. Sitting around in the evening playing board games with people from four different countries, or watching my daughter doing gymnastics with her new friends are memories that will stay with me forever.

**Did you have any dangerous experiences?**

Vietnam health and safety laws are a little different to the UK! There are practically no seat belts and the roads are <u>chaotic</u>. We did take the kids on a motorbike tour of Hanoi City, which they absolutely loved, and the riders taught my 11-year-old son to ride an old-fashioned Russian motorbike!

We also found out that the <u>poisonous</u> Box jellyfish (the deadliest in the world) lives in the waters around Halong bay! My kids spent a lot of time diving into the water and we made sure we were always sitting on the side of the boat so we could see if there were any jellyfish close to them. We had to get the kids out of the water a few times!

**Have you planned next year's holiday yet?**

We are looking at Costa Rica and Borneo. We have a real taste for backpacking now and have a lot of the world left to see!

 017

**1** Work in small groups. Discuss the questions.
  1 Where do you prefer to stay on holiday? Hotels, villas, camp sites or homestays with local families? Why?
  2 Have you ever been on a backpacking holiday? Where would you like to go backpacking?
  3 What do you know about Vietnam?

**2** Read the interview. Choose the correct words to complete the sentences.
  1 Nina and her family went to the *north* / *south* of Vietnam.
  2 Paul is Nina's *son* / *husband*.
  3 John is a *tourist* / *homestay owner*.
  4 Luke and Sophie are Nina's *friends* / *children*.

**3** Work with a partner. What can you remember? Answer the questions. Then check in the interview.
  1 Where did the family go in 2017?
  2 How long is Vietnam's coastline?
  3 How many rooms were there in the homestay?
  4 What did they use to clean their teeth?
  5 What is Nina's family doing for the two little girls they met?
  6 What are Nina's favourite memories?
  7 What were the two dangerous situations?
  8 Where are they planning to go next?

**4** Match the underlined adjectives in the interview to the definitions.
  1 very big ...........
  2 used by more than one person ...........
  3 damaged or ruined by too many buildings, tourists, cars, etc. ...........
  4 likely to make you ill or die ...........
  5 easy to remember ...........
  6 with no order and no rules ...........
  7 done every day ...........
  8 not together with others – individual ...........
  9 simple, with only what is necessary ...........

**5** Work in groups. Discuss the questions.
  1 What were family holidays like when you were a child? How do they compare with Luke and Sophie's holiday?
  2 What are your favourite holiday memories?
  3 Would you like to go to Vietnam? Why?
  4 What are the positives and negatives of tourism for a country?

19

# 2D Holiday experiences

> ▶ Speaking: *Staying in a hotel*
> ▶ Pronunciation: *Intonation in polite questions*
> ▶ Writing: *A blog post about a travel experience; Time sequencers*

## Speaking

1. Read the text and do the quiz. Then work with a partner and compare your answers. Did you tick the same things?

2. ▶018 Listen to three conversations and answer the questions.
   1. Which nights does the woman book?
   2. What kind of room does she want and how much does it cost?
   3. What's her name and email address?
   4. What's her room number?
   5. What time does the hotel serve breakfast?
   6. What two problems does the woman have?
   7. What does she want at 6.30 the next morning?

3. ▶018 Complete the phrases in the *Key Language* box with the words in the box. Listen again and check.

   > do  go  have  included  isn't  like
   > reserved  tell  there's  would

   **KEY LANGUAGE** Staying in a hotel

   **Booking a room**
   1. I'd .................. to book a room for three nights from … till …
   2. Do you .................. any rooms free for those nights?
   3. Could you .................. me the price for that room?
   4. Can I .................. ahead and book it, then?

   **Checking in**
   5. I have a room .................. in the name of King.
   6. Is breakfast ..................?
   7. .................. you have free WiFi?

   **Dealing with problems**
   8. .................. a problem with the WiFi …
   9. … the hairdryer in my room .................. working.
   10. .................. it be possible to have an alarm call tomorrow?

4. ▶019 Listen to four polite questions from the conversations. Notice the intonation.

5. ▶019 Listen again, repeat and practise.

## YOUR TURN

6. Work with a partner. Student A turn to page 126. Student B turn to page 128.

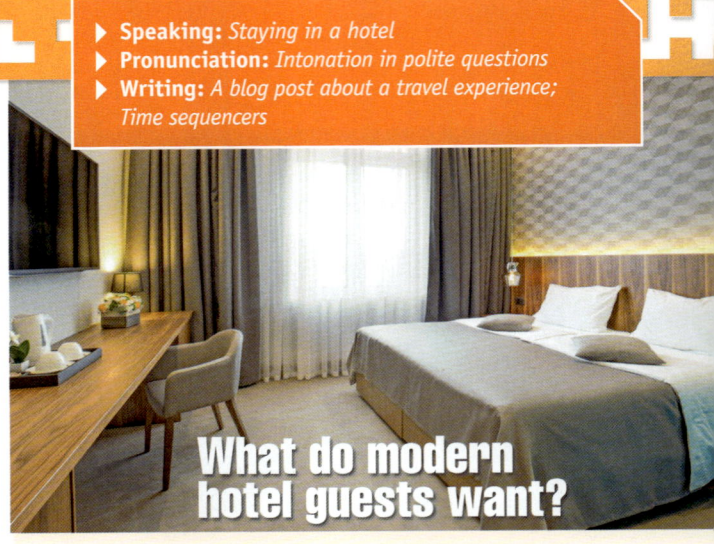

## What do modern hotel guests want?

In the past, hotel guests were happy with a clean room, clean bedsheets, a hot shower, and a comfortable bed. But now, guests are asking for much more from the hotels they stay in … **and** they want it to be free! Top demands include free WiFi, free parking, free late check-out, and even a free mini-bar!

### Quiz

Tick (✓) the things you expect to be included in your room price. Put a cross (✗) next to the things you don't expect.

☐ Free WiFi
☐ Free parking
☐ A safe for your money and passport
☐ Hairdryer
☐ 24-hour reception
☐ Air conditioning
☐ Bathrobe and slippers
☐ Desk
☐ Tea and coffee-making facilities
☐ Gym
☐ Swimming pool
☐ Spa
☐ Free late check-out
☐ Free snacks
☐ Room service
☐ TV

7. Work with a partner. Take turns to be the hotel guest and have the following conversations.
   1. Book a hotel room using your own name and email address.
   2. Check in to the hotel and ask questions.

8. What problems have you had in a hotel? What happened? Tell the class.

# Writing

1. Read the information about the Lake District. Then work with a partner and discuss the questions.
   1. Where is the Lake District?
   2. What can you do there?
   3. Would you like to go there? Why?

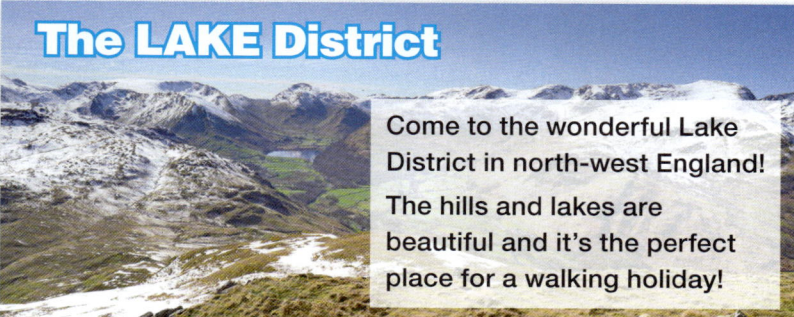

**The LAKE District**

Come to the wonderful Lake District in north-west England! The hills and lakes are beautiful and it's the perfect place for a walking holiday!

2. Lucy is on holiday in the Lake District with her boyfriend, David. Read her blog post. What walk did they try? What happened?

## Day 3 – The walking just got harder!

We started the day with a delicious breakfast in our hotel. After that we went back to our room to plan our day. We decided to try the walk from Ambleside to the top of Red Screes – a 16.6 km walk. While I was looking at the map, David packed our bag with water and food. Then we left the hotel.

Not long after we joined the path it started to snow a little bit! There were lots of other walkers around us, so we weren't worried. We walked through a field of sheep, and soon after we began to climb the hill. After three hours we finally reached the top – and the views were amazing! Then it was time to come down, but before that we sat down, enjoyed the views, and ate our sandwiches to give us some energy. Meanwhile, the snow was getting heavier and heavier. The view was suddenly gone – all we could see was snow! At the same time we realized we couldn't see any other walkers! It was really cold and I started to panic, especially when David fell over in the snow. We decided the best way down was to sit on the snow and slide down. After four hours of sliding then walking, we eventually reached the bottom!

3. Read the *Key Language box*. Then underline all the time sequencers in Lucy's blog.

> **KEY LANGUAGE** Time sequencers
>
> | then | soon after | finally |
> | before that | after | at the same time |
> | eventually | while | not long after |
> | after that | meanwhile | |

4. Work with a partner. Which time sequencers can you use to talk about what happened …
   1. … next?
   2. … earlier?
   3. … at the same time?
   4. … in the end?

5. Choose the correct time sequencers to complete the paragraph.

> We left the hotel and ¹*finally / after that* we walked to the city centre. ²*Then / at the same time* we had breakfast in the main square. ³*Soon after / While* eating our breakfast, we went to an art gallery. ⁴*After / Then* we had lunch in a pizza restaurant and ⁵*after that / while* we were eating, we watched all the people walking past. ⁶*After that / At the same time* we went shopping for four hours and ⁷*before that / finally* we went back to the hotel.

## YOUR TURN

6. Think of a holiday that you enjoyed.
   1. Choose one day and write a blog post about it.
   2. Use time sequencers from the *Key Language* box.
   3. Swap blog posts with a partner and check for mistakes.

# Video 1: Vietnam

## 1 Vietnam

1 Work with a partner and discuss the questions.
  1 Which countries in the world would you most like to visit? Why?
  2 What activities do you most enjoy doing on holiday?

2 Read the article and complete the sentences with the correct words.
  1 ................ is the god of the kitchen. He tells another god about each ................ every year.
  2 Only ................ produces more coffee than Vietnam.
  3 Cashew nuts are the ................ of a plant, and they have much more vitamin C than an ................ .
  4 ................ is the most popular surname in Vietnam.
  5 The points on the star on the Vietnamese flag represent different groups of ................ .
  6 The Dong Tam snake farm helps to ................ snakes and tries to find ................ against their poison.
  7 In the past only the ................ and their servants could enter the Forbidden Purple City.
  8 Ha Long Bay has ................ islands and thousands of ................ go there each day.

# 8 Facts about Vietnam

**For anyone thinking of travelling to Vietnam, here are eight facts that might interest you.**

## FOOD

1 **The kitchen god** Food is so important to Vietnamese people that they actually have a god of the kitchen – Ong Tao. Ong Tao appears just before the Vietnamese New Year and he reports to the God of Heaven on a family's behaviour.

2 **Coffee** People who love this drink will enjoy being in Vietnam as coffee is very cheap and tasty. Vietnam is the second largest producer of coffee in the world, second only to Brazil. In the hot months, try the iced version to cool you down.

3 **Cashew nuts** Over a third of all cashew nuts in the world come from Vietnam. The nuts are actually seeds that grow at the end of the cashew apple. Cashew nuts have 5 times the amount of vitamin C as oranges.

## HISTORY

4 **Names** Ho Chi Minh and Nguyen (pronounced win) are the two most famous names in Vietnam. Nearly half of the population has Nguyen as a surname. Ho Chi Minh was the leader in Vietnam's fight for independence against the French. Ho Chi Minh City is named after him.

5 **The flag** The flag has a red background with a five-pointed star. Each point of the star represents a different thing – farmers, workers, soldiers, academics and young people. The red background is to remember the dead from the wars.

## TOURISM

6 **Museums** Vietnam has many fascinating museums. The Dong Tam snake farm is a living museum. It helps protect snakes and also researches medicines to protect people from their poison.

7 **The Forbidden Purple City** This is a bit like a castle, or a palace. In the past, only the royal family and their servants could go there.

8 **Ha Long Bay** This is one of the New 7 Wonders of Nature and a UNESCO World Heritage Site. There are over 1600 islands in the bay. Thousands of tourists visit the bay every day.

**3** Watch the video. Number the topics in the order they are mentioned.
 a  the main tourist sites
 b  the location
 c  the main cities
 d  the transport

**4** Watch the video again. Are the sentences True or False?
 1  Vietnam has borders with three countries.
 2  Hanoi is the biggest city.
 3  There are more motorbikes than cars.
 4  Ha Long Bay is famous for its dragon bridge.

**5** Can you remember what these adjectives described? Discuss your ideas with a partner, then watch the video again to check.

> ancient   beautiful   biggest   breathtaking   busy
> modern   older   peaceful

**6** Work with a partner and discuss the questions.
 1  What are the biggest cities in your country? Why are they popular with tourists?
 2  Which other locations in your country are popular with tourists?
 3  Which areas of your country do you think are most beautiful? Why?
 4  What do you find most interesting about Vietnam? Why?

# Review

 **LESSON 1A** Write 3 questions you could ask someone about themselves.

 **LESSON 1B** Write 3 sentences using personality adjectives to describe people you know.

 **LESSON 1B** Write sentences to describe a routine or habit and something you are doing now.

 **LESSON 1C** Write sentences about: an embarrassing experience, a stressful experience, an enjoyable experience.

 **LESSON 1D** Look at something you have written in English. Try to find mistakes and correct them.

 **LESSON 1D** Write 3 sentences about someone you know using adverbs and adjectives to describe them.

 **LESSON 2A** Write 2 sentences to describe something you did yesterday or something you were doing at a particular time yesterday.

 **LESSON 2A** Write the Past Simple verb form of 5 irregular verbs.

 **LESSON 2B** Write sentences about places you have and haven't visited. Use *yet*, *already*, *just*, *ever* and *never*.

 **LESSON 2B** Write 3 sentences about things you can book.

 **LESSON 2C** Write the names of places you know that are memorable, chaotic and spoilt.

 **LESSON 2D** List 5 useful phrases for staying in a hotel.

# 3 Work

▶ **Grammar:** *Quantity: much, many, some, any, etc.*
▶ **Vocabulary:** *Work – Benefits and tasks*
▶ **Pronunciation:** *Quantity words*
▶ **Listening:** *Stress at work*

## 3A Stress

1  What things can cause stress at work or college? Order the ideas from 1 (the most stressful) to 5.

> lots of work   not enough time
> boring work   other people   fear of failing

2  Work with a partner. Compare your order and give reasons. What other things can cause stress at work or college?

3  Read the job advert. Match the underlined words and phrases to the definitions below.

### TEAM LEADER

You will <u>be responsible for</u> the day-to-day management of a team of eight sales <u>employees</u>. You will make sure your team meet their sales targets. Your <u>tasks</u> will also include reporting to the management on the team's performance. For the right person we offer:

- an excellent <u>salary</u> of £60,000 per year.
- the chance to earn a <u>bonus</u> when you meet targets.
- <u>flexible working hours</u> so you can start and finish when you want.
- an excellent <u>pension</u> ready for when you retire.
- six weeks <u>paid holiday</u> plus public holidays.

Join our team and have some excellent <u>colleagues</u> to work with.

1  ............... the money you earn for your work
2  ............... the people who work in a company
3  ............... the people you work with
4  ............... the things you have to do at work
5  ............... to be in control of someone or something
6  ............... the money you get when you are older and stop work
7  ............... paid time off when you are free to do what you want
8  ............... not having fixed times to start and finish work
9  ............... extra money you get for doing your job well

4  Work with a partner. Which things in exercise 3 are most important in a job? Why?

> *I'm not worried about my salary. For me, the colleagues I work with are really important.*

5  ▶ 022 Listen to David talking about his job. Put a tick (✓) next to the things he likes about his job and a cross (✗) next to the things he dislikes.
1  the hours he works
2  the number of things he is responsible for
3  his colleagues
4  his salary
5  his paid holidays
6  the tasks he has to do

Work

**6** ▶023 Complete the sentences with the words in the box. Then listen and check.

> bit   enough   few   lot   many x 2   much x 2   too

1. I have a .................. of work to do!
2. I only have a .................. of time before I have to go back.
3. I'm responsible for too .................. projects.
4. It's too .................. work for one person.
5. A .................. of my colleagues are really friendly.
6. I'm not paid .................. money for the number of hours I work.
7. How .................. holiday do you get?
8. We don't get .................. weeks paid holiday.
9. I'm .................. busy!

**7** Look at the sentences in exercise 6 again. Answer the questions. Then check your answers in the grammar box.
1. Which words and phrases for quantity do we use with uncountable nouns? Which do we use with countable nouns?
2. Which words and phrases mean 'more than necessary'?
3. Which phrase means 'not as much as we need'?

**GRAMMAR: Quantity**                                      ▶ PAGE 116

We use *much/a bit of* with uncountable nouns and *many/a lot of/ a few (of)* with countable nouns: *a bit of time, a few of my colleagues*.

When something is more than necessary we use *too* with adjectives, *too much* with uncountable nouns and *too many* with countable nouns: *too busy, too much work, too many projects*

We use *not enough* with nouns when the amount is less than necessary, and *enough* with nouns when it is the correct amount: *I'm not paid enough money.*

**8** ▶023 We usually stress quantity words in sentences. Listen to the sentences in exercise 6 again and notice the stress. Then listen, repeat and practise.

**9** Choose the correct words to complete the sentences.
1. How *many / much* hours do you work each week?
2. I have *a few / a bit of* tasks to do before I can go home.
3. I just have *many / a bit of* work to finish before lunch.
4. Sorry, I'm *too much / too* busy to come out this evening.
5. Do you have *enough / many* free time?
6. We have *a bit of / a lot of* new employees starting today.
7. We need to change. There are *too many / not enough* complaints about our department.
8. There are *not enough / too* minutes in the day!

**10** Complete the tweets with the words in the box.

> enough   few   don't … enough
> too   too many   too much
> not … enough

🐦 **#everydayproblems**

1. I work .................. hours at college. I don't have .................. free time.
2. Some people earn .................. money. It isn't fair!
3. I .................. have .................. experience to apply for a job in management.
4. My colleagues are .................. reliable ................... They never finish their work on time.
5. My younger brother is always .................. careless with his school work. He never gets good marks!
6. I'm never very busy and only have a .................. tasks to do every day.

**11** Choose one of the hashtags below and write three tweets responding to it. Use words and phrases for quantity.
#problemsatwork
#problemsatcollege
#problemsathome

**12** Work in groups. Show your tweets to each other. Ask and answer questions to find out more about the tweets.

*Why do you argue with your family?*

*Why do you have a lot of work at college?*

25

# 3B Is that really true?

- **Grammar:** Something / anything / nothing, etc.
- **Vocabulary:** Work – Experience
- **Reading:** Liar!

# LIAR!

According to Robert Feldman from the University of Massachusetts, 60% of people lie about something in a ten-minute conversation. Not just one lie, but two to three lies in ten minutes! So, what are some of the most common lies?

'I'm nearly there.' In fact, you aren't <u>anywhere</u> near there yet. 'I'm five minutes away.' It's probably closer to twenty minutes.

'The email went into my spam folder.' You actually opened it, read it and haven't done anything about it yet.

'My phone wasn't working.' Somebody phoned you but you didn't answer your phone because you didn't want to speak to them.

'Yes, I remember you.' Maybe you met them somewhere, but you really don't remember them at all.

'I'm fine.' Nobody is fine all the time, but this is what we always say to anybody we meet, just to sound positive.

'I go to the gym four times a week.' You probably went nowhere near the gym last week.

'Sorry, I've got plans that day.' No, you haven't. You have nothing planned. You just don't want to meet that person.

1 Work with a partner. Discuss the questions.
  1 In which of these situations is it OK to lie?
    a Your friend is wearing new clothes and asks for your opinion. You don't like the clothes.
    b Your friend just gave a very boring presentation and asks you if it was good.
    c You didn't finish a piece of work yesterday because you went out with your friends.
  2 When was the last time you weren't completely honest with someone?
  3 What lies do you think people tell at work or college?

2 Read the article. Have you told any of these lies? Do you know anyone who has?

3 Read the article again and answer the questions.
  1 How many minutes will you have to wait for somebody who says they are 5 minutes away?
  2 Why do people sometimes not answer their phone?
  3 Why do people always say, 'I'm fine'?
  4 Why does somebody say they have plans if it isn't true?

4 Look at the underlined word in the article. Underline eight more words that end in -thing, -body and -where.

5 Complete the table in the grammar box with the correct words.

**GRAMMAR:** Something / anything / nothing, etc. ▶ PAGE 117

| | | | |
|---|---|---|---|
| **People** | somebody / someone | ¹................ / anyone | nobody / no one |
| **Things** | ²................ | anything | nothing |
| **Places** | somewhere | anywhere | ³................ |

We use *somebody, someone, something, somewhere* in positive sentences, and in offers and requests: *There's somebody on the phone. Would you like something to eat?*

We use *anybody, anyone, anything, anywhere* in negative sentences and questions: *I can't see anybody. Is there anything in the box?*

We use *nobody, no one, nothing, nowhere* with a positive verb: *There's nobody here.*

**6** Complete the sentences with words from the grammar box.
1 I'm not doing .................. on Friday.
2 Have you seen Tom ..................?
3 I'd like to go to the cinema but there's .................. on I want to see.
4 I've sent five emails but .................. has replied.
5 Can you buy .................. for dinner on your way home?
6 I'd like to speak to .................. about my order.
7 Why isn't .................. answering the phone?
8 Let's do .................. fun tonight!
9 I didn't go .................. at the weekend.

**7** Use the prompts and words from the grammar box to make questions. Then ask and answer the questions with a partner.
1 You / doing / interesting / this evening?
2 You / go / nice / last weekend?
3 You / meeting / next weekend?

**8** How many people do you think lie on their CV when they apply for a job? What kinds of things do they lie about? Read the text and check your ideas.

## EXCELLENT AT …

**According to one survey, 85% of companies have found people lying on their CV. Here are some of the most common lies:**

- Saying 'Knowledge of…' or 'Excellent at…' is one of the easiest lies to put on a CV because in an interview nobody will test your ¹ .................. but one day they will find out the truth.
- Some people lie about the results they got at school. Other people lie and say they have a ² .................. such as a degree when they don't have one.
- Many people lie about their ³ ................... Just because you managed one small project, can you really say you have done project management?
- Your ⁴ .................. can quickly be found out when the interviewer says 'Shall we do this part of the interview in French?'
- Are you really a Team Leader or just the most experienced person in the team? A surprising number of people create a ⁵ .................. to make themselves sound more important.

**9** Complete the text with the words in the box. Which facts in the text do you find most surprising?

> awards   experience   foreign language ability
> job title   personal interests   qualification   skills

**10** ▶ 024 Listen to three people talking in job interviews. What is each one lying about?

**11** Read the questions and think about your answers. Plan true answers to three questions and a lie for the other one.
1 Did you do anything interesting at work or college last week?
2 What foreign languages do you speak? How well do you speak them?
3 What are your personal interests?
4 What work experience do you have? Where? What were you responsible for?

**12** Work with a partner. Ask and answer the questions in exercise 11. Try to guess which answer your partner is lying about.

- According to one survey, 20% of employees create ⁶ .................. for themselves, such as Salesman of the Year.
- Lots of people want to sound educated or interesting and so they often put 'reading' under ⁷ ................... They haven't actually read a book all year.

# 3C Getting rich on Instagram

> **Reading:** *Making money from Instagram*
> **Vocabulary:** *Work and social media*

1. Work with a partner. What jobs can you make a lot of money from? Would you like to do these jobs? Why? / Why not?

2. Read the article quickly. Choose the best title.
   A The dangers of becoming an Instagram influencer
   B The child Instagram influencers who make more than you
   C How to become an Instagram influencer

In 2016, Madison and Kyler Fisher had a difficult time. After a business idea went wrong, the couple from Los Angeles ran out of money. Today their two-year-old daughters, Taytum and Oakley, have 2.2 million followers on Instagram, and make a six-figure-sum. They've been in adverts, a feature film, and appeared several times on the soap opera *Days of Our Lives*. Their parents, both actors, are now producing their own movies and running a family YouTube channel, which has 2.7 million subscribers. Both parents are influencers in their own right, and getting contracts from companies such as Olay and Hyundai on their personal Instagram pages.

### Instagram marketing
The influencer marketing industry is worth about $5 billion to $10 billion, and children are a growing part of Instagram's influencer economy. These kids typically sell children's clothes and toys, but can also appeal to other kinds of companies which are trying to reach their customers. Young parents already shop on Instagram, and this makes it a perfectly natural place for brands trying to reach them. 80% of Instagram's 800 million users follow a business, and the company reports that more than 60% of these people say they discover new products on Instagram.

### Instagram families
What does it mean to have a child who's an Instagram influencer? It might look just like being a regular adult influencer, where companies pay for product placement in photos. But there are also important differences, such as the fact that the kid might be the pretty face in the pictures, but it's their parents who are managing their children's career like a full-time job.

Families of Instagram children can make money, a lot of money, when they share posts. A kid influencer can get about $100 per 1,000 followers when they post on Instagram. A child with 500,000 followers in their network would earn about $5,000 for a single image. The prices go up from there, especially if a brand buys a campaign, which could include multiple posts, Instagram Story updates, and even an event appearance.

Twins Taytum and Oakley get between $15,000 and $25,000 for a single post on their Instagram account. Yet the Fishers say they still don't get many brand deals yet, because the girls can't really follow instructions. Once they're old enough to repeat what their parents (and the brands paying them) want, they could make even more. When the Instagram money is added to their money from modelling, adverts and movies, these kids start to look like

**3** Read the article again. Are the sentences True or False?
1 Taytum and Oakley are Instagram and TV stars.
2 Most Instagram users don't follow companies.
3 People with 1,000 followers can make $5,000 for just one post.
4 The two girls are likely to make more money in the future.
5 Their mum is worried about the girls being on Instagram.
6 Their mum wants them to become movie stars.

**4** Read the article again and answer the questions.
1 How do Madison and Kyler earn money?
2 How much is Influencer marketing worth?
3 How much do the twins make for each post?
4 How did their mum feel about being on Instagram herself?
5 What sometimes happens when the girls are walking in a street?

**5** Add the underlined words in the article to the correct category.
Work/Money ........................
Social media ........................

**6** Complete the texts with the correct form of words from exercise 5. Sometimes more than one answer is possible.

I was working ¹............ in a job I hated. So, I ²............ enough money to go travelling. When I ³............ of money, I got a job working on a farm in Australia. This allowed me to ⁴............ so I could carry on travelling.

Many social media ⁵............ become very famous online. It's possible to make a lot of money, and some stars make ⁶............ or more from ⁷............ photos on Instagram. People such as Selena Gomez, Kylie Jenner and Cristiano Ronaldo have millions of ⁸............. When they ⁹............ a photo on their ¹⁰............ they are paid hundreds of thousands of pounds.

Your ¹¹............ does not need to be big to make money. With 1,000 followers you can earn £40 per post.

**7** Work with a partner. Discuss the questions.
1 Which social media sites do you use? Who do you follow?
2 Do you buy products because famous people promote them? Why / Why not?
3 Is it right that people make so much money on social media? Why? / Why not?

the next generation of child stars. The families are able to give their children a good life now and <u>save up</u> for their future as well.

## Social media problems
While these families are making a lot of money, being an Instagram star does also present problems. Parents want to teach their children to be kind and good people, but they're putting them in a digital world where their value is measured in likes and comments. Fisher, mum of the two-year-old twins Taytum and Oakley, is worried about how Instagram could impact her girls' view of themselves as they get older. Her worries are partly due to her own experience. "I find myself getting depressed sometimes over Instagram likes or comments … I don't want them to think about who's liking them," Fisher says.

## The future
But the family is certainly taking advantage of the popularity now. Fisher has bigger plans for her daughters than Instagram and YouTube. They might already be social media stars that make lots of money at age two, but Fisher hopes that they'll have success on movie screens, too. They're already famous, after all – she says that people stop her girls on the street all the time, asking for photos.

# 3D Skills and interests

> ▶ **Speaking:** *Talking about likes and dislikes*
> ▶ **Writing:** *A formal email; Starting and closing an email*

## Speaking

1 What features are most important to you in a job? Put the things in order of importance.

> earning money   reaching a high position
> making a difference   following your interests / dreams
> using your talents and abilities

2 Work with a partner. Compare your order and discuss your reasons.

3 Read the questions. For each one, score yourself from 1 (= not at all) to 5. Then compare with a partner.
   1 How creative are you?                              1 2 3 4 5
   2 Do you enjoy maths?                                1 2 3 4 5
   3 Do you enjoy sports?                               1 2 3 4 5
   4 How much do you like to work with your hands?      1 2 3 4 5
   5 How good are you at solving problems?              1 2 3 4 5
   6 How much do you like communicating with people?    1 2 3 4 5
   7 How much does science excite you?                  1 2 3 4 5
   8 How much do you like being in charge of people?    1 2 3 4 5

4 Work with a partner. Look at the jobs in the photos. What features from exercise 1 does each one have? What skills from exercise 3 does each one need?

5 ▶026 Listen to three people talking about their likes and dislikes at work. Match each person to a job in exercise 4.
   1 Nick ..................
   2 Tanya ..................
   3 Jake ..................

6 ▶026 Complete the phrases in the *Key Language* box with the words in the box. Listen again and check.

> absolutely love   can't stand
> don't like   hate   keen on   like
> not very keen on   passionate about

### KEY LANGUAGE  Likes and dislikes
1 I .................. performing in front of people.
2 I also .................. writing songs although I'm not the main writer for our group.
3 The one thing I .................. is all the travelling.
4 I'm .................. sport and living a healthy life.
5 The one thing I'm .................. is the early starts and late finishes.
6 To be honest I .................. my job.
7 I .................. working with cars.
8 I'm .................. working in something more creative

## YOUR TURN

7 Talk about what you like and dislike about your current job or course. Use phrases from the *Key Language* box.

> *I love helping people and feeling like I make a difference.*

> *I can't stand doing a boring job. I'm keen on using my talents more.*

8 Imagine your dream job. What would it be? Why would you enjoy it? Why would you be good at it?
   *I'd be a ... because...*

an accountant

a musician

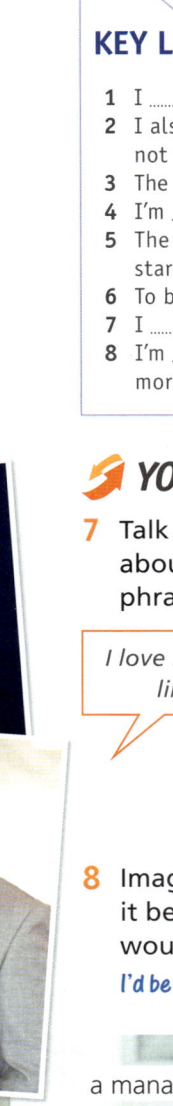

a fitness instructor

a sales person

a vet

a manager

a mechanic

# Writing

**1** How many emails do you send a week? Who to? What for?

**2** Write the phrases in the correct column in the *Key Language* box.
1. Dear Jake
2. Kind regards
3. Thanks for your email.
4. Hope this helps.
5. Dear Ms Zoisin
6. Your sincerely
7. I'm writing with reference to…
8. If you require any further assistance, please do not hesitate to contact me.

### KEY LANGUAGE  Starting & closing an email

| Greeting | First line |
|---|---|
| Hi Dorota, | Got your message thanks. |
| …………… | …………… |

| Closing line | Sign-off |
|---|---|
| Get back to me if you need anything. | Cheers, |
| …………… | …………… |

**3** Which expressions in the *Key Language* box are formal?

**4** Complete the covering email for a job application with phrases from the *Key Language* box.

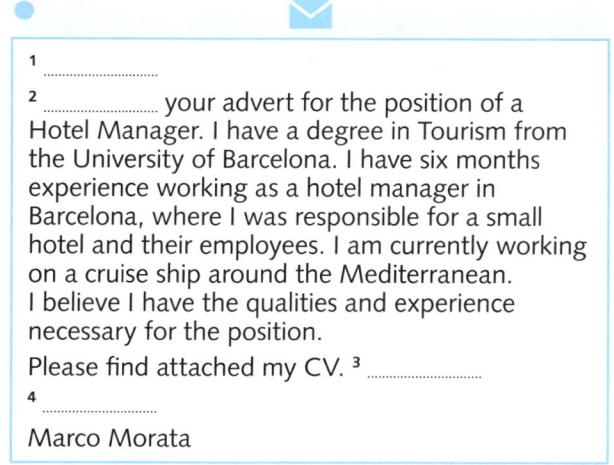

¹ ……………

² …………… your advert for the position of a Hotel Manager. I have a degree in Tourism from the University of Barcelona. I have six months experience working as a hotel manager in Barcelona, where I was responsible for a small hotel and their employees. I am currently working on a cruise ship around the Mediterranean.
I believe I have the qualities and experience necessary for the position.
Please find attached my CV. ³ ……………
⁴ ……………

Marco Morata

**5** Find formal words and expressions in the email with these meanings.
1. The job of a Hotel Manager
2. I have worked for six months as …
3. I was in charge of …
4. At the moment, I am …
5. I've got all the skills the job needs.
6. I'm sending you my CV.

## 🔶 YOUR TURN

**6** Read the job advert and plan your covering email.

**TRAVEL WRITER**
Top travel writers needed.
• 5 years travel writing experience
• Experience managing a team
• A degree

Send your CV and a covering email to Daniel Dalot, d.dalot@recruitment.com

**My qualifications**
……………………………………
……………………………………

**My experience**
……………………………………
……………………………………

**My skills**
……………………………………
……………………………………

**7** Write your covering email to apply for the job. Use phrases from the *Key Language* box and use formal words and expressions.

# 4 Childhood

> - Vocabulary: *Kitchen equipment*
> - Grammar: *Used to*
> - Pronunciation: *Used to*
> - Listening: *Childhood memories*

## 4A How we lived

**1** Match the words in the box to pictures 1–10. Check your answers with a partner. Which items can you see in kitchens A and B above?

| dishwasher | fridge | hob | kettle | microwave |
| oven | pan | sink | toaster | washing machine |

**2** Work with a partner. Think about your kitchen now and in the past. Discuss the questions.
1. What can you remember about your childhood kitchen?
2. What do you like about your kitchen now? What don't you like?
3. How much time do you spend in your kitchen? Would you like to spend more?

**3** Look at kitchens A and B again. Which do you think is from the 1930s and which from the 1960s? Why?

**4** ▶028 Read sentences about Pat's and Brian's childhood. Which do you think are True and which are False? Listen and check your ideas.

1. Pat's childhood kitchen had electricity.
2. She toasted her bread in the oven.
3. Pat's mum had a modern washing machine.
4. Pat's family bought milk in the shops.
5. Brian's childhood kitchen had an electric kettle.
6. He used candles for light in his bedroom.
7. His mother hand-washed some of their clothes in the sink.
8. Brian's family kept meat and milk in the fridge.

# Childhood

**5** 🔊 029 Can you remember what Pat and Brian said? Complete the sentences with the verbs in the box. Then listen and check.

> used to wash   used to light   didn't use to own
> used to keep   didn't use to have   used to deliver

**Pat**
1 We ………………………… an electric kettle.
2 A milkman ………………………… milk to our house every day.
3 We ………………………… all our meat, milk and cheese in our fridge.

**Brian**
4 We ………………………… candles in the bedrooms.
5 My mother ………………………… all the clothes on a Monday.
6 We ………………………… a fridge.

**6** Choose the correct words to complete the grammar box.

> **GRAMMAR: Used to**   ▶ PAGE 117
>
> We use *used to* to talk about ¹past / present situations or habits: *We used to light candles in the bedrooms.*
>
> We use ²*hasn't / didn't* + ³*use to / used to* in the negative form.
>
> We can use the ⁴*Past Continuous / Past Simple* instead of *used to*: *A milkman **used to deliver** milk. A milkman **delivered** milk.*

**7** Rewrite the sentences using *used to* and the underlined verbs. Then check your answers with a partner.
1 My grandparents <u>didn't have</u> a telephone!
   **My grandparents didn't use to have a telephone.**
2 They <u>didn't have</u> a bathroom – they only <u>had</u> an outside toilet.
3 There <u>were</u> only three TV channels when my grandma was a child.
4 They <u>didn't have</u> a car so they <u>took</u> the bus.
5 My nan <u>wrote</u> a letter to my dad every week after he left home.

**8** Work with a partner. What do you know about your grandparents' or parents' childhoods? What things did they use to do and have? What things didn't they use to do or have?

**9** Read what four people say about their childhood. Match the questions with the people.
1 What did you use to do for fun?
2 Did your family use to do anything annoying?
3 What technology did you use to have in your living room?
4 What did you use to hate about your childhood home?

**ADAM** "Yes! My parents and all my aunts and uncles used to smoke in our living room! My eyes used to hurt and it made all our furniture and clothes smell bad!"

**CLARE** "It used to be freezing cold in winter because we had no central heating – only two fires downstairs. There used to be ice on the inside of my bedroom window when I woke up! It was awful!"

**ROY** "Well, we didn't use to have a TV, but we used to play a lot of games together, like card games. I also used to play the piano and we all read a lot of books."

**LISA** "We had a TV and video player … and we had a cassette player, but we didn't use to have a remote control for the TV! We had to get up and walk across the living room to change channels!"

**10** Look at the questions in exercise 9. How do we form questions with *used to*?

**11** 🔊 030 Listen to the sentences with *used to* and *didn't use to* and notice the pronunciation. Then listen, repeat and practise.
1 My eyes used to hurt.
2 It used to be freezing cold in winter.
3 We didn't use to have a TV.
4 We didn't use to have a remote control.

**12** Rewrite the questions using *used to*. Ask and answer them in pairs.

When you were a child …
1 What did you do for fun?
   **When you were a child, what did you use to do for fun?**
2 What did you have in your kitchen? What didn't you have?
3 What did you have in your living room? What didn't you have?
4 What did you like and dislike about your house? Why?

# 4B School days

> **Vocabulary:** School/Studying collocations
> **Grammar:** Modals: can, have to, must
> **Pronunciation:** Have to
> **Listening:** School rules

**1** Work with a partner. Discuss the questions.
1. How big was/is your school?
2. What do/did you like and dislike about your school? Think about the ideas in the box and your own ideas.

> homework   exams   rules

**2** Complete the school collocations with the verbs in the box.

> make   give   fail   ~~do~~   follow
> take   get   break   pass

*do* 
............
............ **homework**
............

............
............ **an exam**
............

............
............ **the rules**
............

**3** 🔊 031 Complete the sentences with the correct form of the verbs in exercise 2. Listen and check.

"Rosie's a good girl. She always ¹............ her homework. She ²............ all the school rules and she ³............ every exam!"

"I'm your form teacher for the year. Remember, I ⁴............ the rules! I also like to ⁵............ you a lot of homework – but that's only because I don't want any of you to ⁶............ the end-of-year exams!"

"My school is really strict. We ⁷............ a lot of homework and we have to ⁸............ exams every month! And anyone who ⁹............ the rules will be sent home!"

**4** Read the article about a school in Birmingham. Why are parents angry? Why did the school send Ryan home?

## Is this the strictest school ever?
### Parents criticize crazy new rules!

**Parents are angry about the new rules at Field School in Birmingham, UK.**

'The new head teacher started two months ago, and since then he's sent hundreds of kids home for breaking the rules! 'It's madness!' said Laura Baxter, mum of Ryan, 14. 'Yesterday, Ryan was sent home for looking at the clock in a lesson! They really <u>don't have to</u> be so strict!'

**So what are these new rules? Students told us they include the following:**

1. You <u>have to</u> walk to school or come by car. You <u>can't</u> cycle because bikes are too dangerous.
2. You <u>can't</u> wear make-up or jewellery, but you <u>can</u> wear a watch.
3. You <u>must</u> walk everywhere. You <u>can</u> only run in P.E. lessons.
4. You <u>have to</u> eat a carrot or an apple as a snack. You <u>can't</u> eat any unhealthy snacks.
5. You <u>mustn't</u> say, 'I don't know,' when someone asks you a question.
6. You <u>mustn't</u> high-five or hug anyone.
7. You <u>can't</u> look out of the window or look at the clock during lessons.
8. You <u>have to</u> go to the toilet in break times. You <u>can</u> only go during lessons 3 times a week.

**Headteacher, Mr Warren**

**5** Read the article again. Choose the correct words to complete the sentences.
1. Students *are / aren't* allowed to cycle to school.
2. You *are / aren't* allowed to run in P.E. lessons.
3. It *is / isn't* necessary for snacks to be healthy.
4. You *are / aren't* allowed to say, 'I don't know,' when someone asks you a question.
5. You *should / shouldn't* only go to the toilet during break times.

**6** Match the underlined modal verbs in the article to the meanings 1–4. Then read the grammar box to check your answers.
1. necessary: ................., .................
2. not necessary: .................
3. possible/allowed: .................
4. not allowed: ................., .................

> **GRAMMAR: Modals: can, have to, must**  ▶ PAGE 118
>
> We use *have to* and *must* to say that something is necessary: *You **have to** walk or come by car to school. You **must** walk everywhere.*
>
> The past form is *had to*.
>
> We use *can* and *can't* to say what is allowed or not allowed: *You **can** wear a watch. You **can't** wear make-up.*
>
> The past form is *could/couldn't*.
>
> Notice the different meanings of *don't have to* and *mustn't*: *You **mustn't** high-five anyone.* (= not allowed). *They **don't have to** be so strict.* (= not necessary).

**7** ▶ 032 Listen to these sentences with *have to* and notice the pronunciation. Then listen, repeat and practise.
1. They really don't have to be so strict.
2. You have to walk or drive to school.
3. You have to eat a carrot or an apple as a snack.

**8** Complete the sentences with the correct form of a modal verb and the verb in brackets. Use the prompts to help you. Sometimes more than one answer is possible.
1. *Can you take* mobile phones into school? (take) PRESENT – ALLOWED?
2. You .................. in the corridors between lessons. (run) PRESENT – NOT ALLOWED
3. I .................. an entrance exam to get into my school. (pass) PAST – NECESSARY
4. .................. your hand up before speaking? (put) PRESENT – NECESSARY?
5. .................. make-up when you were at school? (wear) PAST – ALLOWED?
6. When I was at school I .................. a school uniform. (wear) PAST – NOT NECESSARY
7. You .................. the correct school shoes. (wear) PRESENT – NECESSARY
8. You .................. any electronic toys into school. (bring) PRESENT – NOT ALLOWED

**9** Work with a partner. Look at the signs and make sentences using modal verbs.

1   2   3  4

*You can park here.*
*You don't have to …*

**10** ▶ 033 Listen to Katie and John discussing the school in Birmingham. Who agrees with the school rules? Who disagrees?

**11** ▶ 033 Listen again. Then work with a partner and answer the questions.
1. What rule does Katie want to know about?
2. Why does Katie disagree with the rules?
3. Why does John disagree with Katie?

**12** Work in small groups. Discuss the questions.
1. What do you think of the school rules in the article?
2. Do you agree with Katie or John about the school? Why?

**13** Answer the questions about your school. Then discuss your ideas in groups and use modal verbs where possible.
1. What was/is not allowed?
2. What was/is allowed?
3. What happened/happens if children broke/break the rules?

# 4C Childhood then and now

> ▶ **Reading:** Why childhood is better now
> ▶ **Vocabulary:** Synonyms
> ▶ **Listening:** Kids in the UK

1 When do you think was the best time to be a child? Do you think your childhood was better than your parents' childhood? Why? / Why not?

2 Journalist Tim Lott compared his childhood with his daughter's. Read the article quickly. What two things does he say never happened in his childhood?

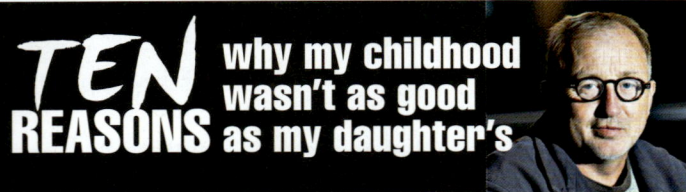

### My kids are at the centre of family life – I was on the edge of my parents' universe.

Louise, my daughter, asked me: "What was it like when you were a child, Daddy?" I told her that my childhood was much worse than hers.

Then she said: "But, Daddy, I read a news story that says British children are the most <u>miserable</u> in the western world."

"Oh," I said, "I always thought life was pretty good for you."

"Well, that isn't what this news story says," she replied. "Things were much better in the 1950s and 1960s when you were growing up."

I thought I might explain a few differences between my childhood and hers. But she turned away, and started playing with her Nintendo. So I'll <u>complete</u> the discussion here.

### My childhood compared with my children's:

1 **Holidays** They were <u>terrible</u>. We spent them in England. It was cold and wet and we stayed in Bed and Breakfasts where you had to get out of the building <u>straight</u> after breakfast. My children have been to far more <u>unusual</u> <u>locations</u>. Yes, we're quite rich, but almost everyone can afford a holiday abroad <u>these days</u>.

2 **Being bored** My children are never bored. They have iPods, mobile phones, PCs, games consoles, TV on demand, child-friendly free museums and exhibitions. OK, we're not poor, but even families on lower salaries can afford basic modern technology.

3 **Sleepovers** When did that happen? I never once slept at a friend's house overnight as a kid.

4 **Getting hit** Like most kids in my childhood, my parents hit me now and then. My children don't get hit. It's very <u>rare</u> <u>nowadays</u>.

3 Read the article again and answer the questions. Then check your answers with a partner.
1 Why was Louise surprised when her dad told her his childhood was awful compared with hers?
2 Why didn't Louise listen to her dad's list of reasons?
3 Why does Tim think it is easier for families to go on better holidays now?
4 What example does Tim give to show he was not at the centre of his parents' universe?
5 Why does Tim think the Children's Society report shows that children are happier nowadays?
6 What were two bad things about football in Tim's childhood?
7 Why was the food awful in Tim's childhood?

4 Match the underlined words in the article to the synonyms.
1 adjective – *bad* (x4): ................
2 adjective – *very sad*: ................
3 adjective – *doesn't happen very often*: ................
4 adjective – *strange*: ................
5 plural noun – *places*: ................
6 adverb – *now* (x2): ................
7 adverb – *immediately*: ................
8 verb – *finish*: ................

5 ▶ 035 Listen to a radio programme. What are the people discussing? Choose A, B or C.
A How to improve schools in the UK.
B Why parents in the UK work so hard.
C Why children in the UK are not happy.

Childhood

**5 Importance** I was not the centre of my parents' lives. I had to fit in with what they did. Sitting in the pub car park with a packet of crisps was as good as it got. My children are at the centre of family life.

**6 Happiness** A Children's Society report found that one in 11 young people aged between eight and 15 don't feel very happy in life. But that means 10 out of 11 are happy with their life!

**7 School** Children in Britain report higher levels of satisfaction with school than almost any other European country!

**8 Football** When I went to a football match I had to listen to <u>horrible</u>, racist shouting from frightening men. And that was just the footballers! Also, the football itself was a very low level compared with today.

**9 Food** It was <u>awful</u> – cooked too long in water – all of it. We never ate out. I went to my first restaurant on my 18th birthday.

**10 TV** It was terrible. Now it's good.

So what was life like in the "old days", Louise? It was <u>rubbish</u>!

▶ 034

**6** ▶ 035 Listen again and answer the questions.

1 What number was the UK on Unicef's list?
2 Which countries were at the top of the list?
3 What are parents doing or not doing that could make their children unhappy?
4 What are schools doing or not doing that could make their students unhappy?

**7** Work in groups. Discuss the questions.

1 Can you think of any other reasons why UK children might be unhappy?
2 How happy do you think children are in your country?
3 Do you think Tim's daughter is really having a better childhood than him? Why?
4 What can governments, schools and parents do to make sure children enjoy their childhood?

# 4D Life decisions

▶ **Speaking:** Giving and responding to advice
▶ **Writing:** A paragraph about a big decision; Structuring a paragraph; Reasons and results

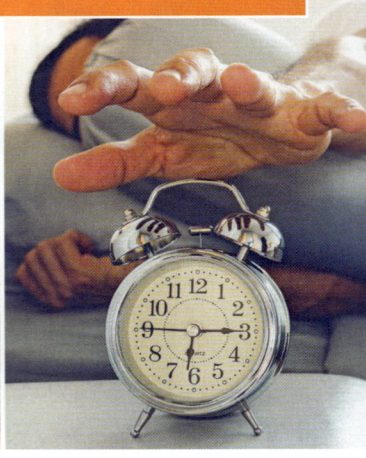

## Speaking

**1** Look at the life changes people often want to make. Which changes have you tried to make? Which do you want to make in the future?

- read more
- save money
- get more sleep
- exercise more
- learn a new skill
- start a new hobby
- spend more time with family/friends
- make new friends

**2** 🔊 036 Listen to three conversations. Which changes in exercise 1 does each person want to make?

Emma ........................................................
Simon ........................................................
Robert ........................................................

**3** 🔊 036 Complete the phrases in the *Key Language* box with words in the box. Then listen again and check.

> better   should   doing   were   don't   worth

### KEY LANGUAGE Giving advice

1 If I ................ you, I would turn off all screens an hour or two before bed.
2 It's probably ................ eating something healthier!
3 It's much ................ to try to meet people with similar interests.
4 I think you ................ start using one of those dating apps.
5 Why ................ you go for a run?
6 How about ................ some weights at home?

**4** Work with a partner. Which of the advice in exercise 3 do you agree with? What other advice would you give to Emma, Simon and Robert?

**5** 🔊 037 Listen and complete the phrases in the *Key Language* box. Practise saying them with a partner.

### KEY LANGUAGE Responding to advice

1 Really? I'm not ................ about that.
2 I ................ you're right.
3 No, I haven't. That's a ................ idea!
4 Seriously? I don't ................ so.
5 ................, but I really don't enjoy running.
6 That's so ................! I could fit that in easily.

**6** Add the phrases from the *Key Language* box to the correct column.

| I agree strongly | I agree a bit | I disagree |
|---|---|---|
| That's a great idea! | | |

## YOUR TURN

**7** Work with a partner. Student A turn to page 126. Student B turn to page 128.

**8** Think of a real or imaginary problem that you have. Then work with a partner and take turns to do the following.
1 Tell your partner about your problem.
2 Give and respond to advice.

# Writing

**1** Work with a partner. Look at the list of possible decisions in life. Answer the questions.

- a university subject
- a career
- a career change
- where to live
- who to go on a date with
- to get married or not
- to have children or not

1 What big decisions have you made? Were they good decisions?
2 Which decisions do you think you'll make in the next five years? What will help you make the right decisions?

**2** Put the sentences in the correct order to make two paragraphs about big decisions.

Paragraph 1
a) A few years ago, it was really obvious a colleague at work liked me and one day he asked me out on a date. ......1......
b) I'm so happy I did because now we're happily married with two amazing children. ..........
c) However, we had a lot of fun at an office party, so when he asked me out again I said yes. ..........
d) At first, I said no because I didn't think it was right to date someone I worked with. ..........

Paragraph 2
a) However, after some help from my parents I finally did it and I know that starting my own business was a brilliant idea because now I love going to work. ..........
b) I used to have a well-paid job in a bank, but I didn't like the work and the hours were long, so I left. ..........
c) One of the best decisions I ever made was to quit my last job. ..........
d) After leaving the bank I wanted to start my own business but I didn't at first, because I was worried about how hard it would be. ..........

**3** Match the sentences in each paragraph in exercise 2 to the types of sentences below.
1 Topic sentence – the main idea of the paragraph.
2 Supporting sentences – sentences that give further details, examples or reasons.
3 The concluding sentence – the sentence that summarizes what the paragraph was about.

**4** Find the reason and the result in each sentence.
1 I didn't start my own business because I was worried about how hard it would be.
2 We had a lot of fun at the party, so I said yes.

**Childhood**

**5** Complete the *Key Language* box with *because* and *so*.

> **KEY LANGUAGE** Reasons and results
>
> 1 We use .................... to introduce a reason.
> 2 We use .................... to introduce a result.

**6** Join the sentences together in two different ways using *so* and *because*.
1 I didn't like my job. I left the company.
   *I left the company because I didn't like my job.*
   *I didn't like my job so I left the company.*
2 She changed her course. It was boring.
3 I moved to a big city. There were more job opportunities.
4 We sold our car. We wanted to do something for the environment.
5 I started running. I lost lots of weight.
6 We wanted our children to see the world. We took them out of school and travelled for a year.

## YOUR TURN

**7** Think about a big decision you have made in your life. Answer the questions and make notes. Then write a paragraph about your decision.
1 What was the decision?
2 What was the reason for the decision?
3 What were you doing before?
4 What was the result of the decision?

**8** Swap your paragraph with a partner. Discuss the questions.
- Are the sentences in a logical order?
- Has language for reasons and results been included?
- Do you think your partner made the right decision? Why? / Why not?

# Video 2: The good old days

## 2 The good old days

1 Work with a partner and discuss the questions.
  1 What decade did you grow up in?
  2 How was this decade different to the decades your parents and grandparents grew up in?
  3 What decades in the past do you think were most or least fun to grow up in? Why?

2 Read the article and answer the questions.
  **1950s**
  1 What day did people usually have a bath?
  2 What kinds of people had a car?
  3 How often did people go to restaurants in the 1950s?
  4 What snack did people get once a week?
  5 How long was the typical family holiday?

  **1970s**
  6 What kinds of takeaway food did people start to eat?
  7 What did parents do if the teacher hit their child?
  8 Why did people work three days a week?
  9 What changed for women during the 1970s?
  10 What happened in 1976?

3 Watch the video in which people talk about their childhood. Complete the sentences with one or two words.
  1 Chris spent the summer in the ............... with his ............... . They would ride ............... and ............... in ponds.
  2 Diane liked living in ............... and especially liked ............... . She also enjoyed being part of a large ............... and having lots of people in their home.
  3 Lauren played bulldog and a lot of ............... as a child.
  4 Simon felt ............... as a child.
  5 James moved a lot and lived in ............... and ............... . He also moved around Britain a lot.

## 5 SIGNS YOU GREW UP IN THE...

Depending on where you grew up, there are some clear signs as to what decade you grew up in. If you were in the UK, these are some of the things that would show the decade you grew up in.

### 1950s

- You used to have a weekly bath. No one had a shower and you only ever had a bath on a Sunday before you went back to school.
- There was no traffic. Well, not exactly no traffic, but only very wealthy people had a car. Everyone walked or cycled everywhere.
- You used to eat home-cooked food every day. Processed food didn't really exist. People ate out maybe once a year and the only takeaway was fish and chips.
- You hardly ever had any snacks or treats. If you were lucky, you might get one piece of chocolate a week. You ate your meals and had nothing between them.
- You had ice cream once a year. The family holiday was a day trip to the coast. As a special treat you were allowed an ice cream.

### 1970s

- People ate less fresh food. The sound of the microwave pinging was a common sign dinner was ready. You ate at least one takeaway a week. If your family was adventurous, this was an Indian or Chinese takeaway.
- Your teachers were allowed to hit you. Any bad behaviour in school meant the teacher would probably hit you. Rather than be angry at the teacher hitting you, your parents probably hit you again for behaving badly.
- Your parents only worked three days a week. The coal miners in the UK were often on strike for better pay. In 1974, to deal with the electricity shortage, the government limited people to working three days a week for a period of three months.
- There were a lot of stay-at-home mums. At the start of the decade, 45% of mums stayed at home. By the end of the decade, it was just 25%.
- You experienced a drought. 1976 was the driest year in over 200 years. Many water supplies to homes were turned off and people had to get water from pumps in the street.

**4** Watch the second part of the video in which people talk about things they didn't like about their childhood. Answer the questions.
1. What didn't Chris like doing with his family?
2. What didn't Cathy like about the TV?
3. What was difficult for James in his childhood?

**5** Watch the last part of the video in which people discuss whether children today have an easier or harder time. Write the name of each person in the correct column.

Diane   James   Joanne   Lauren   Louis
Michelle   Shana   Simon

| An easier time | A harder time | Both easier and harder |
|---|---|---|
|  |  |  |
|  |  |  |

**6** Which person from exercise 5 talks about each of these topics? Watch the video from exercise 5 again and check your answers.

freedom   opportunities   school pressure
being protected   technology   social media

**7** Work with a partner and discuss the questions.
1. What did you like about your childhood?
2. What didn't you like about your childhood?
3. Do you think life is easier for children today? Why? / Why not?

# Review

**LESSON 3A** List 5 benefits you get from work.

**LESSON 3A** Write 3 sentences using quantity words to describe your work life.

**LESSON 3B** Write 3 sentences you could put on your CV to describe your work experience.

**LESSON 3B** Write 3 sentences using *something / anything / nothing*, etc. about your plans for this weekend.

**LESSON 3C** Write down 3 things you do online.

**LESSON 3D** Write about 5 things you like and dislike doing.

**LESSON 3D** Write a short email applying for a job as a tour guide.

**LESSON 4A** List 5 things you find in a kitchen.

**LESSON 4A** Write 3 sentences about things you used to do as a child.

**LESSON 4B** Write 3 sentences about rules in your work or college.

**LESSON 4B** Write 3 verbs that collocate with the word *exam*.

**LESSON 4C** Write 3 synonyms of the adjective *bad*.

**LESSON 4D** List one phrase for agreeing, one for disagreeing and one for agreeing a bit.

**LESSON 4D** Write 2 sentences showing reasons and results using *so* and *because*.

# 5 Health

- **Vocabulary:** Health and fitness: collocations and phrasal verbs
- **Grammar:** Will for decisions, offers and promises
- **Reading:** Three health plans
- **Listening:** Healthy habits

## 5A Fit and healthy

1. Work in small groups. Discuss the statements. Do you agree or disagree with them? Why?

   **MODERN LIFESTYLES ARE UNHEALTHY**

   **EXERCISE IS MORE IMPORTANT FOR YOUR HEALTH THAN DIET**

   **WE SHOULD NEVER EAT PROCESSED FOOD AND DRINKS, LIKE CAKES, BURGERS, COLA, ETC.**

2. Read the article about three plans to improve your health. Which plan …
   1. means no white bread?
   2. means a late breakfast?
   3. means no meat?

3. Match the underlined collocations and phrasal verbs in the article to the definitions.
   1. starting to do something regularly
   2. become healthy and strong
   3. become heavier
   4. reduce the amount of something
   5. stop eating something completely
   6. uses fat in your body for energy
   7. stop doing or using something
   8. become lighter

## THREE PLANS TO IMPROVE YOUR HEALTH

Modern lifestyles are not always healthy. We spend hours looking at screens, and we don't always have enough time to eat well. Exercise can help us <u>get fit</u>, but changing the way we eat can improve our health faster than <u>taking up</u> a new sport. Here are three plans that could help you get healthy.

**GOING VEGAN**
This is a huge trend and it's never been easier to become vegan. It can mean big changes though, because you have to <u>cut out</u> all animal products, not just meat – so that means no cheese or eggs! Fans of vegan diets say that you will have more energy and your skin will look better. We also know that eating plant-based food is better for the environment and it's better for your heart, too.

**CLEAN EATING**
Modern food production means a lot of the food we buy today is full of added sugar. Eating this kind of food everyday can make us <u>put on weight</u> and feel unhealthy. Clean eating means eating food that is as close to its natural form as possible. So this means lots of fresh fruit and vegetables, but meat and fish are also allowed. Cutting out processed foods that are full of added sugar and chemicals, will help you feel healthier and happier. It could also help you <u>lose weight</u> if you want to be lighter.

**16:8**
Did you know that giving your body a break from food can help you sleep better and improve brain function? The 16:8 fasting plan is simple – you don't have to <u>give up</u> any foods, but in a 24-hour period, you can only eat during eight of those hours. So if you finish eating at 6pm, you can't eat again until 10 a.m. the next day. During the 16-hour fast, your body doesn't have to deal with any food in your stomach, so you sleep better and your body <u>burns fat</u>. It's also a good way to <u>cut down on</u> the amount of sugar you eat. This reduces your blood sugar highs and lows – which means you can concentrate better during the day.

Health

**4** Work with a partner. Take turns to say sentences using vocabulary from exercise 3 and the prompts below.
1 … can help you get fit / lose weight / burn fat.
2 … can make you put on weight.
3 I want to cut down on / cut out / give up / take up …

> Training for a 5k race can help you get fit.

> I agree. It can also help you lose weight.

**5** 039 Listen to Larissa and Thomas talking about their health. Answer the questions.
1 What plan will Thomas follow?
2 What plan does Larissa decide to follow?
3 What exercise do they agree to do together?

**6** 039 Work with a partner. Who said these sentences? Write L (Larissa) or T (Thomas). Listen again and check.
1 I'll never give up meat.
2 I'll cook for you.
3 I'll show you this article on my phone.
4 I think I'll try it.
5 I think I'll follow that plan.
6 I won't go swimming with you … but I'll go running with you.
7 I'll come to your house at 7 a.m.
8 I promise I'll run slowly at first.
9 I'll cancel our table at Pizza Express …

**7** Choose the correct words to complete the rules in the grammar box.

---
**GRAMMAR: Will**  ▶ PAGE 119

We can use will + infinitive (without to) for:
- decisions made ¹in the past / at the time of speaking: I think **I'll try** it.
- ²instructions / offers: **I'll cook** for you.
- promises: I promise **I'll run** slowly at first.

The negative of will is ³won't / willn't.

---

**8** Complete the conversations with will/won't and the verbs in the box.

| ask | help | come | stop | have | give |

1 **A:** Dad, you have to do something about your health!
   **B:** Look, I ............... smoking in the New Year, I promise.
2 **A:** I booked a taxi to the station, but it's still not here!
   **B:** Don't worry, I ............... you a lift.
3 **A:** Emma never comes out with us, does she?
   **B:** No, never! I ............... her again. There's no point!
4 **A:** What would you like to order?
   **B:** Oh, I really don't know! Erm, OK, I ............... the chicken burger.
5 **A:** You want me to run ten kilometres? It's impossible!
   **B:** I'm a fitness trainer – this is my job! I ............... you get fit and then it'll be easy!
6 **A:** We're going out for drinks later. Would you like to come?
   **B:** Er … look, thanks for the offer, but I ............... this time. I'm trying to save money.

**9** 040 Listen and check. Then practise the conversations with a partner.

**10** How can you improve your health? Think about these ideas and make notes.

- diet and food
- bad habits to stop
- exercise
- good habits to start

**11** Work with a partner. Take turns to tell each other your ideas in exercise 10. Offer or promise to help your partner.

> I think I'll go vegan, so I'll cut out meat, fish, eggs and milk products.

> Good idea. I'll help you plan some meals and I'll take you shopping.

# 5B Food in the future

> - **Vocabulary:** Word families
> - **Grammar:** Future forms: will, be going to, Present Continuous
> - **Pronunciation:** Word stress
> - **Reading:** Can we feed the world?

1 Work with a partner. Why do some people in the world not have enough to eat? Discuss the ideas in the box and your own ideas.

> politics   food waste   meat production   population

2 Look at the photos and read the introduction to the article. What ideas do you think the article will mention? Read it and check.

## CAN WE FEED THE WORLD?

One in nine people in the world do not have enough food for a healthy active life! That's crazy, especially when we know that many people throw food away every day! Will we see improvements to this situation? Unfortunately, I don't think so, and here's why:

**Population:** The population of the world is going to grow. There will be 1.3 billion extra people to feed by 2050 and we simply cannot produce enough food!

**Meat production:** We give a lot of food and water to animals, rather than eating and drinking it ourselves. Meat production also increases $CO_2$ levels, which causes climate change. But people still want to eat meat and are happy to pay for it, so farmers are going to continue producing it until this changes.

**Climate:** Scientific research shows that there is going to be an increase in temperatures of at least 1.5°C by 2050. And we know this is going to create big problems for food production. Flooding and heatwaves both lead to damaged plants in the fields.

**WE MUST ACT NOW TO MAKE SURE WE CAN FEED THE WORLD, BOTH TODAY AND IN THE FUTURE.**

3 Read the article and answer the questions.
  1 What is going to happen to the global population?
  2 What does meat production use? What does it increase?
  3 The writer talks about two problems caused by climate change. What are they?

4 Work with a partner. Complete the table with words from the article.

| VERB | NOUN |
| --- | --- |
| improve | .................. |
| populate | .................. |
| .................. | growth |
| produce | .................. |
| research | .................. |
| increase | .................. |
| .................. | creation |
| .................. | action |

5 Practise saying the words in exercise 4. Which syllables do you think are stressed?

im**prove**

6 ▶ 041 Listen and check. Then listen again, repeat and practise.

7 Complete the sentences with the correct form of words from exercise 4. Then work in groups and discuss the questions.
  1 There are 66 million people in the UK. What's the p.................. of your country?
  2 What kind of products does your country p..................?
  3 How can your government i.................. the environment in your country?
  4 What changes can lead to the c.................. of new jobs in a city?
  5 Will the population i.................. or decrease in your country in the next 10 years?

44

# Health

**8** 🔊 042 Listen to some comments from people who read the article. Match the people to what they plan to change.

1 Prisha    a their garden
2 Rob    b nothing
3 Jürgen    c their diet
4 Nicole    d their holiday plans
5 Ed    e their house

**9** 🔊 042 Use phrases a–l to complete the sentences the five people say. Then listen again and check.

a I'll go
b I'm going to stop
c are going to go
d I'm going to buy
e is coming
f I'm going to become
g we're driving
h will help
i we're going to grow
j it's going to be
k we'll probably save
l I'm not going to do

**PRISHA**
Look at the statistics on world population – ¹_____ impossible to feed everyone! That's why ²_____ a vegan.

**ROB**
We have to stop climate change and I want to help with that! ³_____ solar panels for our roof. In fact, a salesman ⁴_____ to my house next week to arrange it.

**JÜRGEN**
⁵_____ flying. ⁶_____ to our holiday home in Italy this summer – no planes this time.

**NICOLE**
⁷_____ fruit and vegetables in our garden so we won't need to buy so much food shipped from other countries. So ⁸_____ money as well because we know food prices ⁹_____ up. In fact, I think ¹⁰_____ to the garden centre right now to buy some seeds.

**ED**
¹¹_____ anything. I don't think all these small decisions ¹²_____.

**10** Read the grammar box. Match the answers in exercise 9 with rules 1–5.

**GRAMMAR: Future forms** ▶ PAGE 119

*will* and *be going to* for predictions

1 We can use *will* to make predictions about the future: *We'll probably save money*.
2 When we have more evidence for our prediction, we use *be going to*, not *will*: *Look at the statistics … (EVIDENCE) – it's going to be impossible to feed everyone!* (PREDICTION)

*be going to* for intentions

3 We can also use *be going to* to talk about our plans or intentions for the future: *I'm going to stop flying*.

Present Continuous for future arrangements

4 We can use the Present Continuous to talk about arrangements and appointments in the future: *A salesman is coming to my house next week*.

*will* for spontaneous decisions

5 Remember, we also use *will* for decisions about the future, made as you are speaking.

**11** Choose the correct verb forms to complete the sentences.

1 I *'ll meet* / *'m meeting* my teacher at 10 a.m.
2 Look at those black clouds! It *will* / *'s going to* rain.
3 What can I have for breakfast? … Oh, I know, I *'ll* / *'m going to* have eggs.
4 In the future I think some humans *are living* / *will live* on the moon.
5 I've thought about it carefully and I've decided I'm *going to* / *'ll* quit my job.
6 We're playing against a great team tomorrow, so we probably *aren't winning* / *won't win*.

**12** Work with a partner. What do you think people will eat in the future? Give reasons for your opinions.

*We're not going to have enough … because*
*I think we'll eat more/less … because*

**13** Work in small groups. Discuss:

1 your plans and intentions for the future
   *I'm going to travel around India after university.*
2 an arrangement or appointment that you have
3 a prediction about young people, your country, or your own future

45

## 5C Are we healthier or unhealthier now?

▶ Reading: *Modern-day health problems*
▶ Vocabulary: *Nouns for diet and illness*

1. Do you agree or disagree with the quote? Why?
   "We are now living healthier lives than ever before."

2. Read the introduction to the article. Why *should* we be healthy now?

3. Work in two groups. Group A: read text A. Group B: read text B. Answer your questions.

   **Group A**
   1. What percentage of the food that UK families buy nowadays is 'ultra-processed'?
   2. What are the reasons for putting additives into food?
   3. Why do our bodies like processed foods?
   4. What problems can we have if we eat too much processed food?

   **Group B**
   5. How many people use the internet to find out what is wrong with them?
   6. How might using Dr Google make you worry?
   7. Why should we not always trust an online diagnosis?
   8. What happened to the patient whose doctor didn't agree with Dr Google, but was wrong?

4. Work with a partner from the other group. Take turns to tell each other about your text.

5. Work with a partner. Match the underlined nouns in the texts to the definitions.
   1. natural chemicals in food and drink that we need to be healthy
   2. when a doctor tells you what is wrong with you
   3. the number of these show how much energy you are getting from food
   4. feelings or signs that tell you that you have an illness
   5. chemicals added to food to make it last longer or look better
   6. a worried feeling that makes it difficult for you to sleep or work
   7. something in foods like meat, fish and eggs that we need in order to to grow and be healthy
   8. an opinion on the best thing to do

6. Work in small groups and discuss the questions.
   1. In a normal day, how much of the food that you eat is processed?
   2. What can parents, schools and governments do to help young people eat less processed food?
   3. Have you or someone you know ever researched symptoms online? If so, was it a good or bad experience? Why?
   4. Do you think online symptom-checkers save money for the health system? Why? / Why not?

## MODERN-DAY health problems

In the developed world we're living longer than ever before. We have clean water, warm homes, enough food to eat and access to healthcare when we need it. So why are so many of us still unhealthy – in both body and mind? Here are two ways the modern world has created brand-new health problems.

Health

**TEXT A**

# A love of highly-processed foods

Did you know that half of all the food that UK families buy today is 'ultra-processed'? This means food that is made in a factory where lots of different chemicals are added to it. These extra ingredients are known as additives and they are often not very good for us.

## Why use additives?

Adding extra salt, sugar, fats, or chemicals to food can help it stay fresh for longer. This means that it will be cheaper than fresh food because shops can store it for longer. Additives are also used to improve how food looks and tastes so that people are more likely to buy it, enjoy it, and then buy more of it!

## Why do we love processed food?

Most processed food has added sugar and fat – and our bodies are designed to like these foods. Biologically, our bodies would like us to get as many calories as we can, as quickly as we can. Processed foods are perfect for this – they're high in calories, they're easy to eat, and the additives make them taste good too. Plus, they're usually cheaper than fresh food, and they're easy to prepare – which is helpful for people with busy modern lives.

## What changes should we make?

The problem with processed food is that it doesn't have as many nutrients per 100g as natural, unprocessed foods. Our body needs a balance of nutrients – we need proteins from meat, fish, eggs, beans, etc., we need vitamins and minerals, and we need good quality carbohydrates and fats. If we eat too much processed food, we won't get the nutrients that we need and with all the added sugar, fat and salt, we are more likely to put on weight and suffer from heart disease, diabetes or even cancer. So next time you're in the supermarket, try to only buy food that has fewer than 10 ingredients … and then the time after that, buy food with fewer than 5 ingredients. Before long, you'll be able to cut processed food out of your diet entirely!

**TEXT B**

# Doctor Google

Have you ever felt ill and typed your symptoms into Google? As many as one in five people now look for a diagnosis online. I'm sure we've all done it at some time or other, and why not? It's much quicker than making an appointment with your doctor. So, what's the problem?

## Are you worrying too much?

The problem is health anxiety. This happens when you begin to worry too much about any symptoms you have and you start to believe you have a serious illness. So, you wake up with a headache and your eye hurts, you Google it, and an online symptom-checker says you might have a terrible illness! Then you research the illness and read about other symptoms … and suddenly you start to feel those symptoms too! The information can be really frightening. And worrying about it can take over your life!

## Can you trust an online diagnosis?

The chances of online symptom-checkers diagnosing incorrectly are high. A recent study found that the internet only gave the correct diagnosis 34% of the time, compared with 72% for doctors who saw their patient face-to-face. And what if the information we read tells us to take a medicine that will make us feel worse? It could even be dangerous. It's also true that patients using Dr Google ask their doctor for more expensive hospital tests – and these tests are often completely unnecessary.

## Is it always wrong to use Dr Google?

But what about when Dr Google is right? There are examples where a patient has self-diagnosed online, their doctor has disagreed, the patient lives with the symptoms for many months before finally their doctor decides the patient was right! So it can in fact be useful to use Dr Google, but if you think you have a health problem, it's always best to see a real-life doctor and get their advice.

043

# 5D Getting better

▶ **Speaking:** Talking about health and illness
▶ **Pronunciation:** Pronouncing difficult words
▶ **Writing:** A New Year plan; Connecting contrasting ideas

## Speaking

1. Work with a partner. Match the photos to the health problems.
   1. He feels sick/nauseous.
   2. He has a sore throat.
   3. He has a headache.
   4. He has diarrhoea.
   5. He has a cold.
   6. He has a rash.
   7. He has a fever/high temperature.
   8. He has a stomach ache.

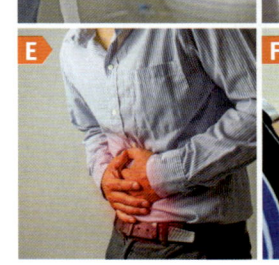

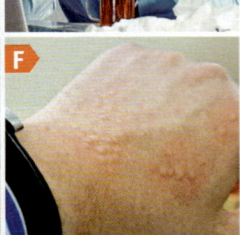

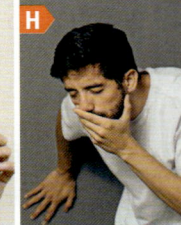

2. ▶044 Listen to four people talking to a doctor. Complete the chart with each person's symptoms and illness.

   **Symptoms**

   > a stomach ache   being sick
   > a rash   a cough   ~~a sore throat~~   a headache

   **Illness**

   > flu   food poisoning   an allergy   ~~a bad cold~~

   | | Symptoms | Illness |
   |---|---|---|
   | 1 | _a sore throat_ , ............ sneezing | _a bad cold_ |
   | 2 | ............, diarrhoea, ............ | ............ |
   | 3 | a fever, ............, feel sick | ............ |
   | 4 | ............ | ............ |

3. ▶044 Listen again and complete phrases in the *Key Language* box.

   ### KEY LANGUAGE Talking about health and illness

   1. Come in. So, how can I ............ you today?
   2. I ............ very well. I ............ a sore throat, a cough and I ............ sneezing.
   3. OK, ............ a bad cold so ............ some paracetamol and …
   4. I ............ a really bad stomach ache and diarrhoea … and I ............ sick.
   5. Is anyone else ............ in your family?
   6. Well, it ............ like food poisoning.
   7. What ............ to be the problem?
   8. I ............ terrible! I ............ a fever, a headache and I ............ a bit sick.
   9. I've got a rash on my arms. It's really ............ .
   10. Take this ............ and it should get ............ .

4. Look at the phrases in the *Key Language* box again. Which are for …?
   a. finding out what's wrong
   b. describing what's wrong
   c. giving a diagnosis or advice

5. Work with a partner. Do you know how to say these words? The spelling doesn't help!

   > cough   diarrhoea   stomach   fever
   > temperature   headache

6. ▶045 Listen, check and repeat.

7. Turn to p142 and practise the conversations in audio 044.

## YOUR TURN

8. Work with a partner. Student A turn to page 126. Student B turn to page 128.

9. Work in small groups. Think of a time when either you, someone you know or your pet was ill. Tell your group about it.
   1. What were the symptoms?
   2. Did you/they go to the doctor's/vet's?
   3. What was wrong?
   4. Did you/they take any medicine?
   5. How long did it take to feel better?

## Writing

**1** Work with a partner. Discuss the questions.
1. Do you make New Year plans or resolutions?
2. What could you do next year to improve your life?

**2** These sentences all have the same meaning. Underline the differences you can see.
1. Last year was great, but I hope next year will be even better!
2. Last year was great. However, I hope next year will be even better!
3. Although last year was great, I hope next year will be even better!

**3** Work with a partner. Look at the sentences in exercise 2 again. Then complete the rules in the *Key Language* box with *but*, *although* and *however*.

> **KEY LANGUAGE** Connecting contrasting ideas
>
> We can use *but*, *although* and *however* to contrast two different ideas.
> 1. .................. always needs a comma after it.
> 2. .................. and .................. can start a sentence.
> 3. .................. and .................. go between the two different ideas.
> 4. .................. goes before the two ideas.

**4** Join the contrasting ideas in different ways using *but*, *although* and *however*.
1. I knew I was unfit. I didn't want to join a gym.
   *I knew I was unfit, but I didn't want to join a gym.*
   *Although I knew I was unfit, I didn't want to join a gym.*
   *I knew I was unfit. However, I didn't want to join a gym.*
2. I went to see the doctor. She didn't know what was wrong with me.
3. I hate exercise. I go running three times a week to stay fit.
4. I know sugar is bad for me. I can't give it up.

### Health

**5** Read Tara's New Year plan. Choose the correct words to complete it. What future verb form does she use to talk about her plans?

> **My NEW Year plan**
>
> Last year started badly ¹*because / so* I had flu for the first two weeks of the year. Luckily, work was good ²*because / but* we were so busy that I stayed in the office until 8 p.m. most days! ³*However, / Although* I sat in front of a computer all day at work, I always spent the rest of my evening at home online! Things have to change! So here are my plans:
>
> - I'm going to spend much less time online. ⁴*So / However*, I won't stop completely because social media helps me keep in touch with old friends.
> - I'm going to reduce my working week to four days. I'm going to spend that extra day doing exercise ⁵*although / because* I want to get fit. ⁶*But / And* I'm going to leave the office at 6 p.m. every work day.
> - I want to see the Grand Canyon, ⁷*because / so* I'm going to book a holiday to America.
> - ⁸*But / Although* I really want to help the environment, I can't give up my car because I need it for work, ⁹*because / so* I'm going to stop eating meat instead.

**6** Work with a partner. Would you like to do the same as Tara? Why? / Why not?

### YOUR TURN

**7** Think back to your answers in exercise 1. Then write your New Year plan. Use words from the Key Language box where possible.

**8** Swap New Year plans with a partner. Suggest ways to help your partner achieve their goals.

# 6 City Life

▶ **Vocabulary:** Describing towns and cities
▶ **Grammar:** Comparatives
▶ **Listening:** Comparing places

## 6A Calm or crowded?

**1** Work with a partner. Ask and answer the questions.
1. What do you like about where you live?
2. What's your favourite place to go on holiday? What do you like about it?
3. Imagine you could live in a small, quiet village or a large, busy city. Which would you choose and why?

**2** Read the texts about Walberswick and Bristol. Match the sentences to the places.
1. This place is full of things to do in the evening. ............
2. This place is great for creative people. ............
3. This place is great for people who love the countryside. ............
4. A lot of creative people were born here. ............

**3** Match the underlined adjectives in the texts to the definitions.
1. ............ from a long time ago
2. ............ peaceful and quiet
3. ............ attractive and easy to like
4. ............ beautiful and making you think of love
5. ............ relating to traditions and people's way of life
6. ............ interesting and exciting
7. ............ very exciting to look at
8. ............ making you feel worried or nervous

### A Walberswick

Set on the Suffolk coast in the East of England is the <u>charming</u> village of Walberswick. The village sits on the banks of the river Blyth and has a long, sandy beach on the <u>calm</u>, but cold North Sea. It is ideal for a peaceful <u>romantic</u> break. Nearby is a pretty nature reserve, ideal for a relaxing walk in the country. The beautiful village attracts artists and people from the film and media industry who want to escape the <u>stressful</u> life of large cities.

### B Bristol

Located in the South West of England, Bristol is a <u>lively</u> city with a population of around half a million people. Bristol is an <u>ancient</u> city with a strong <u>cultural</u> history and is full of <u>spectacular</u> buildings. Many famous poets, artists and musicians were born here or lived here, including the famous street artist, Banksy. The city is also well-known for its music scene and excellent nightlife.

City Life

**4** Use the adjectives to tell your partner about a place you know.

**5** ▶047 Listen to Amy having a conversation about visiting her friend Tom in Walberswick. Tick the things she liked about Walberswick.

The local community ☐
The local facilities ☐
Walking in the countryside ☐
Relaxing on the beach ☐

**6** ▶048 Listen to Tom having a conversation about visiting Amy. Tick the things he liked about Bristol.

The location of all the things to do ☐
How peaceful and relaxing it was ☐
The street art and things to do in the evening ☐
The culture and the historic sites ☐

**7** ▶049 Complete the sentences with the words and phrases in the box. Listen and check.

| as convenient as   as relaxing as |
| calmer   livelier   simpler |

1 It isn't ............... living in a big city.
2 I'd much rather live somewhere ............... .
3 It wasn't ............... I wanted.
4 I just prefer somewhere ............... with a ............... way of life.

**8** Read the grammar box and complete the rule.

**GRAMMAR: Comparatives**  ▶PAGE 120

We use comparatives when we compare two things.

To make a comparative, add ............... to one syllable adjectives: *calm* → *calmer than*

Add *-r* to adjectives ending in *e*: *simple* → *simpler than*

For one syllable words ending in a vowel + consonant, double the final consonant: *hot* → *hotter than*

For two syllable adjectives ending in *-y* change the *y* to *i* and add *–er*: *lively* → *livelier than*

For other two syllable adjectives put *more* before the adjective: *more romantic than*

*Not as* + adjective + *as* shows that two things are not equal: *not as calm as*

Some adjectives are irregular: *good* → *better than* / *bad* → *worse than*

**9** Complete the sentences with the correct comparative form of the adjective in brackets.
1 Berlin has a ............... (lively) nightlife than Hamburg.
2 Cambridge isn't ............... (charming) as Oxford.
3 It's beautiful here, but the views from the other side of the river are ............... (spectacular) than from here.
4 Life in a big city is ............... (good) than life in a small town.
5 Bristol is ............... (close) to the coast than my town.
6 Life is ............... (simple) in a small village, but it isn't ............... (convenient) as living in a town or city.
7 It's ............... (stressful) living here, but there's more to do.
8 This place is big and cold! The last holiday house we rented was ............... (cosy) than this one!

**10** Work in small groups. Who do you think lives in the better place, Amy or Tom? Why?
*I prefer where Tom / Amy lives because ...*

**11** Look at the pictures of Benidorm and Villajoyosa. Work with a partner:
• Which place is better for a holiday? Why?
• Compare two places that you know. Tell your partner about them.

Benidorm

Villajoyosa

## 6B The best city in the world

> - **Vocabulary:** Recommending places
> - **Grammar:** Superlatives
> - **Reading:** Vienna

**1** Look at the top ten cities to live in. What do you know about these cities?

1 **VIENNA**, Austria
2 **MELBOURNE**, Australia
3 **OSAKA**, Japan
4 **CALGARY**, Canada
5 **SYDNEY**, Australia
6 **VANCOUVER**, Canada
7 **TORONTO**, Canada
8 **TOKYO**, Japan
9 **COPENHAGEN**, Denmark
10 **ADELAIDE**, Australia

**2** Read the article and match a heading to each section.

Drink here   Shop here   See this   Walk here   Stay here   Try this

**3** Which things in the text would you like to do? Why?

# Make VIENNA your next CITY break

Vienna is frequently voted one of the best cities in the world to live in, but many more tourists go to Paris, London and Barcelona. However, for a great weekend away Vienna is hard to beat.

**A** ...........................
Hotel Am Stephansplatz is in the heart of the city and a perfect base to go shopping, sightseeing and use public transport. Many of the major sights such as Mozart House, Hofburg Palace and the State Opera are within walking distance of the hotel. It is also good value for money for such a central hotel. However, it isn't the quietest place I have ever stayed in, as it is on one of the busiest squares in Vienna. For a quieter location, try the Hilton Vienna Danube Waterfront on the banks of the Danube, the second longest river in Europe.

**B** ...........................
From the hotel, there are lots of exciting places to explore on foot. Across the road from the hotel is Stephansdom cathedral. A ten-minute-walk away is Der Graben, one of the most famous and oldest streets in Vienna. Within easy reach of the street is Ankerhaus, the home of the architect Otto Wagner. Finally, make your way to Petersplatz to see the beautiful Peterskirche.

**C** ...........................
Vienna is home to the Kunsthistorisches Museum, one of Europe's best kept secrets. It is as good as the Louvre in Paris, but gets only a tenth of the visitors. Or go to the Belvedere Palace on the edge of the city centre to see an amazing collection of paintings by the artist Klimt.

**D** ...........................
Vienna is one of the easiest cities to walk around, but why not sit back and enjoy the views as the tram takes you through the historic centre?

**E** ...........................
The historic old town is well-known for small independent and local shops. Don't miss Meinl am Graben – probably the best place to buy local fine foods.

**F** ...........................
The rooftop bar of Hotel Lamee is the ideal place to relax with a drink and enjoy magnificent views of the city centre. Stephansdom can clearly be seen just across the road.

**City Life**

**4** Complete the sentences with the underlined phrases in the article.
1. Madrid is .................. perhaps the most famous football team in the world.
2. For a .................. restaurant, go away from the main square. The food is cheaper and excellent quality.
3. Take a trip to the top of the Shard, the tallest building in Europe, for .................. of London.
4. The town is .................. for its sandy beaches.
5. This small hotel is the .................. explore the old city.
6. Palermo is the .................. explore the north and the west of Sicily.
7. The beautiful island of Kythnos is one of Greece's .................. .
8. For the perfect romantic weekend away, Paris is .................. .

**5** Use the phrases from exercise 4 to write four top tips for visitors to a city you know.

**6** Read the grammar box, then find examples of superlatives in the text.

### GRAMMAR: Superlatives ▶ PAGE 120

We use superlatives when we compare three or more things.

| Adjective | Comparative | Superlative |
|---|---|---|
| old | older | the oldest |
| hot | hotter | the hottest |
| busy | busier | the busiest |
| famous | more famous | the most famous |
| good | better | the best |
| bad | worse | the worst |
| far | further | the furthest |

We often use superlatives with the Present Perfect and *ever*: *It's the best film I've ever seen.*

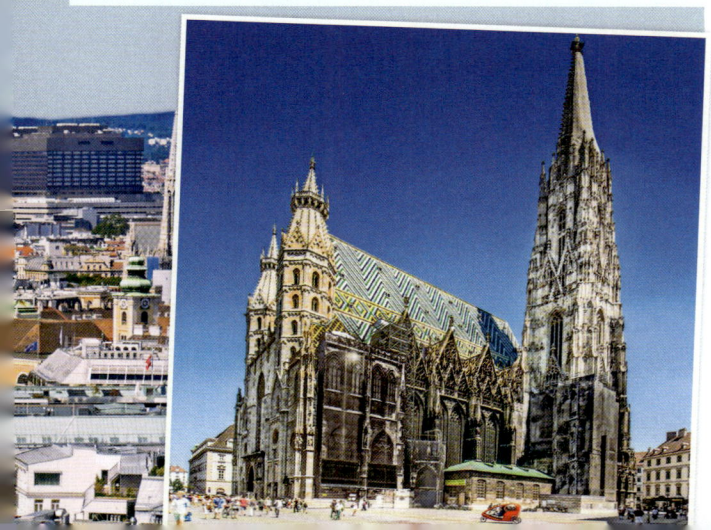

**7** Complete the sentences with the correct superlative form of the adjectives in brackets.
1. India has some of the .................. (polluted) cities in the world.
2. February is the .................. (bad) time of year to visit England as it's so wet and cold.
3. Zurich is one of the .................. (expensive) cities in the world to live in and visit.
4. Many people think Florence in Italy is one of the .................. (pretty) cities in the world.
5. The .................. (far) I've ever flown is to New Zealand.
6. The .................. (hot) country I've ever visited was the UAE.

**8** Use the prompts to write sentences with superlatives + Present Perfect + *ever*.
1. it / bad hotel / stay in
   *It was the worst hotel I have ever stayed in.*
2. He / friendly person / I / meet
3. It / busy / museum / I / be to
4. They / had / expensive / meal / they / eat
5. It / dirty / hotel / I / stay in
6. Madrid / good city / I / live in
7. Daisy / intelligent person / I / work with

**9** Work with a partner. Tell your partner about:
- the busiest place you've ever been to
- the most dangerous place you've ever been to
- the most expensive area to live in your city
- the most beautiful place you've ever been to

*The busiest place I've ever been to was Tokyo. The underground was crazy!*

**10** Look back at the text on Vienna. Find useful phrases for talking about places.
in the heart of the city

**11** Work with a partner. Write sentences for a guide to your city. Include adjectives comparatives and superlatives, to describe towns and cities, and phrases for talking about places.

*The most romantic hotel to stay in is…*
*It has magnificent views of the river and it is also within easy reach of the city centre.*

**12** Share your guide with another pair of students. How similar or different are they?

53

# 6C Changing cities

▸ **Reading:** *Changing cities*
▸ **Vocabulary:** *Adjectives to describe cities*

1. Work with a partner. What makes a city a great place to live in? Think about:

   | job opportunities | culture | environment | education | nightlife |

2. Read the two articles. Which city changed after one event?

## The Lion city

**A** Singapore is one of the richest countries, and people there live some of the longest lives in the world. However, this wasn't always true. It was once a city with thousands of tiny boats <u>crowded</u> along a dirty river. Now there are far fewer boats and most are brightly lit for tourists. While it is now a rich, international city, the old, <u>historic</u> parts are still there. The river isn't as dirty as it once was and is now the best way to explore the heart of the city.

**B** One of the most famous historic centres is Chinatown. The <u>traditional</u> buildings and old-fashioned tea houses sit next to <u>modern</u> restaurants and cafes. Other local areas have also improved. The Bugis district with its old shophouses opposite the modern shopping malls is a great place for shopping. The night life is also unique, with the world's oldest night zoo and the first ever night race in Formula 1.

**C** Singapore has one of the highest number of people living in one of the smallest places on Earth, but it is greener than many people think. There isn't as much green space on the ground as before, but there are gardens on balconies, bridges and roofs. Gardens on the 26th and 50th floors connect a group of seven 50-storey buildings, and residents can jog around them. In the future, people will be based in Smart Work Centres – offices shared with other companies. These will be nearer to people's homes so that people travel less and the roads and subway aren't as busy as now. Singapore is a city that never stops changing!

▶ 050

3. Read the texts again. Match each sentence to a paragraph.
   1. Very few tourists visited it before this event. ...............
   2. Unusual spaces are being used to add green areas to the city. ...............
   3. The river was once the main way to travel. ...............
   4. More people got jobs after the changes. ...............
   5. An area once full of factories is now a regular tourist destination. ...............
   6. There are old buildings next to new developments. ...............

4. Read the texts again and answer the questions.
   1. What are the boats used for now in Singapore?
   2. What examples of old buildings in Singapore does the text give?
   3. What two things did Singapore have before any other city?
   4. What unusual place can people use for exercise?
   5. What do some people think there are too many of in Barcelona?
   6. When was the beach built?
   7. Which region had few jobs?
   8. What were three of the benefits of spending $9 billion?

City Life

### The Mediterranean city

**D** One of the largest cities in the Mediterranean and the most visited in Spain, Barcelona is a city full of tourists. Some people think there are too many tourists and have even started to protest about it, but just a few years ago, that was not true. Before the Olympic games, very few people visited the city. In the past, many Olympic cities only spent money on the event, but Barcelona also improved the transport connections, the quality of life and made the city a beautiful place for tourists to visit.

**E** The city is on the coast, but it had no beaches until the 1992 Olympics. The area was full of industry and no local people or tourists ever visited. Using sand from Egypt, they built a two-mile beach with many bars, restaurants and shops, including an ice bar with lots of ice sculptures. Another former industrial area that has become more fashionable is the neighbourhood of Poblenou. Once one of the least attractive areas of the city, because of closed factories and high unemployment, it is now a beautiful place to live and visit.

**F** There are now much better roads around the city and many more parks and fountains. There are nearly 80% more public open spaces than before the Olympics. All of this means the city is a much more enjoyable space to live in. It's also home to the largest city park in the world – 22 times the size of Central Park in New York. All these changes cost around 9 billion US dollars, but unemployment fell a lot, tourism more than trebled and even the local sports teams became more popular!

**5** Match the underlined adjectives in the texts to the definitions.
1 ................ with a lot of factories
2 ................ important in the past
3 ................ beautiful
4 ................ full of people
5 ................ fun
6 ................ from the present time
7 ................ popular at a particular time
8 ................ done in a way that has not changed for a long time

**6** Use the adjectives from exercise 5 to describe different parts of a city you know.

*Soho is a fashionable part of London to meet friends and go for a drink.*

**7** Tick the statements you agree with.
"It isn't important to keep old buildings." ☐
"People who want more green spaces shouldn't live in cities." ☐
"Cities need to plan for the future and not think about the past." ☐
"Tourism brings more advantages than disadvantages." ☐

**8** Compare your choices with a partner. Give reasons for your choices.

*Lots of tourists means more money.*

# 6D Places

> **Speaking:** Asking for and giving directions
> **Writing:** A description of your hometown; Describing and recommending places

## Speaking

1 Look at the four statements. Which one is true for you or for someone you know?

**One in ten men won't ask for directions**

**25** Two thirds of people under 25 can't read a map

**50%** Nearly fifty per cent of people give up on a journey because their satnav stops working

**A third of people don't trust the directions people give them**

2 ▶051 Listen to three conversations. Mark the routes on the map. Label these places on the map.

Via Roma   Piazza San Marco   Hotel Tre Fontana

3 ▶051 Listen again and complete the phrases in the *Key Language* box.

### KEY LANGUAGE Asking for and giving directions

1 Could you ................ me, is there ...?
2 ................ a look at this map.
3 I'm ................ for the Piazza ...
4 Is this the right ................ to ...
5 Turn back and go the ................ you came.
6 Is it ................?
7 Sorry to ................ you ...
8 How do I ................ to ...?
9 Keep ................ until you reach ...

4 Match the phrases with the pictures.

1 turn right
2 go straight on
3 in front of you
4 cross a bridge
5 turn right at the crossroads
6 take the second turning on the right
7 go through the (park)
8 keep going until you reach (the end of the road)
9 go around the roundabout and take the third exit
10 take a left at the traffic lights

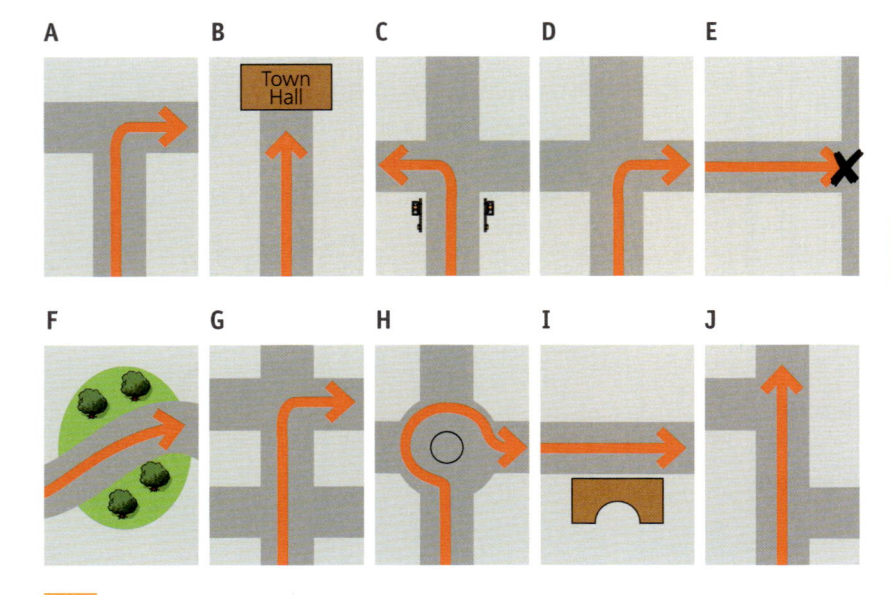

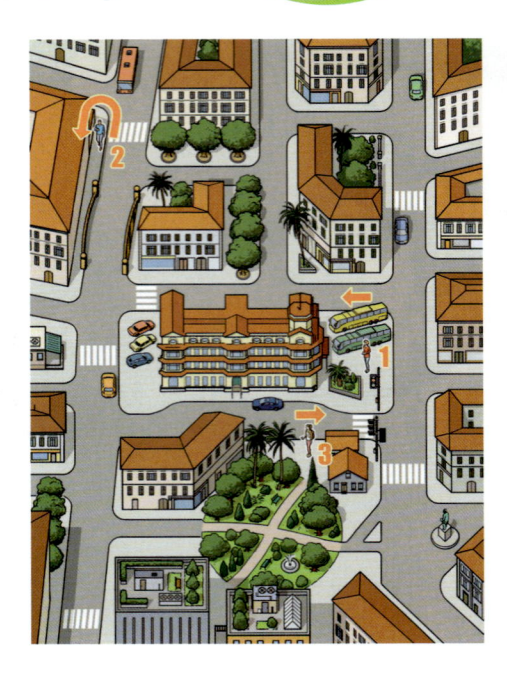

A  B  C  D  E
F  G  H  I  J

## YOUR TURN

5 Work with a partner. Student A turn to page 127. Student B turn to page 129.

6 Work with a partner. Give directions to places in your town or city. Then swap roles.

*Can you tell me how to get to...?*

**Student A** Think of a place in the town or city where you are now. Tell your partner where you are and where you want to go.

**Student B** Give Student B the directions they need.

56

City Life

## Writing

1 Read the description of Palermo. Match the topics to the paragraphs.
   a When to visit    b A day out    c Location    d Where to eat    e Ancient Palermo

## Palermo

**1** ..................
Palermo is the main city of the Mediterranean Island of Sicily. Sicily is the largest island in the Mediterranean and is located at the southern tip of Italy, just a few miles from the North African coast. Just under 700,000 people live there and 1.3 million people live in the metropolitan area. Palermo is located in the north west of Sicily.

**2** ..................
Palermo is one of the busiest and liveliest places you could visit in the Mediterranean. In the past, many different countries controlled Sicily and it is a fantastic place for architecture because of this. The Norman Palace is one of the best places to see this. The Arabs built it, then the Normans and the Spanish expanded it at different times. Throughout the city you can see other examples of architecture from all the countries and cultures that lived there.

**3** ..................
One of the best ways to experience Palermo is through its food. Sicily has a strong culture of keeping traditional foods alive and using local ingredients. Head to the streets markets of Ballaro, Il Capo and Vucciria which is famous for the local Sicilian pizza known as sfincione.

**4** ..................
Sicily has lots of places of interest for people who like culture and history, including eight locations listed on the UNESCO World Heritage Sites. However, if you want to go on a day trip, take the train to the town of Cefalu. The town is located on the northern coast of Sicily. As well as the fantastic beaches, there is an ancient Norman cathedral and beautiful streets to wander around.

**5** ..................
The weather makes Palermo a fantastic city to visit at any time of the year, however, spring and autumn are perhaps the best seasons to visit the city. It isn't as busy as the summer and although it is warm, the hottest you will experience is probably around 28 degrees.

2 Read the *Key Language* box. Find examples of the *Key Language* in the description of Palermo.

> **KEY LANGUAGE** Describing and recommending places
>
> **Describing places**
> … is the capital / main city of …
> … is located on / at …
> … is in the middle / north / south / east / west of …
> … lies on the banks of …
>
> **Recommending places**
> From… you can enjoy great views of the city.
> If you want to go on a day trip, go to …
> … is a fantastic place for …
> … is famous for …

3 Complete the sentences about Madrid with phrases from the *Key Language* box.
   1 Madrid is the .................... Spain.
   2 It .................... middle .................... Spain
   3 It .................... on the .................... of the Manzanares river.
   4 If you want to ...................., go to the ancient walled city of Toledo.
   5 El Rastro market is .................... for shopping.

## YOUR TURN

4 Choose a town or city that you know well. Make notes on:
   • the location
   • history and interesting places to visit
   • where to eat
   • a day trip
   • when to visit

5 Use your notes to write a description of your town or city. Use the *Key Language* box to help you.

# Video 3: Parkrun

## 3 Running for fun

1 Work with a partner and discuss the questions.
 1 When was the last time you went for a run?
 2 What's the furthest you have ever run?
 3 Have you ever heard of Parkrun? What do you know about it?

2 Read the text and answer the questions.
 1 How many runners have taken part in Parkrun?
 2 How old was Eileen when she did her first Parkrun?
 3 Why did Eileen attend the first Parkrun?
 4 Did Eileen plan to run her first event?
 5 How did she feel after her first Parkrun?
 6 What did she try to run between on her second Parkrun?
 7 How much faster was her second Parkrun?

3 ▶ Watch the video. Are the sentences True or False?
 1 Norman has always lived in Australia.
 2 Running helps him to forget about other things.
 3 Norman's son thinks the running isn't good for his father's health.
 4 Norman plans to give up running soon.

### NEVER TOO OLD TO PARKRUN!

Parkrun was founded by Paul Sinton-Hewitt on 2 October 2004 at Bushy Park in London, England. The first event had just 13 runners and was run over 5 kilometres. Since then there have been over 125,000 events involving just under 4 million walkers and runners in nearly 2,000 locations around the world.

Eileen Bartlett began her journey at Lee-on-the-Solent Parkrun as a volunteer when she was 72.

"Volunteering as the event photographer brought me to Parkrun initially because I wanted to learn how to photograph moving people. One day though, just before the start, something came over me and I decided I was going to take part instead."

She spoke to the volunteers and even though she wasn't wearing running clothes, she joined in at the back of the race where the Tail Walker was helping the slower runners. The Tail Walker was really supportive and Eileen loved every second of the race.

"After that first Parkrun I couldn't stop smiling all day. I wanted to tell everyone on the bus home that I'd just done 5k! Deep down I was worried I would be in pain the following day, but I wasn't, so the following week I returned to Parkrun more comfortably dressed. I started out with the Tail Walker who suggested I try running from one park bench to the next. So, I did. Park bench to park bench. I left him behind, pushed on and finished six minutes faster than the previous week. That is how it continued, steadily improving my times week on week."

Since then, Eileen has completed 59 Parkruns and volunteered more than 90 times.

**4** Work with a partner. Can you remember what these numbers refer to?

92   99   100   1986   10

**5** ▶ Watch the video again and complete the sentences.
1 Norman is ................. years old.
2 He started running in ................. .
3 The local ................. used to organize a run for charity.
4 Norman's ................. introduced him to Parkrun.
5 Norman doesn't worry about ................. any more.
6 Norman's son thinks it inspires people to get off ................. and start moving.
7 Norman is going to run until he ................. .

**6** Work with a partner and discuss the questions.
1 What do you think Norm means when he says, 'I'm going to run till I drop.'?
2 Would you like to take part in a Parkrun? Why / Why not?
3 Do you prefer exercising on your own or with others? Why? / Why not?
4 Which older people do you find inspiring? Tell your partner something about them.

# Review

| LESSON 5A | List 5 phrasal verbs or collocations connected to health. |
| LESSON 5A | Write 3 sentences offering to help someone with something. |
| LESSON 5B | Write 2 sentences for each word, one using the noun form and one using the verb form. *improve   create   grow* |
| LESSON 5B | Write one sentence about a prediction about your life and one sentence about a plan you have. |
| LESSON 5C | Write 2 health changes you would like to make. |
| LESSON 5D | List 5 different illnesses. |
| LESSON 6A | Use *however*, *but* and *although* to write three sentences. |
| LESSON 6A | List 5 adjectives to describe towns or cities. |
| LESSON 6A | Write 3 sentences comparing two places you know well. |
| LESSON 6B | Write 3 sentences using vocabulary to make recommendations. |
| LESSON 6B | Write 3 sentences describing some of the best experiences you've ever had. |
| LESSON 6C | Write 2 sentences about a place you know that has changed. |
| LESSON 6C | List 5 useful expressions for giving directions. |
| LESSON 6D | Write a recommendation about a place you think someone should visit. |

# 7 Connections

▶ **Grammar:** Tense review
▶ **Listening:** Thinking about the past, present and future

## 7A Time

1 Do you agree with the statements below? Give each one a score from 1 (strongly disagree) to 5 (strongly agree). Compare your answers with a partner.

> 1 Familiar sights, sounds and smells often bring back wonderful memories.
> 2 I often think about bad decisions I made in the past.
> 3 I don't worry about the future. There is nothing I can do about it.
> 4 When I want to achieve something, I set goals for the future.
> 5 The most important thing is to have excitement in my life now.

2 ▶053 You are going to listen to a radio programme on whether thinking about the past, present or future makes us happier. Listen to the first part. What type of person does the professor talk about?

3 ▶053 Listen again and answer the questions.
   1 Why are traditions such as national holidays important to some people?
   2 What do some people like to collect?

4 ▶054 Listen to the rest of the radio show. Are the sentences True or False?
   1 Thinking about wanting to change our past is bad for our happiness.
   2 People often think about the past or future too much.
   3 We should think about our future.
   4 Professor Jackson believes that fate controls our life now and in the future.
   5 To be happy, we need to live only in the present.

5 Work with a partner. Look back at your answers to the quiz in exercise 1. Discuss the questions.
   1 How important is it for you to 'live in the moment' and enjoy time with family and friends?
   2 How focused are you on your future goals? Do you think you spend so much time thinking about the future, that you do not enjoy your life enough now?
   3 Do you believe in fate?

**6** Match the underlined verb forms in sentences from the listening (1–8) to the uses a–h in the grammar box.

1 Traditional holidays are very important to these people and they <u>celebrate</u> them every year.  **a**
2 They <u>enjoyed</u> these holidays as a child and they were happy times for them. ..........
3 For example, they think about the boyfriend they <u>were going out with</u> when they were at university. ..........
4 It's important to think about what we <u>are doing</u> now. ..........
5 We<u>'ll be happier</u> in a bigger flat. ..........
6 I<u>'m going to buy</u> a flat next year. ..........
7 I<u>'ve done</u> that before. ..........
8 Don't worry. I<u>'ll do</u> that from now on. ..........

| GRAMMAR: Tense review | ▶ PAGE 121 |
|---|---|

a Things that happen always or usually  **Present Simple**
b Things happening now or in the near future ..........
c Finished actions in the past ..........
d Actions in progress at a time in the past ..........
e Future plans ..........
f Predictions ..........
g Offers, promises and decisions ..........
h Past experiences not in a specific time ..........

**7** Write the names of the tenses in the grammar box.

**8** Complete the conversations with the correct form of the verbs in brackets.

1
A: What .......... we .......... this weekend? (do)
B: I .......... away with Kate, Debbie and Rita. (go)
A: But you .......... up with them last weekend. (meet)
B: I know but we .......... away this weekend every year together. (go)
A: Fine. I .......... my own plans then! (make)

2
A: You're late! Where .......... you ..........? (be)
B: Sorry. I .......... ready at home when my mum .......... me. (get / call)
A: Why .......... it .......... so long? (take)
B: She thinks she .......... her job. (lose)

**9** ▶055 Choose the correct words to complete the questions. Listen and check.
1 What *are you usually doing / do you usually do* at the weekend?
2 *Are you watching / Do you watch* any good TV series at the moment?
3 Where *did you go / do you go* on holiday last year?
4 What *did you do / were you doing* at 7 o'clock last night?
5 What *are you doing / do you do* this weekend?
6 Do you think you *will be / are being* rich one day?
7 *Have you ever seen / Did you see* Beyoncé in concert?
8 *Did you enjoy / Have you enjoyed* traditional holidays when you were a child?

**10** Work with a partner. Ask and answer the questions in exercise 9.

**11** Work in groups. Take turns to talk about:
- a positive memory or experience from your past.
- a bad decision that you made.
- something new that you have started and are enjoying doing.
- a goal you want to achieve in the future.

# 7B Relationships

> **Vocabulary:** Relationships
> **Grammar:** Present Perfect: for and since
> **Reading:** Childhood sweethearts

**1** Work with a partner. Read the comment and discuss the questions.

> "There are billions of people in the world. I just haven't met the right person yet. The perfect person is waiting for me. I just have to keep trying."

1 Do you believe there is one perfect person for everyone? Why / Why not?
2 What type of person would be your ideal boyfriend / girlfriend?

> They need to be really good looking. I want someone who is fit and strong.

**2** Read the article and answer the questions.
1 When did Jenifer and Dwayne first meet?
2 Where did she finish the relationship with him?
3 When did they get married?
4 Where did Dwayne ask Jenifer to marry him?

**3** Complete the sentences with the correct form of the underlined words and phrases in the article.
1 Dan and Ellie ................ in a castle in Scotland. The wedding was amazing!
2 She ................ me by text message. It was so rude!
3 I ................ Freddie at a friend's party, but at first we didn't get on that well.
4 We ................ to different restaurants and then I knew she was the person I wanted to marry.
5 I was so nervous when I ................ her ................ , but luckily she said yes!
6 Paul and I separated for six months but then we ................ again.
7 They are always ................ . I'm surprised they're still together.
8 Ana is on her own at the moment. She doesn't ................ a boyfriend.

**4** Work with a partner. Ask and answer questions using the words and phrases in exercise 3.

> Do you have a boyfriend / girlfriend?
> When did you meet your partner?
> When did you get married?

## CHILDHOOD Sweethearts

Have you ever thought back to when you <u>had</u> your first <u>boyfriend</u> or <u>girlfriend</u> and wondered where they are and what they are like now? Well for some people, a second chance can happen.

Jenifer and Dwayne have known each other since they were sixteen years old. They <u>met</u> when they were in a school play together. Dwayne <u>asked</u> Jenifer <u>out</u> and they quickly got together and became childhood sweethearts. However, things started to go wrong and after a few weeks of <u>arguing</u>, Jenifer decided to <u>break up with</u> Dwayne - at the end of the school prom! Both went their separate ways and had different boyfriends and girlfriends for years, but then in 2012 they reconnected on Facebook. After messaging on Facebook and speaking on the phone for a while, they <u>went on a few dates</u> and soon <u>got back together</u>. They <u>got married</u> a few years later, in 2016. "We've been married for three years now," said Jenifer. "We've known each other for ages but we spent 10 years apart. I feel so lucky that we reconnected." Dwayne added, "I actually asked her to marry me on the high school steps where she broke up with me. A slightly happier experience this time!"

**5** Look at the pairs of sentences. Do they have the same meaning? Which tense does each one use?
  1 a We got married three years ago.
    b We've been married for three years.
  2 a Jenifer and Dwayne met when they were sixteen.
    b Jenifer and Dwayne have known each other since they were sixteen.

**6** Look at the sentences in exercise 5 again. Complete the rules in the grammar box with the words in the box.

> for   past   present   since

### GRAMMAR: Present Perfect: *for* and *since*   ▶ PAGE 121

We use the Present Perfect to talk about something that started in the ¹............................ and continues in the ²............................ .

We use ³............................ for periods of time.

We use ⁴............................ to say when something started.

**7** Complete the table with the words and phrases in the box.

> ~~2015~~   ~~ages~~   February   a long time
> Monday   three weeks/months/years
> this morning/afternoon   lunchtime
> last weekend   I was a child

| For | Since |
|---|---|
| ages | 2015 |

**8** Complete the sentence beginnings with the past participle of the verbs in brackets.
  1 I've ............... (live) in…
  2 I've ............... (work) at…
  3 I've ............... (have) this phone…
  4 I've ............... (know) my best friend …
  5 I've ............... (own)…
  6 I've ............... (play)…
  7 I've ............... (study)…
  8 I've ............... (like)…

**9** Complete the sentences in exercise 8 so that six are true for you and two are false.

**10** Work with a partner. Read your sentences from exercise 9 to each other. Ask questions to find out which of your partner's sentences are false.

> *I've had this phone for three years.*

> *Really? Where did you buy it?*

**11** Use the prompts to write questions.
  1 have / a car? How long / it?   **Do you have a car? How long have you had it?**
  2 be / in a relationship? How long / together?
  3 live / a flat? How long / there?
  4 be / married? How long / married?
  5 have / job? How long / work / there?
  6 be / vegetarian? How long / vegetarian?
  7 have / interesting hobbies? How long / interested?

**12** Move around the room and ask the questions in exercise 11 to other students. If they answer *yes* to the first question, ask them the second question. Think of one more question each time to find out more information.

> *Do you have a car? How long have you had it? What kind of car is it?*

# 7C The story behind the place

> **Reading:** A historic building and the people who lived there
> **Vocabulary:** Society

## Highclere Castle

Highclere Castle in the south of England has a long and interesting history. It has become well-known recently as the location for filming *Downton Abbey*, a popular TV series about life in a wealthy British family in the early 1900s. Viewers have enjoyed watching the interesting characters in the series, but the real-life Highclere characters are just as interesting.

*George Herbert*

*Alima Wombwell*

### A USEFUL MARRIAGE

George Herbert, the fifth Earl of Carnarvon, was born at Highclere in 1866. By 1895, he had a lot of debts, a very expensive home to run and staff to pay. Like many wealthy aristocratic men at that time, he turned to 'new money' to solve his problems. He married Almina Wombwell. She was born in France, but was a daughter born outside marriage of the wealthy Alfred de Rothschild, a member of the powerful banking family.

As part of the marriage contract, all the Earl's debts were paid and Rothschild agreed to pay Almina £12,000 a year for life. This amount would be worth £6.5m today. George and Almina were soon enjoying an exciting lifestyle involving yachts and foreign travel. Almina's money not only paid for this lifestyle, but it even paid for her husband's adventures in Egypt with Howard Carter, where the two men discovered the tomb of Tutankhamen.

### THE TV VERSION OF ALMINA

*Downton Abbey's* Lady Cora is, like Almina, a foreign heiress who marries into the higher classes of British society. And there were dozens of wealthy heiresses who did this in real life. Most of them came from the new millionaires that were created by the growth of industry in the 19th century in the United States. In the same year as Almina's marriage, nine American heiresses married English men from high social classes. By 1900, about a quarter of the British House of Lords had an American connection. Overall, about 350 American heiresses had married into the British high society pre-1914.

Many British families from the higher social classes actually had very little wealth left at this time. They had huge expensive homes, but they did not have much income. However, they had a position in society, along with a title such as Earl, Count or Duke that was attractive to these young, rich American women.

### HIGHCLERE TODAY

Highclere is now looked after by Lady Fiona Carnarvon, the eighth Countess, and she has more modern ideas about how to bring money into the family. The house is open to visitors and Lady Carnarvon believed that using the house to film *Downton Abbey* might attract more. "We certainly hoped having *Downton Abbey* here would improve our profile," she says, "and we have noticed more visitors to the estate." Before the first series was shown, there were 100 coach parties a year; afterwards, 600.

*The stars of Downton Abbey*

# Connections

**Highclere Castle**

The present estate is very different to the one that Lady Cora is in charge of in *Downton Abbey*. 150 years ago, the estate had 100 workers; it now has a full-time staff of just seven, including a butler and a cook. Does Lady Carnarvon think that places like Highclere are just historic locations, or do they still have a place in a modern society? "Actually, I think they've found a place in the modern world," she says. "So many big houses were destroyed in the 1950s and '60s, but today there's a sense of wanting to feel grounded and people wanting to understand their history, and houses like this are living history with a real personal connection to the past."

Lady Carnarvon knows her family is lucky, but believes it is more important to spend their wealth helping local charities rather than buying <u>status symbols</u> such as Ferraris and yachts.

### Glossary
**heiress** a woman who gets money from an older relative when they die
**duke** a title given by the king or queen. Other titles in order of importance include count, countess, duchess, marquess, marchioness, earl, viscount, viscountess, baron and baroness
**House of Lords** the upper chamber of the British Parliament

056

**1** Work with a partner and discuss the questions.
  1 Does your country have a royal family? Did it have one in the past? What do you know about them?
  2 Look at the titles in the glossary. Are there similar titles in your country? Are they still important today?
  3 What periods of your country's history are often shown in films and TV dramas? What was life like at that time?

**2** Read the article. Then work with a partner. What can you remember about…
  Highclere            Lady Cora
  Almina Wombwell      Lady Fiona Carnarvon
  George Herbert       Downton Abbey

**3** Find these numbers in the article. What do they refer to?

  ~~£12,000~~   350   8th   100   600
      7   1950s and 60s

£12,000 – the money given to Almina every year

**4** Read the article again and answer the questions.
  1 What things did Almina and the fifth Earl of Carnarvon enjoy in life?
  2 What did the Earl and Howard Carter discover?
  3 How did American heiresses get their money at this time?
  4 Why did members of British high society need American money?
  5 What happened at Highclere after they filmed *Downton Abbey* there?
  6 Why does Lady Carnarvon think buildings like Highclere are important?

**5** Complete the questions with the underlined words in the article.
  1 Are there different .................... in your country? Is it easy to guess someone's family background? Why?
  2 Why do you think people are interested in the .................... of rich and famous people?
  3 Do you think it is right that some people have a higher .................... in society because of who their parents are?
  4 Do you think rich people should use their .................... to help other people?
  5 Are ...................., such as cars, designer clothes and a big house important to you? Why? / Why not?
  6 Why do some people find money, status and titles ....................?

**6** Work with a partner. Discuss the questions in exercise 5.

65

# 7D Events

> **Speaking:** Reacting to news
> **Pronunciation:** Sounding enthusiastic and sympathetic
> **Writing:** An invitation; Key language for invitations

## Speaking

1 Look at the events in the box. What do you say in your own language when someone tells you about one of these events?

> getting engaged    a pet dying
> breaking up with their partner
> losing a job    having a baby
> getting a new job

*If someone tells me they are getting engaged, I say …*

2 ▶057 Listen to 6 short conversations. Match each conversation to an event in exercise 1.

1 ........................
2 ........................
3 ........................
4 ........................
5 ........................
6 ........................

3 ▶057 Listen again and complete the phrases in the *Key Language* box.

### KEY LANGUAGE  Reacting to news

**Reacting to good news**
1 I'm .................. for you!
2 Wow! .................. !
3 That's .................. news!

**Reacting to bad news**
4 Oh, .................. to hear that.
5 If there's anything I can do, just .................. know.
6 I'm .................. for your loss.
7 Any time you need to talk, just .................. .

4 ▶058 Read and listen to the conversations below. Notice how the speakers show they are enthusiastic or sympathetic.

1 **A:** I passed my driving test!
  **B:** Congratulations! Good for you!
2 **A:** Well, I don't have a job any more.
  **B:** Oh no! What are you going to do?

5 Work with a partner. Practise the conversations in exercise 4. Try to sound enthusiastic or sympathetic.

6 Add a follow-up question from the box to each piece of news.

> ~~Is it a boy or a girl?~~    What happened between you?
> How did he propose?    When do you start?
> What are you going to do?

1 **A:** My wife has had our baby.
  **B:** Congratulations! **Is it a boy or a girl?**
2 **A:** Steve and I have got engaged.
  **B:** That's great news! ..................
3 **A:** I got the job!
  **B:** That's fantastic news! ..................
4 **A:** I don't have a job any more
  **B:** Oh no! ..................
5 **A:** I've broken up with Jimmy.
  **B:** Oh, sorry to hear that. ..................

## YOUR TURN

7 Work with a partner. Think of some exciting news in your life, or invent some exciting news. Try to think of at least three events.

8 Move around the room telling people your news. React in an enthusiastic way to the news you hear and ask a follow-up question each time.

# Writing

**1** Work with a partner. When was the last time you went to one of these events? Tell your partner about the event.

wedding

birthday

house-warming

leaving do

baby shower

**2** Put the four parts of the invitation and response in the correct order. Which day do Debbie and Paula agree to meet?

**A** Hi! I'd love to but I've already got plans on Friday. Are you free next week?
Paula ........

**B** I'm free Wednesday or Friday. Are you free on either of those days? ........

**C** Hi Paula, How are you? <u>I'm meeting</u> Kaye and Charlotte on Friday in town <u>for</u> drinks. <u>Would you like to come along?</u>
Debbie 1

**D** Friday works well for me. I'll text you next week and we can plan where to go. XXX ........

**3** Read the invitation below and answer the questions.
1 What is the event?
2 Who is invited?
3 When is it happening?
4 Where are the people meeting?
5 What does Maria want to check?

Dear Karen,
How are you? How's the new job?
I just thought I'd let you know, <u>we're planning a small house-warming on Friday 27th</u>. <u>I was wondering if you're free and wanted to come?</u> It's just a small group of friends – neighbours, colleagues and some old university friends. We're planning to start around 8 p.m. in our new house – 24 Duke Street. There's no need to bring anything. We'll provide drinks and a buffet. <u>Can I just check, do you have any allergies at all?</u>
Hope you can come!
Love, Maria XXX

**4** Add the underlined phrases from exercises 2 and 3 to the *Key Language* box.

### KEY LANGUAGE Invitations

**Describing an event**
We're organizing a lunch for... ¹ .................. ² ..................

**Inviting people**
We'd be delighted if you could join us.
Are you free next week? ³ .................. ⁴ ..................

**Checking needs**
Do you have any special dietary requirements?
What can I bring? ⁵ ..................

## YOUR TURN

**5** Use the questions to plan an event.
- What are you celebrating?
- When is the celebration?
- Who do you want to invite?
- Where are you going?

**6** Write an invitation to your event. Remember to describe the event and check people's needs. Use phrases from the *Key Language* box.

**7** Swap invitations with a partner. Write a reply to your partner.

# 8 Stories

- **Vocabulary:** *Types of books*
- **Grammar:** *Past Perfect*
- **Reading:** *Agatha Christie*
- **Pronunciation:** *Contractions*

## 8A A famous writer

1 Work in groups and discuss the questions.
   1 How often do you read books?
   2 What type of books do you like best? Why?
   3 Do you prefer e-books or paper books? Why?
   4 What was the last book you read? Was it good?

2 Complete the definitions of types of books with the words in the box.

| biography   classic   detective story   novel |
| romance   science fiction |

   1 A ............... is a book that tells a made-up or fictional story – it's not true.
   2 A ............... is a story about love and relationships.
   3 A ............... is a very famous and much-admired story, usually from the past.
   4 A ............... is a book about crimes and the people who solve them.
   5 A ............... is a book about a real person's life – it's true.
   6 A ............... story often includes aliens, space travel and future technology.

3 Work with a partner. Can you think of an example for each type of book in exercise 2?

4 What do you know about Agatha Christie? What type of books was she famous for? Have you read any of them? Read the article and check your ideas.

### Agatha Christie: best-selling novelist of all time!

**Agatha Christie is famous for her detective stories. She wrote over 80 novels and has sold over 2 billion books worldwide! So, what do we know about her life?**

She was born in Torquay, England in 1890. Her parents ¹............... her older sister to school, but her mother decided to teach Agatha at home. She loved reading and writing.

Life changed for the family when Agatha was 11. Her father ²............... very ill for some time, and he died in November 1901. Her mother then sent her to school.

In 1910, she wrote her first novel, *Snow Upon the Desert*. It was set in Cairo, Egypt, where she ³............... three months earlier that year with her mother. Unfortunately, the book publishers didn't like it.

She returned to England and by this time, she was keen to get married. She ⁴............... to find a husband in Cairo, but with no success. Finally, she met army officer Archibald Christie at a dance, they married in 1914 and had a daughter, Rosalind, in 1919.

Her first detective story, *The Mysterious Affair at Styles*, which she ⁵............... in 1916, was published in 1920. The main character in the book was *Hercule Poirot* – a Belgian detective. She published many more stories about him during her lifetime.

**Hercule Poirot**

68

Stories

**5** Find these dates in the article. What happened in these years?

1890   1901   1914   1920   1930   1976

**6** Read the article again. Complete it with the verbs in the box.

had been   had died   had fallen   had met
had sent   had spent   had tried   had written

**7** Look at the underlined verbs in the pairs of sentences. In each pair, which action happened first? Number the actions 1 and 2.

Her parents <u>had sent</u> her older sister to school. ☐
Her mother <u>decided</u> to teach Agatha at home. ☐

Her father <u>had been</u> very ill. ☐
He <u>died</u> in November 1901. ☐

She <u>married</u> her second husband in 1930. ☐
They <u>had met</u> only six months earlier. ☐

In 1926, not long after her mother **⁶**............., her husband told her that he **⁷**............. in love with his secretary! Agatha divorced Archibald, but she kept his surname for her writing. She married her second husband, archaeologist Max Mallowan, in 1930. They **⁸**............. only six months earlier during a trip to Baghdad on The Orient Express! They had a happy marriage and she continued to write for the rest of her life, until her death in 1976.

*"An archaeologist is the best husband a woman can have. The older she gets, the more interested he is in her."*

**8** Complete the grammar box with the correct words.

before   had   not   past participle

**GRAMMAR: Past Perfect**  ▶ PAGE 121

We form the Past Perfect with **¹**............. + **²**..............

We use the Past Perfect to show that a past action happened **³**............. another past action: *Her husband **told** her that he **had fallen** in love with his secretary.*

We form the negative Past Perfect with *had* + **⁴**............. + past participle.

**9** ▶060 Work with a partner. Answer the questions about Agatha Christie using the Past Perfect. Then listen and compare.

1 Why is it surprising that Agatha's mother taught her at home?
   *Because she had sent Agatha's older sister to school.*
2 Why did Agatha Christie set her first novel in Cairo?
3 Why was it not surprising that her father died?
4 Why did Archibald and Agatha get divorced?
5 Why was it surprising that Agatha married Max in 1930?

**10** Complete the sentences with the correct Past Simple or Past Perfect form of the verbs in brackets.

1 I ............. (give) my copy of *Murder on the Orient Express* to Ben because I ............. (read) it before.
2 My parents ............. (be not) very happy with me because I ............. (fail) my exams.
3 Most people ............. (leave) by the time we ............. (arrive) at the party.
4 I ............. (leave) my books at college so I ............. (not do) my homework.
5 We ............. (want) to go to Venice on holiday because we ............. (not be) there before.

**11** ▶061 Listen to the conversations and check.

**12** ▶062 Underline the contractions and practise the sentences. Then listen, repeat and practise again.
1 I'd read it before.
2 I hadn't studied enough.
3 We'd been stuck in traffic.
4 We hadn't realized how busy and crowded it is.

**13** Complete the sentences with your own ideas and a verb in the Past Perfect. Then tell a partner.
1 I wanted to read … on holiday because …
2 When I woke up this morning I felt … because …
3 I wanted to go to … on my last holiday because …

## 8B Fact is stranger than fiction

▸ **Vocabulary:** *Connecting words*
▸ **Grammar:** *Narrative tenses*
▸ **Reading:** *A real-life cave rescue*

**1** Work with a partner. Discuss the questions.
1. Do you prefer reading non-fiction (true stories) or fiction (made-up stories)? Why?
2. What surprising or interesting true stories have you read about recently?

**2** Look at the photos and the title of the article. Do you know about this story? What can you remember? Read the article quickly to check your ideas.

**3** Read the article again. Complete it with the Past Simple, Past Continuous or Past Perfect form of the verbs in brackets.

### Thai boys found alive in cave after 9 days!

On June 23, the Wild Boars football players ¹ _were training_ (train) with their coach, Ekkapol Chantawong. <u>After</u> they ² _____ (finish) training, they ³ _____ (decide) to go into the nearby caves in Chiang Rai. The boys wanted to go to the end of the cave, write their names, and come back.

They ⁴ _____ (visit) the cave the day before, but they hadn't gone in very far, so they ⁵ _____ (not know) how much water was in there. It was raining when they arrived at the cave and <u>as</u> they ⁶ _____ (explore) the cave, more rain began to fall. Soon the cave was full of water <u>so</u> the 12 boys and their coach were trapped!

<u>When</u> they didn't come home, the families of the boys became worried. They ⁷ _____ (realize) the boys were in the cave <u>because</u> they ⁸ _____ (leave) their bags, bikes and shoes outside the cave entrance.

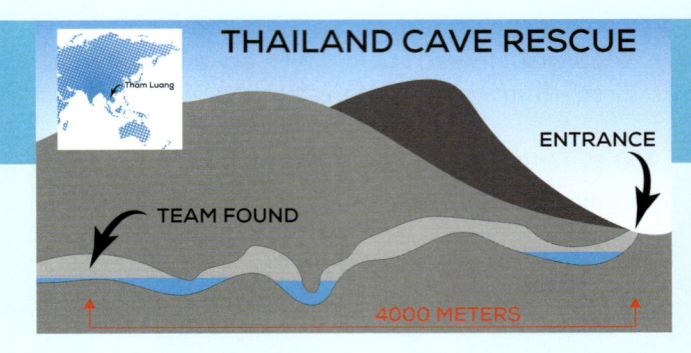

<u>Amazingly</u>, on July 2, two divers found them alive! They ⁹ _____ (be) in the cave for nine days and they ¹⁰ _____ (be) hungry and weak. When one boy asked when they could get out of the cave, the diver replied, 'Not today. You have to dive.'

Over the next few days, 90 experienced divers came to help get the boys out. <u>While</u> they ¹¹ _____ (plan) the rescue mission, some divers took food and oxygen to the boys. <u>Sadly</u>, on July 6, diver Saman Kunan died while he ¹² _____ (take) oxygen tanks into the cave.

<u>Fortunately</u>, there was a happy ending for the team. On July 8 the rescue mission began. All 12 boys, plus their coach were brought safely out of the cave.

**THAILAND CAVE RESCUE**
Tham Luang
ENTRANCE
TEAM FOUND
4000 METERS

**4** ▶ 063 Listen and check your answers.

**5** Complete the grammar box with *Past Simple*, *Past Continuous* or *Past Perfect*.

> **GRAMMAR: Narrative tenses** ▶ PAGE 122
>
> The Past Simple, Past Continuous, and Past Perfect are called narrative tenses because we use them when we tell stories or describe what happened.
>
> We often use the ¹................... to give the background to a story. We also use it to talk about actions in progress in the past: *The Wild Boar football players* **were training** *with their coach.*
>
> We use the ²................... with the Past Simple to show which order things happened in. Actions in the ³................... happened before actions in the ⁴...................: *After they* **had finished** *training, they* **decided** *to go into the nearby caves.*

**6** Read the article again. Complete the questions with the Past Simple, Past Continuous or Past Perfect form of the verbs in brackets. Then ask and answer them with a partner.
1 What **were** the Wild Boars **doing** on June 23 (do)
   They were training with their coach.
2 What ............ they ............ the day before? (do)
3 What happened as they ............ the cave? (explore)
4 How ............ the families ............ that the boys were in the cave? (know)
5 How long ............ they ............ in the cave when they were found? (be)
6 What ............ Saman Kunan ............ when he died? (do)

**7** Work with a partner. Study the sentences. Which tense is used in the second part of each one? How does this change the meaning?
1 When I arrived home, my dad was making coffee.
2 When I arrived home, my dad made coffee.
3 When I arrived home, my dad had made coffee.

**8** Complete the three sentences with your own ideas. Use three different tenses. Then compare with a partner.
1 When I arrived home, ................................................
2 When I arrived home, ................................................
3 When I arrived home, ................................................

**9** Complete the sentences with the Past Simple, Past Continuous or Past Perfect form of the verbs in brackets. Sometimes more than one answer is possible.
1 I was angry with my sister because she ............ all my chocolate. (eat)
2 The man was running because he ............ the bus at the top of the road. (see)
3 It all began on a summer's day. The sun ............ and the birds ............. (shine/sing)
4 I ............ to the cinema with Ben because I had already seen the film. (not go)
5 I ............ a shower when my phone rang, so I didn't answer it. (have)
6 He couldn't find his mobile phone because he ............ it in a taxi! (left)

**10** Look at the underlined connecting words in the article. Which …
1 tell you when something happened: ............, ............, ............, ............
2 gives you a reason: ............
3 gives you a result: ............
4 are adverbs that show a good feeling: ............, ............
5 is an adverb that shows a bad feeling: ............

**11** Think of something that happened to you last week. Write a short blog post about it. Use all three narrative tenses and some connecting words from exercise 10.

**12** Swap blog posts with a partner. Ask questions to find out more information. Then tell the class what you can remember about your partner's blog post.

Stories

# 8C The Problem of Thor Bridge

▶ Reading: The *Problem of Thor Bridge*
▶ Vocabulary: *Adjectives*

1 Look at the title and the pictures and answer the questions.
   1 Who wrote the story? What kind of story is it?
   2 Who are the two main characters? What do you know about them?

2 Read the story quickly and answer the questions.
   1 Who was murdered?
   2 Who do the police think was guilty?
   3 Who asks Sherlock Holmes to help? Why?

3 Read the story again. Answer the questions.

   1 Why was Holmes happy?
   2 What did Holmes know about Neil Gibson?
   3 What two facts suggest that Miss Dunbar was guilty?
   4 What did Holmes and Watson find out from Mr Bates?

   5 Why was Gibson angry with Holmes?
   6 What was the truth about Mr Gibson?
   7 What did Miss Dunbar ask Gibson to do?
   8 What was Gibson's explanation of the murder?

   9 Who did Sergeant Coventry think was guilty? Why?
   10 What did Holmes see on the bridge?
   11 Why did Miss Dunbar go to Thor Bridge? What did she leave in the garden?
   12 What two things did Holmes need for his test?

4 Find these underlined adjectives in the story. Match them to the definitions.

   | brutal | curious | furious | jealous | mean | serious |

   1 strange or unusual
   2 extremely cruel
   3 unhappy because someone else has something you want
   4 unkind
   5 not joking
   6 extremely angry

5 Work in small groups and discuss the questions.
   1 What do you think happened to Maria Gibson? Why do you think so?
   2 Turn to page 130. Read the end of the story – were you right?
   3 What is your opinion of these the characters in the story? Why?
      • Dr Watson
      • Sherlock Holmes
      • Neil Gibson
      • Maria
      • Miss Dunbar

**1** *You have a case, Holmes?*
*Yes, I have a case.*

Dr Watson came downstairs to have breakfast. Sherlock Holmes was already in the dining room – he had been bored and depressed for a month, but today he looked happy. Watson wanted to know why.

**5** *I wish you good morning.*
*What the devil do you mean by this?*

Bates left, and not long after, Gibson arrived. Holmes asked Gibson if he was having a relationship with Miss Dunbar. Gibson was angry and said he was just her employer and nothing more. Holmes told Gibson he was a liar and asked him to leave.

**9** *One of a pair? Where is the other?*

The next day, Holmes and Watson travelled to Thor Place. There they met a local policeman, Sergeant Coventry. Coventry said he thought Neil Gibson may be guilty. The gun was Gibson's. It was one of a pair and they hadn't found the other gun yet.

# THE PROBLEM OF THOR BRIDGE,
## by Sir Arthur Conan Doyle

**2**

Dear Sherlock Holmes

I can't see the best woman God ever made go to her death without doing all that is possible to save her. I can't explain things, but I know that Miss Dunbar is innocent. All I know and all I have and all I am are for your use if only you can save her.

Yours faithfully,

Neil Gibson

After breakfast, Holmes showed a letter to Watson to explain the new case. It was from a rich American gold miner called Neil Gibson. Someone had murdered his wife, Maria, and the police thought that his children's teacher, Miss Dunbar, was guilty.

**3**

Watson asked Holmes to explain further. He told Watson that Maria's body was found at Thor Bridge, half a mile from the house. Someone had shot her in the head. She was holding a letter from Miss Dunbar, and a gun was later found in Miss Dunbar's wardrobe.

**4**

*He was brutal to her – yes, sir, brutal!*

A guest arrived. It was Mr Bates – Neil Gibson's manager. He wanted to tell Holmes about Gibson, before Gibson himself arrived. He told Holmes that Gibson was a horrible man who was mean to his wife and no longer loved her.

**6**

Gibson left, but then returned to tell the truth. He had met his wife, Maria, in Brazil. She was beautiful and they were in love. As she became older, he no longer loved her. Then he fell in love with Miss Dunbar and told her so!

**7**

*You have more money than you need. You should use it for good.*

Gibson explained what had happened between him and Miss Dunbar. She was shocked when he told her about his feelings. She wanted to leave the house immediately. But she stayed – only because he promised to give money to charities that she cared about.

**8**

Gibson then gave his explanation for the death of his wife. Maria knew that he loved Miss Dunbar and she was jealous. She wanted to scare Miss Dunbar with a gun, but the gun had fired by mistake and killed Maria.

**10**

*This is curious.*

The three men walked to Thor Bridge, where the body had been found. They spoke about the note from Miss Dunbar that was found in Maria's hand. Holmes then noticed some damage to the bridge.

**11**

*She hated me, Mr Holmes.*

Next, Holmes and Watson visited Miss Dunbar in prison. She said she had received a note from Mrs Gibson requesting a meeting on Thor Bridge and asking for a written reply to be left in the garden. When they met, Maria was furious and shouted. Miss Dunbar ran off.

**12**

*My dear Holmes, you are joking.*

*No, Watson, I am very serious.*

After the meeting with Miss Dunbar, Holmes and Watson took a train back to Thor Place. Holmes was excited and asked if he could borrow Watson's gun for a test on Thor Bridge. He also wanted some string.

# 8D Feelings and events

- **Speaking:** Talking about feelings
- **Pronunciation:** Emphasizing feelings
- **Vocabulary:** Adjectives ending in -ed and -ing
- **Writing:** A short story; Adverbs

## Speaking

1 Work with a partner. Look at the photos. How are the people feeling?

2 ▶066 Listen and match the people to the photos. Were you right about their feelings?

Jill .................... Claire ....................
Mark .................... Jess and Dan ....................

3 ▶066 Listen again and complete the phrases in the *Key Language* box.

### KEY LANGUAGE  Talking about feelings

1 I'm .................... worried.
2 We were .................... excited.
3 I was .................... frightened.
4 I was .................... shocked.

4 ▶067 Listen to the sentences in the *Key Language* box again and repeat. Which words come before the feeling adjectives? Do they make the feeling weaker or stronger?

5 Complete the social media updates with adjectives from the box. Use *so* or *really* to make the feeling stronger.

> worried   nervous   excited   bored
> delighted   upset   shocked   frightened

1 Jack is feeling .................... .
  I've got my science exam tomorrow!
2 Lucy is .................... .
  I'm going on holiday to Australia tomorrow!
3 Mandy is .................... .
  Just heard someone trying to get into the house through the back window! The police are on their way!
4 Debbie is .................... .
  Nothing to do and nowhere to go! Even the TV is rubbish today!
5 Peter is feeling .................... .
  We've just sold our house! We're moving next month!
6 Neil is .................... .
  Just got another gas bill – no idea how I'm going to pay it!
7 John is feeling .................... .
  Maria just broke up with me after five years together!
8 Molly is .................... .
  Just seen the awful news! Can't believe what's happened!

6 Work with a partner. Underline the two adjectives in each sentence and discuss the differences in meaning.
1 The news was shocking. I was shocked.
2 Jorgé is so worried about money. It's really worrying that he doesn't have anything in the bank.

7 Correct the adjectives in the sentences. Sometimes the word is wrong, sometimes the ending is wrong.
1 I'm so boring! When will this lesson finally end?
2 I was upset to hear that my daughter had passed all her exams.
3 The story was so excited, I didn't want it to end!
4 I felt so delighted before my presentation – I couldn't sit still.
5 I was so shocking by the ending of that Agatha Christie story!
6 I thought someone was following me – it was a really boring experience!

## YOUR TURN

8 Work with a partner. Student A turn to page 127. Student B turn to page 129.

9 Work in small groups. Take turns to talk about a time in your life when you were …
1 really frightened    4 so nervous
2 so shocked           5 really worried
3 really bored         6 so excited

> I was really frightened when …

# Writing

**1** Look at the photo. What do you think is happening?

**2** Look at the paragraph structure for a short story. Then read the paragraphs from *Toby's nightmare day*. Put them in the correct order.

1. Introduction
2. Background information
3. Main events
4. More main events
5. Conclusion

## Toby's NIGHTMARE DAY

**A** ☐ He left the house at 9.20 a.m. and walked to the train station. When he arrived, he discovered he had missed his train! Luckily there was a bus outside the station, so he jumped on.

**B** ☐ He <u>finally</u> arrived at the office at 10.05 a.m. He took a deep breath and walked <u>confidently</u> into the interview room. 'Good morning, Mr Hopwood, - you're late!' said the interviewer. 'Let's hear your presentation.' Toby was <u>carefully</u> putting his memory stick into his laptop when he realized his mistake – he had brought his flatmate's memory stick! He nervously explained what had happened. The interviewers were not impressed – <u>unfortunately</u>, Toby didn't get his dream job.

**C** ☐ It was a cold winter's morning, and Toby <u>sleepily</u> reached out to check his phone. It was 9 o'clock – he had forgotten to set his alarm! Suddenly he remembered why today was an important day. He had a job interview at the local newspaper at 10 a.m.

**D** ☐ Toby had wanted to be a journalist since he was 7 years old, so he desperately didn't want to mess this up. He showered quickly and put on his best suit.

**E** ☐ Toby got off the bus and took out his mobile phone – he wanted to use Google maps to help him find the newspaper office. His battery had run out and his phone wasn't working! He asked an old lady to help and fortunately she knew where he wanted to go.

**3** Work with a partner. Read the story again and discuss the questions.
1. What three things went wrong for Toby?
2. Can you find examples of the Past Simple, Past Continuous, and Past Perfect?

**4** Work with a partner. Read the *Key Language* box and complete it with the underlined adverbs in the story. Then think of more adverbs for each category.

> **KEY LANGUAGE** Adverbs
>
> **Adverbs of time**
> eventually, firstly, soon, already, ..............................
>
> **Adverbs to describe actions**
> carefully, nervously, desperately, quickly, ........................., ........................
>
> **Adverbs to comment on a whole sentence**
> luckily, fortunately, ..............................

**5** Complete the sentences with suitable adverbs from the *Key Language* box.
1. ........................, we don't have any of those jackets in your size, sir.
2. He walked ........................ to the front of the class – his legs were shaking.
3. She ........................ wanted to go the concert, but her parents wouldn't allow it.
4. Holmes ........................ opened the old suitcase – he didn't want to break it.
5. I left my lunch at home, but ........................, my husband brought it to the office.

## YOUR TURN

**6** You are going to write a short story for a competition. Choose a situation and plan five paragraphs.
- A nightmare day
- A mystery
- A frightening experience

**7** Write your short story. Use narrative tenses and adverbs.

**8** Cover the final paragraph of your story, then swap stories with a partner. Can you guess the ending to your partner's story?

# Video 4: Film locations

## 4 Film locations

1 Work with a partner and discuss the questions.
  1 What good films have you seen recently?
  2 What are your favourite TV shows? What do you enjoy about them?
  3 Do you recognize any of the places in the pictures? Do you know what films or TV shows were filmed there?

2 Read the article. Are the sentences True or False?
  1 The planet Crait that we see in the film is actually part of Bolivia.
  2 Nothing lives on Salar de Uyuni.
  3 There is a hotel made from salt in Bolivia.
  4 The place where Harry Potter first learns to fly a broom is in Scotland.
  5 The bridge that the Hogwarts train goes over is in Northern England.
  6 The *Harry Potter* locations in Oxford are far apart.
  7 They filmed part of *Black Panther* in the British Museum.
  8 The Iguacu Falls are completely in Brazil.

3 ▶ Watch the video about *Game of Thrones*. Tick the topics it mentions.
  1 locations around the world that are used in *Game of Thrones*
  2 the main story of the show
  3 the benefits to Northern Ireland of the series
  4 the main characters from the show
  5 locations in Northern Ireland that are used
  6 jobs for local people
  7 the number of people who watched *Game of Thrones*

## THE WORLD is a film set

### STAR WARS

In *Star Wars: The Last Jedi* the last battle happens on the imaginary planet of Crait. However, unlike many of the scenes that they made using computer images, they filmed the battle scenes on the salt plains of Bolivia. There are salt plains all over the world, but to get some really amazing images they filmed the scenes on the largest salt plain on Earth – Salar de Uyuni. High in the Andes mountains, these salt plains cover an area of 4,000 square metres. Very few things can live there, although you can see giant cacti, flamingo birds and a type of fox. For tourists, there is even a hotel – Palacio de Sal that is made completely from salt. The luxury hotel has facilities such as a golf course, a sauna and a steam room to relax in.

### HARRY POTTER

There are some amazing locations across the UK for fans of the *Harry Potter* movies to visit, including the Glenfinnan Viaduct in Scotland – the famous bridge the train travels across on the way to Hogwarts. Alnwick castle, in the North of England is the castle where Harry Potter first learns to fly a broom. And a visit to Oxford allows you to see three locations from the *Harry Potter* movies. The Bodleian library was also the Hogwarts library. Next door is the Divinity School – in the movies this was the Hogwarts hospital. A short walk away is Christchurch College with The Great Hall, which is the location for the Hogwarts dining room and the place we first meet many of our favourite characters.

### MARVEL MOVIES

The Marvel film series is one of the most successful in recent years. Five of the films are in the top ten movies of all time. One of these is the *Black Panther* film, set in the imaginary country of Wakanda. The film's main character, Erik Killmonger, visits the imaginary Museum of Great Britain. In real life, the museum is called the British Museum. Rather than taking everyone working on the film to the UK, they actually filmed these scenes in the High Museum of Art in Atlanta, Georgia. When someone wants to become the King of Wakanda, they must challenge the old king to a fight at Warrior Falls. The actual location for this was the Iguacu Falls on the border between Argentina and Brazil.

**4** ▶ Watch the video again. Complete the sentences with one or two words.
1. *Game of Thrones* was filmed in Croatia, Malta, Morocco, .................. and Northern Ireland.
2. They filmed most of the show in .................. .
3. The film studio is also the location where they built the .................. ship.
4. Northern Ireland Screen paid .................. of the series budget.
5. *Game of Thrones* was worth .................. for the Northern Irish economy.
6. The actors and crew spent money and .................. in Ireland.
7. Local people have received a lot of .................. to work on the show.

**5** Work with a partner and discuss the questions.
1. Can you think of any famous films or TV shows that were filmed in your country? Where did they film them?
2. Have you ever visited a famous film location? Where was it? What was it like?
3. What TV shows are you currently watching? What are they about?

# Review

| LESSON 7A | Write sentences in 3 different tenses to describe events in your life. |
| LESSON 7B | Write 5 words to describe events in a relationship. |
| LESSON 7B | Write one sentence using *for* and one using *since* to describe how long events or situations have continued in your life. |
| LESSON 7C | Give 3 examples of a status symbol. |
| LESSON 7D | Write 2 phrases for reacting to good news and 2 for reacting to bad news. |
| LESSON 7D | Write a short invitation to an event. |
| LESSON 8A | Name 5 different types of books. |
| LESSON 8A | Write the past participles of 5 irregular verbs. |
| LESSON 8B | Write sentences telling part of a story using *so*, *as* and *because*. |
| LESSON 8B | Write a paragraph of a short story using 3 narrative tenses. |
| LESSON 8C | Name 3 adjectives ending -*ous*. |
| LESSON 8D | Write 4 sentences about how you feel in different situations, using *so* or *really* + adjective. |

# 9 Opportunities

- **Grammar:** Infinitive with to
- **Pronunciation:** Weak forms of to
- **Vocabulary:** Negative prefixes
- **Reading:** You make your own luck

## 9A Luck

**1** Look at the pictures. Which ones represent good luck or bad luck in your culture? What other things do people think are lucky or unlucky in your culture?

**2** ▶069 Listen to three people talking about things that happened to them. Match each person to their lucky event.

| | | | |
|---|---|---|---|
| 1 | Liam | a | getting a promotion |
| 2 | Michaela | b | meeting their partner |
| 3 | Sam | c | avoiding an accident |

**3** ▶069 Listen again and answer the questions.
1 Why did Liam decide to speak to some new people?
2 Which two groups of people did he speak to?
3 Why does Michaela try to walk a different way every day?
4 Who did she meet while walking?
5 Who was Sam driving to see?
6 Why did Sam leave the motorway?

**4** Why do you think Liam, Michaela and Sam were lucky? Was it just chance, or was it based on their actions or personality?

**5** Read the article and choose the best heading for each section.
1 Changing your luck
2 Trying new things
3 Dealing with bad luck
4 Keeping an open mind

## You make your own luck

**Why do some people seem so unlucky and other people seem to have all the luck? Over ten years, Richard Wiseman researched luck to try to find out why some people are luckier than others.**

**A** ..................
Wiseman found that lucky people often have more interesting opportunities than unlucky people. However, they have these opportunities because of their personality. People who are unlucky often worry more, are uninterested in news experiences and feel dissatisfied with life. These people are very careful and plan a lot. For example, if you ask an unlucky person, 'Why did you go to the party?' they might answer, 'To find the perfect partner.' But because they have a fixed plan, these people miss other chances, like making good friends. They only look for a certain job online and miss other possible good jobs. Lucky people are more open and relaxed and see lots of different things, not just the thing they were looking for. To be lucky, you need to be ready to take chances that appear.

**B** ..................
Lucky people also try to do different and unusual things. When you do the same things every day, your chances of having a lucky experience get much smaller. If you always go on holiday to the same place every year, walk the usual way to work or speak to the same people, you will not have as many new opportunities.

**C** ..................
Lucky people and unlucky people also deal with bad luck differently. When lucky people have an unlucky experience, they think, 'It wasn't that bad. It could be worse.' Unlucky people think, 'Typical! Just my luck!' Lucky people turn a negative experience into a positive one.

**D** ..................
So, can you learn to be lucky? Richard Wiseman taught a group of unlucky people to behave like lucky people. Afterwards, they were all happier and more satisfied, and they felt luckier. Make these changes in your life to become a luckier person:
- You need to create and see opportunities.
- Start to have a positive view on life. Don't think things are impossible to achieve.
- Be ready to make decisions based on your feelings and not think about them too much.
- Remember to see bad luck in a positive way.

*Why not give it a try?*

**6** Read the article again. Complete the sentences with the correct information.

According to Richard Wiseman, …

1. Lucky people have more chances due to their ……………………
2. Unlucky people get more worried and ……………………
3. Unlucky people …………………… everything they do, but lucky people take …………………… when they can.
4. Unlucky people do not have as many chances because they do the …………………… all the time.
5. Lucky people make a bad experience a …………………… one.
6. Unlucky people can be taught to be the same as …………………… people.

**7** Work with a partner. Which sentences in exercise 6 do you agree with? Why?

**8** Complete the adjectives in the sentences with the correct negative prefixes in the box. Check your answers in the article. Can you think of any more adjectives that use these prefixes?

| un- x 3   im-   dis- |

1. I try to encourage my friends to have new experiences, but they are always completely …………… interested.
2. It's not fair! I'm always so …………… lucky in life!
3. I'm really …………… satisfied at work.
4. I try to have new and …………… usual experiences every day.
5. I think it's …………… possible to change your luck.

**9** Look at the underlined infinitives in the sentences. Then match the uses of the infinitive to the rules in the grammar box.

1. Be ready <u>to make</u> decisions based on your feelings.
2. You need <u>to create</u> and see opportunities.
3. Make these changes to your life <u>to become</u> a luckier person.

> **GRAMMAR: Infinitive with *to*** ▶ PAGE 122
>
> We use the infinitive with *to*:
> a after some verbs such as *need*, *try* etc. ……………
> b after adjectives. ……………
> c to give a reason for doing something. ……………
>
> Infinitives with *to* can be positive or negative. *It's important **to be** on time. Try **not to be** late.*

**10** Match the sentence halves.

1. When you cook, it's important
2. I know you always see the bad side, but try
3. I joined the running club

a to be positive.
b to have fresh ingredients.
c to meet new people.

**11** 🔊 070 Complete the sentences with *to* + the verbs in the box. Listen and check your answers.

| not be   do   drive   email   help |
| finish   go   ~~meet~~   quit   rain |

1. Nice *to meet* you.
2. What are you planning …………………… this weekend?
3. I hope …………………… this by Friday.
4. Just my luck! It has started ……………………!
5. I need …………………… Maria about the meeting.
6. It's important …………………… out with friends and relax.
7. I've decided …………………… my job and find a new one.
8. The trains aren't working this weekend. You'll need …………………… to London.
9. My parents have offered …………………… me buy a new car.
10. I promise …………………… late again!

**12** 🔊 070 Listen again and repeat the sentences. Notice how *to* is pronounced.

**13** Choose two events or activities. Write two sentences for each one with ideas about how to be successful at it. Use the infinitive with *to*.

> get a good deal when shopping
> manage your time   get fit and healthy
> make a good impression on your partner's parents
> learn a language

*It's useful to download an app to record your diet and exercise.*

**14** Work in groups. Tell your classmates your ideas. Which ideas do you think are the best? Why?

# 9B Happiness

> **Grammar:** *Gerunds*
> **Vocabulary:** *Verbs + gerund or infinitive with to*
> **Reading:** *Being happy*
> **Listening:** *Things that make me happy*

1 Work with a partner. Look at the pictures. Which activities make you happy? Which would you include in your perfect weekend? Why?

## BEING HAPPY

### FEELING GOOD
What do you imagine when you think of your perfect weekend? Reading a book? Playing with your children? Not according to one study called Mappiness, which found something very different. Users were asked to download an app which sent them a 'ping' at different times of the day. Users had to record what they were doing and how happy they felt. The activities that made people happiest were nearly always ones you do with other people, such as going to the theatre or an exhibition, or socializing. The activities were also nearly always outdoors, such as playing sports, going for a run, hiking or fishing.

### FEELING BAD
So, what makes us unhappy? Well, largely work. We can't stand travelling to work, sitting in meetings or dealing with administration. Not surprisingly, we also hate waiting and queuing or being sick in bed. Researchers were also able to spot the world events, such as election results, that made a lot of people unhappy.

### THE RIGHT DAY
People often assume that Monday is the unhappiest day of the week. It's true that most of us don't look forward to starting work again, but in fact Tuesday is the worst day of the week. Perhaps because the happiest time, the weekend, is a distant memory and the next weekend seems a long way away.

2 Read the article. Which of your ideas are mentioned?

3 Read the article again and answer the questions.
   1 What did the activities that made people happiest have in common?
   2 What six activities made people the least happy?
   3 What type of event can make a lot of people unhappy?
   4 What is the worst day of the week? Why?

4 Work with a partner and discuss the questions.
   1 Do you agree that things you do with other people make you happier?
   2 Are you happier when you are outside? Why?
   3 What activities in your day make you unhappy? Why?
   4 Do you agree that technology is a useful way to research how people feel?

# Opportunities

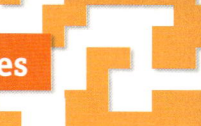

**5** 🔊 071 Listen to four people talking about activities that make them happy or unhappy. Number the activities they talk about in the correct order.
- ☐ hiking
- ☐ going to the theatre
- ☐ travelling to work
- ☐ going to meetings

**6** 🔊 071 Complete the sentences with the words in the box. Listen again and check.

> attending   finding   sitting   taking

1  One of the worst things is ............... meetings.
2  ............... at the top of a hill or mountain is very satisfying after a day of climbing.
3  I hate ............... the train every day.
4  I'm not very good at ............... new things to do.

**7** Match the sentences in exercise 6 to the rules in the grammar box.

### GRAMMAR: Gerunds ▶ PAGE 123

We form the gerund with the base form of the verb + *-ing*: *working*, *hiking*.

We use the gerund:
a  after some verbs such as *like*, *hate*, etc. ...............
b  after a preposition ...............
c  as a noun ...............
d  as the subject of a sentence ...............

The gerund can be positive or negative. *I hate **being** late. I hate other people **not being** on time.*

**8** Complete the sentences with gerunds formed from the verbs in the box.

> buy   do   drive   sunbathe   travel   wait

1  ............... for someone to answer my call in a call centre really annoys me.
2  I love ............... on the beach.
3  My brother is really bad at ............... his car.
4  I'm thinking of ............... a new bike.
5  I really enjoy ............... exercise, especially running.
6  ............... by plane usually involves a lot of queuing and waiting.

**9** Complete the sentences with the gerund or infinitive form of the verbs in brackets.

1  ............... (do) exercise can reduce your levels of stress.
2  I've decided ............... (not buy) my own flat.
3  Be careful ............... (not lose) this phone. It was really expensive.
4  Have you finished ............... (write) the report?
5  We've spent hours ............... (stand) in this queue.
6  I took this job ............... (earn) more money.
7  Promise ............... (call) me when you get there.
8  I don't mind ............... (visit) museums but I prefer art exhibitions.

**10** Complete five of the sentences so that they are true for you. Use a gerund or infinitive.

1  On my last holiday I enjoyed ...............
2  For my next holiday I want ...............
3  At home, I hate ...............
4  At the weekend, I love ...............
5  I spend too much time ...............
6  I dream of ...............
7  This weekend I'm thinking of ...............
8  At work, I would like ...............

**11** Work with a partner. Share your sentences and ask questions to find out more.

> *For my next holiday I want to go to Australia.*

> *Why do you want to go to Australia?*

## 9C Enjoying life

▶ Reading: Getting more out of life
▶ Vocabulary: Phrases for time

1 Write down how much time you spend doing these things each day.

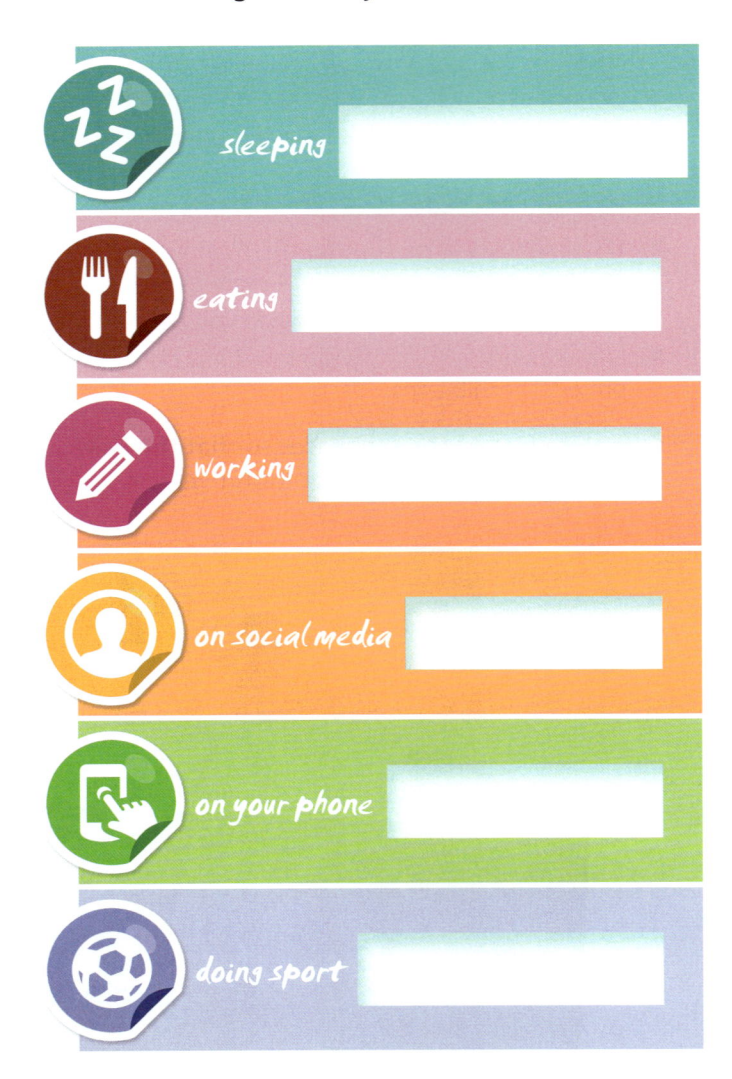

- sleeping
- eating
- working
- on social media
- on your phone
- doing sport

2 Work with a partner. Compare the amount of time you spend doing each activity in exercise 1. Which should you spend more or less time on?

3 Work with a partner. Read the introduction to the article and look at the pictures. What do you think the tips might be?

4 Read the rest of the article and complete it with the correct headings.
   a Lower your aims
   b Stop taking photos
   c Stop looking at your phone
   d Get off social media
   e Stop comparing yourself to others

## Getting more out of LIFE

People often have regular habits and routines, and they do these things without really thinking about how they make them feel. Here are six tips to help you enjoy life more.

**1 Get a hobby**

Working long hours in a stressful job can leave us feeling like we don't have enough energy to do anything else but eat, sleep and work. However, it's important to try to make time for hobbies. Sitting on the sofa watching TV or looking at your phone is a waste of time. Instead, join a sports club, or at least go for a jog or swim before or after work.

**2 ............................**

The average person spends hours every week on social media, but the more you spend time on social media, the worse your mood can get. People worry about how many 'likes' their posts get. They feel jealous of other people's lives. They get into arguments. Even the feeling of wasting time can create a negative mood.

**3 ............................**

People frequently compare themselves to other people. You go to someone's place and you check out their flat, their furniture, their car and their clothes. You look on social media at people's social life and holidays. Doing these things won't make us enjoy our life any more. Save time and energy. Stop comparing yourself to others and enjoy the things you have.

**4** ........................

How we feel each day is not really affected by how well things are going. What is more important is that things are going better than you thought they would. Don't be in a hurry trying to achieve, lots of different things. Set targets that are easier to achieve and you will feel better. Set high targets that are difficult to achieve, and you will feel like a failure. You didn't fail because you aren't good enough, but because the target was unrealistic.

**5** ........................

Phones now do so many different things that it's not surprising people spend hours on them. In fact, on average, people check their phone every 15 minutes. It's often the last thing we see at night and the first thing we see in the morning. Screen time before sleeping and waking in the night to check your phone seriously affect your ability to sleep. A lack of sleep has a serious negative effect on our health and mood.

**6** ........................

Taking photos of important events is nothing new, but modern technology allows us to constantly record everything that is happening. However, according to research, the more photos we take of an event, the less likely we are to actually remember it. Remembering fun times and talking about them with the people who were there is usually a very enjoyable way to spend time. If our memories aren't as strong, then we aren't likely to feel as good. Try living in the moment, not through the camera.

Making these six simple changes will help you to get more out of life.

▶ 072

**5** Read the article again and answer the questions.
1 Name three ways in which social media makes people unhappier.
2 What things do we compare about ourselves and other people?
3 Why isn't it important how well our life is going?
4 What kind of targets should we set?
5 What can screen time affect?
6 What effect does not having enough sleep have on us?
7 What effect does taking photos have on our memory?
8 How can having strong memories affect our happiness?

**6** Work with a partner. Which tips in the article do you agree with? Which ones do you think you should try? Why?

**7** Complete the sentences with the underlined phrases for time in the article. Change the form of the words if necessary.
1 I always feel like I'm ........................ and don't have enough time for everything.
2 Working ........................ is fine. I enjoy my job.
3 I don't spend much time on social media. I think it's a ........................ .
4 I should ........................ friends and family more.
5 Switching off notifications on your phone can ........................ a lot of ........................ .
6 I don't ........................ enough ........................ relaxing and doing the things I enjoy.

**8** Work with a partner. Which statements in exercise 7 do you agree with? Why?

# 9D Opinions

> ▶ **Speaking:** *Agreeing and disagreeing*
> ▶ **Pronunciation:** *Intonation to emphasize your opinion*
> ▶ **Writing:** *An opinion blog; Opinions and reasons*

## Speaking

Taylor Swift

Chris Hemsworth

Serena Williams

Bill Gates

1 Work with a partner. Look at the people in the photos. What do you know about each one? Why do you think they are so successful?

2 ▶073 Listen to two friends discussing why they think people are successful. Which ideas do they mention?

> money   connections   hard work
> luck   family   talent

3 ▶074 Complete the phrases in the *Key Language* box with the words in the box. Listen and check.

> absolutely   agree   but   guess
> so   sorry   sure   true

### KEY LANGUAGE  Agreeing and disagreeing

1 I'm not ............... about that.
2 Yes, ............... he has …
3 I'm ..............., but I don't think that's true.
4 That's ............... .
5 I'm afraid I don't ............... 
6 Really? I don't think ............... 
7 Definitely!
8 Maybe. I ............... people from a rich background …
9 Exactly!
10 You're ............... right!

4 Add the phrases from the *Key Language* box to the table.

| Strongly agree | Agree | Disagree | Strongly disagree |
|---|---|---|---|
| Definitely! | | | |

5 ▶074 Listen and notice how the people use intonation to emphasize their opinions. Then listen again, repeat and practise.

## 🔥 YOUR TURN

6 Look at the opinions below. Which ones do you agree with and which do you disagree with? Why?
   1 People only become successful through hard work.
   2 All successful people have been lucky.
   3 Family and connections have the biggest impact on someone's success.
   4 It is easy for rich people to be successful.
   5 Talent alone is not enough to be successful, you also have to work hard.

7 Work with a partner. Share your opinions from exercise 6. Give reasons why you agree or disagree with your partner.

> *I don't think hard work is enough. You need a lot of other things such as luck and talent to be successful.*

> *You're absolutely right! Working hard won't make someone a success if they don't have much talent.*

## Writing

1. Work with a partner. Look at the quotes. Which ones do you agree with? Why?

   1. **Money is not the only answer, but it helps.**
      *Barack Obama*

   2. **There is no correlation between amounts of money and happiness.**
      *Kesha*

   3. **I think money is essential to happiness.**
      *Wilbur Smith*

2. Read the blog post. What things does the writer think make people happy?

3. Read the blog post and the comments. Add the underlined phrases to the *Key Language* box.

> **KEY LANGUAGE** Opinions and reasons
>
> **Giving opinions**
> *Personally,*   *I think…*   ………………   ………………
>
> **Giving reasons**
> When we express an opinion, we often give a reason to support it.
> *because …*   ………………   ………………

4. Match the sentence halves.
   1. In my opinion, people aren't happier when they are richer because…
   2. I think the important thing is having enough money as…
   3. Because I worked really long hours…

   a. it can be really stressful when you don't.
   b. my health got much worse.
   c. they compare themselves to other people. It means they always want more – a new car, a bigger house, etc.

5. Write a comment in response to the blog post in exercise 2. Give your opinion and a reason for your opinion.

### YOUR TURN

6. Look at the statement below. What reasons can you think of for and against it?
   *Money makes you happier.*

7. Write a blog post. Give your opinion on the statement in exercise 6. Include reasons for your opinion.

8. Work with a partner. Swap your blog posts. Write a comment in response to your partner's blog post.

## RICH and happy?

I asked my son, 'What do you want to be when you grow up?' His answer: 'Rich.' He said he would be happy then because he could have everything he wanted.

Personally, I was quite shocked by this. <u>In my opinion</u>, money doesn't buy you happiness. I understand that everyone needs a certain amount of money to feel safe and secure. When you don't have enough money life can be really stressful and worrying. However, <u>in my view</u>, happiness comes from other things. For example, from spending time with my family and having close friends and the people around me. Being free to make choices and decisions is also really important <u>because</u> I like to feel I'm in control of my own life. Why do so many young people want to be rich? It won't make them happy.

### Comments

I think money does make people happy. I can have and do all the things I enjoy <u>since</u> I have enough money. **Tom**

Young people see the lives of rich people through social media. They want to make money <u>as</u> they think they'll be happy then. It's a real shame. **Hannah**

# 10 Environment

- **Grammar:** Modals of advice
- **Vocabulary:** Environment
- **Listening:** Living a greener life

## 10A Going green

1. How much do you worry about the environment? Rate yourself on the scale. Then compare your rating with a partner and discuss your reasons.

   I worry about the environment...
   not at all  1 2 3 4 5 6 7 8 9 10  a lot

2. Work with a partner. Which of these issues are you the most concerned about? Why?

   air pollution   climate change
   overpopulation   food shortages
   the oceans

3. Look at the picture and read the article. Which place does the picture show?

## MAKING a change

Different countries are coming up with ideas to protect the environment. Here are five changes made in different countries around the world.

1. In Ireland, the government thought that people <u>shouldn't</u> use plastic bags. So they became the first country to charge money for plastic bags.

2. In Norway, the government thinks people <u>ought not to</u> use cars in Oslo, so they are building lots of new cycle paths. By 2025, people will also have to drive electric cars.

3. People <u>could</u> also make changes themselves. In India, Mumbai, local residents cleared over 5 million kilograms of rubbish from a local beach over two years.

4. Some governments think they <u>ought to</u> reward people for helping the environment. In Curitiba, Brazil, local residents can exchange rubbish for bus tokens, food or money.

5. Singapore has one of the largest populations in a small area in the world. However, the government thinks the city <u>should</u> provide green spaces for people to enjoy. Singapore is the greenest city in Asia.

4. Read the article again and answer the questions.
   1. What did Ireland do first?
   2. When will Norway ban petrol cars?
   3. How much rubbish was collected from one beach in India?
   4. What can people exchange rubbish for in Curitiba?
   5. What record in Asia does Singapore have?

**Environment**

**5** Work with a partner. What changes has your country made to help the environment?

**6** Complete the rules in the grammar box with the underlined modal verbs in the text.

> **GRAMMAR: Modals of advice** ▶ PAGE 123
>
> We use **should, shouldn't** to give advice or suggest the right or wrong thing to do.
> We can also use ¹................ / ................ instead of *should/shouldn't*. It has the same meaning.
> We can use ²................ to give advice or make a suggestion that is less certain.

**7** Complete the sentences with *should/shouldn't* or *ought to/ought not to* and the verbs in the box.

| buy   drive   eat   grow   have |
|---|
| watch   turn   use |

1 You ................ your car to work. It's bad for the environment.
2 You ................ less plastic.
3 Why don't you have a bike? You ................ a new bike to travel around the city.
4 You ................ so much meat. It's better to be vegetarian.
5 You ................ holidays in your own country. Flying pollutes the air a lot!
6 You ................ your own fruit and vegetables.
7 You ................ the heating on until winter starts.
8 You ................ so much TV. It uses a lot of electricity. Read a book instead.

**8** Work with a partner. Discuss which advice in exercise 7 you agree with. Which changes should governments help people to make? Which changes should or could you make for yourself?

> *I agree that people shouldn't drive to work. I think governments ought to provide better public transport. I could cycle more, but it's easier to use my car.*

**9** ▶076 Listen to interviews with three people on a radio show *Going Green*. Match each person to a change they have made.

1 Bella         a throw away less
2 Erdem       b use your car less
3 Mable       c eat less meat

**10** ▶076 Listen again. How successful was each person's change?

**11** ▶076 Complete the sentences with the correct form of the verbs in the box. Listen again and check your answers.

| replace   quit   give away   recycle |
|---|
| reduce   repair   reuse   share |

1 Our family decided to ................ eating meat.
2 I ................ normal burgers and sausages with vegetarian ones.
3 I wanted to ................ how often I used my car.
4 I now ................ a car journey to work.
5 I started by ................ things I didn't want.
6 Other people can ................ them and then it's not waste.
7 I ................ a slightly broken table and chairs.
8 It's important to do things like ................ paper and plastic.

**12** Write questions to ask a partner using the verbs in exercise 11. Then work with a partner to ask and answer your questions.

**13** Work with a partner. Talk about things you do that are bad for the environment. Give your partner advice on changes they could make.

> *I always go abroad for my holidays.*
>
> *You could replace one holiday abroad with a holiday in this country.*
>
> *I'm not going to do that! The weather's terrible here!*

# 10B Looking to the future

> **Grammar:** Will, may, might
> **Vocabulary:** Geographical features
> **Listening:** Environmental problems

ocean

1 Look at the pictures. Which of these geographical features do you have in your country? Can you name examples?

2 Complete the fact file with the correct form of words from exercise 1. Which facts do you find the most shocking? Why?

## Our disappearing WORLD

1 _Lakes_ such as the Aral Sea in Uzbekistan are now only ten per cent of their original size.
2 The number of trees people are cutting down in .................. means they will disappear in 100 years.
3 In the Pacific .................. there is an area of plastic three times the size of France.
4 Nearly half of all .................. in the world are not safe to swim or fish in. Many, such as the Yangtze and Mississippi, are polluted by industry and farming.
5 Each year, farming and a lack of water creates an area of .................. the size of Poland.
6 .................. in the Arctic and Antarctic are disappearing quickly and causing sea levels to rise.

rainforests

3 ▶077 Listen to a radio programme on the future of the natural world. What does it say about these things?

| technology | clean water | diets | drugs | sea level |

4 ▶077 Match the sentence halves to complete Professor Brown's predictions. There are two sentence endings that you don't need. Listen again and check your answers.

river

1 Life will improve
2 More people might not have clean water
3 Diets may change
4 We may not have life-saving drugs
5 We might not be able to live in some cities
6 We may need to spend money

a to protect cities from flooding.
b because we have cut down rainforests.
c because of better technology.
d because of air pollution.
e because lakes and rivers are drying up.
f because of rising sea levels.
g because meat needs a lot of water to produce it.
h because the pollution will be too high.

lake

desert

ice cap

**5** Work with a partner. Which of Professor Brown's predictions do you agree with? Why?

**6** ▶078 Complete the sentences with the words in the box. Listen and check.

> may become   may need   may not be
> might help   ~~might not have~~
> will lead   won't

1 In the future over two billion ....might not have.... access to clean water.
2 This dry land ................ to more fires which destroy food, wildlife and homes.
3 In the future, people ................ to eat more vegetables and a vegetarian diet ................ much more normal.
4 There are thousands of plants not tested for how they ................ humans.
5 It ................ possible to live in cities such as Shanghai and Kolkata.
6 Of course money can be spent to protect these cities so that they ................ definitely need to move.

**7** Look at the sentences in exercise 6 again. Then choose the correct words to complete the rule in the grammar box.

> **GRAMMAR: Will, may, might** ▶ PAGE 123
>
> We use *will*, *may* and *might* to make predictions about the future.
>
> *Will* and *won't* are **more / less** certain than *might*, *might not*, *may* and *may not*.

**8** Match the sentences.
1 Eat fewer takeaways. *c*
2 We're a bit late.
3 Where's Michael?
4 I'm packing a few jumpers.
5 Helen wasn't at work today.
6 It's an unusual film.

a Don't worry. He won't be late. He never is.
b She may be ill.
c You will lose weight.
d You may not like it.
e We might not catch the train.
f It might be quite cold.

Harry

Joanna

**Environment**

**9** Look at the two people in the photos. What different opinions might they have on climate change? Complete the sentences with *will/won't*, *might/might not* and the verbs in the box.

> be x 2   fight   find   increase   have   have to   travel

1 Temperatures ................ . Climate change isn't happening.
2 We ................ enough food. Scientists can just develop better farming methods.
3 There ................ fewer flights. Scientists are building solar planes.
4 I don't believe in climate change. Anyway, scientists ................ solutions to all of our problems.
5 We ................ live on another planet because we have destroyed this one.
6 Countries ................ wars about water in the future.
7 Air pollution ................ such a big problem, but more changes are needed.
8 I'm not sure, but I think people ................ to other countries by plane in the future because flying is so bad for the environment.

**10** ▶079 Listen and check your answers.

**11** Work with a partner. Which of Joanna's and Harry's predictions do you agree with? Why?

**12** Tick the sentences that are true for you.
1 I walk or cycle whenever I can.
2 I recycle as much as possible.
3 I try to drive and not fly to go on holiday.
4 I grow my own food.
5 I help with environmental projects like cleaning parks and rivers or planting trees.

**13** Work in groups. Compare your ideas from exercise 12. Then discuss what changes you will or might make to your life to protect the environment.

> I will recycle more.

> I might walk more, but I won't give up my car.

> I might start growing my own food.

89

## 10C Plastic life

> **Reading:** Plastic pollution: The biggest issue facing the world?
> **Vocabulary:** Change

1. Think about all the things you have bought this week. How many do you think contain plastic? Think about coffee cups, bottles, packaging, clothes and anything else. Compare your list with a partner.

2. Read the first two paragraphs of the article. How many pieces of plastic packaging did Daniel Webb buy in a year? What did he do with them?

# The BIGGEST issue facing the world?

One early evening in mid-2016, Daniel Webb, 36, took a run along the coast near his home in Margate, England. As Webb looked down at the beach, he noticed lots of pieces of plastic. "Old toys, probably 20 years old, bottles that must have been from other countries because they had all kinds of different languages on them," he says. Webb decided that he would start a project to keep all the plastic he used in a year, to find out how much there was. He would not <u>change</u> the number of plastic things he bought in that time (although he had already given up buying bottled water), and each item would be carefully washed and put in his spare room.

The result was turned into a huge poster in his home town. "Three days before the billboard went up, we started weighing and counting it all," Webb says. "There were 4,490 pieces in the collection. If you take me as an average person and times it by the UK population, it means we throw away 293 billion plastic items a year." Of those 4,490 individual items, 60% were food packaging – mostly salad and vegetable packaging and bread bags. Ninety-three per cent of the total amount was single-use plastic, and just eight items – mostly coffee cup tops – were made out of biodegradable material. Daniel hopes his project will help <u>raise</u> awareness of the issue of single use plastics. So, how big is the problem around the world and what can be done about it?

### A   A MODERN PROBLEM

People have made plastics for over 100 years, but it was only in the 1950s that we started to produce <u>significantly</u> more plastic. Drinks bottles, and, in recent years, coffee cups are two of the most obvious things we use. However, plastic is in everything from chewing gum to clothes to tea bags. In just seventy years, plastic can now be found everywhere on our planet and it is possibly a bigger problem for humans to face than climate change.

### A GROWING PROBLEM

Unfortunately, nearly every piece of plastic ever made is still here today. This is about 8.3 billion tons, or about the same weight as every single person in the world. Americans use around 500 million plastic straws every day. Shops give out about 2 million plastic bags every minute around the world. People buy one billion plastic bottles every minute globally. <u>Slightly</u> over ninety per cent of this plastic is never recycled.

### WOULD YOU LIKE PLASTIC WITH THAT?

Scientists think that about 8 million tons of plastic ends up in the seas and oceans of the world every year. By 2025, the amount of plastic in the oceans could increase to 160 million tons. The sea is important for food for people and we are killing sea life by polluting the oceans more and more. Nearly 70% of the oxygen produced in the world is actually produced by the sea. Also, scientists have found that people eat nearly 11,000 tiny pieces of plastic every year just by eating fish and shellfish.

**3** Work with a partner. Discuss the question at the end of the second paragraph. Then read the rest of the article. Does it include any of the ideas you discussed?

**4** Read Part A of the article again. What do these numbers refer to? Which numbers and facts do you find the most surprising?
1. 100
2. 1950s
3. 8.3 billion
4. 500 million
5. 2 million
6. One billion
7. 8 million
8. 160 million
9. 70%
10. 11,000

### B  WHAT CAN BE DONE?

There are many simple changes that we can all make to <u>dramatically</u> <u>reduce</u> the amount of plastic we use, from carrying our own water bottles and coffee cups we can use again, to not using plastic straws and bags. There has also been a <u>rise</u> in the number of package free shops around the world. Shops such as Unverpackt in Berlin sell over 600 different products, from jams to pastas to dishwasher powder, all without any packaging.

### NEW SOLUTIONS

Plastic bottles are perhaps one of the biggest problems around the world. Some cities, such as London, plan to introduce more water fountains around the city to reduce the number of bottles people buy. Another possibility is to produce bottles from different materials. James Longcroft, a scientist from the UK, has invented a bottle made from paper and other natural products that will biodegrade in a very short period of time. This could lead to a <u>dramatic</u> <u>fall</u> in the amount of plastic used.

While climate change probably needs governments to agree on what to do, a <u>slight</u> <u>reduction</u> in the amount of plastic we each use could make a huge difference.

**Glossary**
**packaging** the material that things are wrapped in before they are sold
**ton** 1000 kilograms

**5** Read Part B of the article again and answer the questions.
1. What simple changes can people make to reduce the amount of plastic they use?
2. How do shops like Unverpackt help with this?
3. What do some cities plan to build to reduce plastic waste?
4. What has James Longcroft invented?

**6** Work with a partner. Are you worried about the amount of plastic we use? What changes could you make to reduce the amount of plastic you use?

**7** Add the underlined words from the article to the table. Check the meanings.

| Verbs | Adverbs | Nouns | Adjectives |
|---|---|---|---|
| change | | | |

**8** Complete the sentences with words from exercise 7.
1. It's impossible to give up using plastic completely but everyone can .............. the amount they use.
2. Governments need to .............. reduce the amount of single use plastic produced.
3. The .............. in coffee drinking has created a lot more plastic waste.
4. Stopping free plastic bags led to a .............. in the number of people using them.
5. Even a .............. change in behaviour, such as taking a coffee cup to work can help.
6. A .............. of just 10% of the plastic each person uses could make a huge difference.
7. People need to make .............. changes to how they shop, or plastic will become an even bigger problem.

**9** Work with a partner. Which statements do you agree with? Why?

> I am already trying to significantly reduce the amount of plastic I use.

> I will try to change some of my habits to use less plastic.

> I'm not worried about the problem and don't plan to give anything up.

> Governments need to make dramatic changes. People cannot make much difference on their own.

# 10D Structuring ideas

▸ **Speaking:** *Structuring a presentation*
▸ **Writing:** *A summary of survey results; Connecting ideas*

1 waste
2 transport
3 energy

## Speaking

1 Look at the pictures. In what ways does your school / college / company have an impact on the environment? What changes could they make to reduce their impact?

2 ▶081 Listen to a presentation suggesting ways in which a company could be more environmentally friendly. Which of your ideas from exercise 1 does it mention?

3 ▶081 Listen again. Complete the sentences with no more than two words or a number.
   1 The company wants to reduce their carbon footprint by .................. per cent.
   2 The talk will look at changes to the .................. and individual changes.
   3 They plan to add .................. and a garden to the roof.
   4 New energy efficient .................. use 80% less energy.
   5 Turn off .................. at the end of the day.
   6 Turning down the temperature by one degree saves the same amount of energy as it takes to print .................. pieces of paper.

4 ▶082 Complete the phrases in the *Key Language* box with the words in the box. Listen and check.

> divided   firstly   head   move   point
> questions   up   talk

### KEY LANGUAGE  Structuring a presentation

1 Hi, I'm Andre and I am the .................. of facilities management.
2 Today I am here to .................. to you about …
3 My talk is .................. into two parts.
4 .................. I will talk about … then I'll look at …
5 Right, let's .................. on to…
6 This leads to my next .................. , which is …
7 To sum .................. , …
8 Does anyone have any .................. ?

5 Match the phrases in the *Key Language* box to the functions.
   a Introducing the presentation
   b Organizing the ideas
   c Changing the topic
   d Summarizing
   e Inviting questions

## 🔶 YOUR TURN

6 Work with a partner. Brainstorm different ways your school / college / company could reduce its impact on the environment.

> *Perhaps your company could …*
> *One thing my college does is …*
> *Why doesn't your school …*
> *Perhaps your company could do the same?*

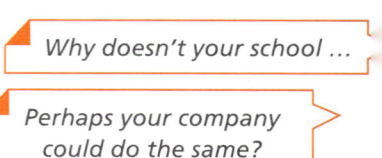

7 Plan a presentation describing changes your school / college / company could make. Use phrases from the *Key Language* box to help you.

8 Work in small groups. Take turns to deliver your presentation. Discuss the best ideas from your different presentations. Report back to the class on the best three ideas.

# Environment

## Writing

**1** Look at the results of a survey into changes a local government plans to make to help the environment. Which changes are the most popular? Which are the least popular?

|  | Number of people who like the idea |
|---|---|
| Turn street lighting off at midnight | 20% |
| Collect bins once every two weeks | 25% |
| Build more cycle paths | 50% |
| Add more recycling points | 70% |
| Create more parks | 80% |

**2** Work with a partner. Which changes would / wouldn't you be happy for your local government to make? Why?

**3** Read the summary of the survey results and answer the questions.
1. What does the local government want to achieve?
2. Who does not want more cycle paths?
3. Why don't people want street lights to be turned off?

### Summary

The local government has spoken with people in the area about possible changes it could make to help the environment. The aim is to make the town a greener and cleaner place for everyone. The response to the ideas was generally positive. The most popular suggested change is creating more parks. <u>In addition</u>, adding more recycling points was a very popular choice. <u>Furthermore</u>, half the people in the survey said they liked the idea of building more cycle paths. However, this idea was much less popular with car drivers. By far the least popular suggested change is to collect bins only once every two weeks. <u>Despite</u> more recycling bins being a popular choice, people still want their rubbish to be collected weekly. As well as changes to rubbish collection being unpopular, residents were not keen on the idea of turning street lighting off at midnight. People want the lights to remain on, <u>otherwise</u> they felt there might be an increase in crime levels.

**4** Complete the *Key Language* box with the underlined words in the summary.

> **KEY LANGUAGE** Connecting ideas
>
> Adding similar ideas – *as well as*, *also*, ................................
>
> Adding contrasting ideas – *however*, *while* ................................

**5** Choose the correct words to complete the sentences.
1. People support charging money for plastics bags. *Despite / Furthermore*, many people are in favour of banning them altogether.
2. *Despite / In addition* more people cycling, there was not much support for more cycle paths.
3. More electric car charging points were a popular idea. *While / In addition*, many people support banning diesel cars from city centres.
4. People want bins to be collected weekly, *otherwise / also* they worry that more rubbish will be left on the streets.

## YOUR TURN

**6** Look at the results of a similar survey in a different town. Which changes are the most popular? Which are the least popular?

|  | Number of people who like the idea |
|---|---|
| Build more cycle pathways | 28% |
| Ban plastic bottles | 28% |
| Collect bins once every two weeks | 35% |
| Add more water fountains | 60% |
| Free solar panels | 92% |

**7** Write a summary of the survey results for the local council. Use words from the *Key Language* box.

# Video 5: Saving the planet

## 5 Saving the planet

1 Work with a partner and discuss the questions.
  1 Where was the last place you flew to?
  2 How many flights do you think you have taken in your life?
  3 Would you ever consider not flying for a year or never again? Why? / Why not?

2 Read the article and answer the questions.
  1 Do you have a word or phrase similar to 'flight shame' in your language?
  2 What do many young people not talk about now?
  3 Are planes more damaging or less damaging to the environment now?
  4 Which types of countries produce more $CO_2$ from flying?
  5 Why might 'green' flights never be possible?
  6 Which flights might France ban?
  7 What does the Green Party in the UK want to do?
  8 What did 15,000 people in Sweden agree not to do?
  9 What might the Swedish government introduce?

3 Work with a partner. You are going to watch a video about Greta Thunberg. Discuss what you know about her.

## SCHOOL Strikes

A new word has emerged in many languages around the world. In English, it is "flight shame", in Swedish "flygskam" and in Dutch "vliegschaamte". Many young people now don't want to tell everyone about the amazing faraway places they have visited. As a result of the school climate strikes that were started by Greta Thunberg, many young people are now trying to fly as little as possible. So, just how damaging is flying and what are some people and organizations doing about it?

Planes are now much less damaging to the environment than they were two or three decades ago. However, the number of flights that are taken is now far higher. As a result, about 2% of all $CO_2$ emissions come from flying. Since wealthy people take more flights in general, the percentage of $CO_2$ that comes from flying is much higher in richer countries and it is closer to 7%. Although many of these countries have made progress with making road travel greener, this may not be possible with air travel because of the amount of power that is needed to get a plane in the air. So, what can be done to reduce the impact of flying?

In France, the government is thinking about banning internal flights between places that are already connected by a train line. The Green Party in the UK has suggested that the government should limit everyone to one return flight per year. They suggest that if someone wants to fly more, they could buy the permit from another person. Individuals are also making changes and having a big effect. Maja Rosen and her neighbour, Lotta Hammar from Sweden started the campaign Flygfritt (no-fly) 2019, and around 15,000 people agreed not to fly that year. In fact, in Sweden, the number of flights that people take is down by 8%, and train travel has increased by a similar amount. As a result, the Swedish government is thinking of introducing more overnight trains to destinations around Europe.

**4** ▶ Watch the video. Choose the correct words to complete each sentence.

1 Greta Thunberg started the protests
   a with some friends.
   b on her own.
   c with her school.

2 Greta hasn't met
   a the Pope.
   b the Russian President.
   c the head of the European Parliament.

**5** ▶ Watch the video again. Complete the sentences with one or two words.

1 Some people try to change the effects of climate change by ................ or using electric cars.
2 Greta Thunberg's mother is a ................ and her father is an ................ .
3 Greta thinks her Asperger's is a ................ .
4 Greta missed school on ................ .
5 On ................ 2019, school strikes happened around the world.
6 Greta has ................ followers on Instagram.
7 Greta's family don't travel by ................ and have become ................ .

**6** Work with a partner and discuss the questions.

1 Have you ever protested about something? What was it? Did it have an effect?
2 Greta said, 'I want you to panic. And then I want you to act.' What actions could individuals or governments take to reduce their impact on the environment?

# Review

| | |
|---|---|
| **LESSON 9A** | Write 3 sentences using the negative prefix *un-*. |
| **LESSON 9A** | Write 3 sentences using an infinitive + *to* to describe reasons for foreign travel. |
| **LESSON 9B** | Use the words *decide*, *like* and *think of* to write 3 sentences including a gerund. |
| **LESSON 9C** | How many phrases for time can you remember from this lesson? |
| **LESSON 9D** | Write 2 phrases to express agreement and 2 to express disagreement. |
| **LESSON 9D** | Write sentences using *as*, *since* and *because* to give reasons why people work. |
| **LESSON 10A** | Give 2 pieces of advice to a friend who needs help. |
| **LESSON 10A** | Write 3 sentences using *recycle*, *reuse* and *reduce* to talk about helping the environment. |
| **LESSON 10B** | Name 3 geographical features. |
| **LESSON 10B** | Make 3 predictions about your own future using *will*, *may* and *might*. |
| **LESSON 10C** | Name a verb, an adverb, a noun and an adjective to do with change. |
| **LESSON 10D** | Write 4 phrases for structuring a presentation. |
| **LESSON 10D** | Name 3 words to add similar ideas and 3 words to add contrasting ideas. |

# 11 Life

- **Vocabulary:** Phrasal verbs
- **Grammar:** First conditional
- **Reading:** *Are you a pessimist or an optimist?*
- **Pronunciation:** Contractions

Megan

Tom

## 11A Optimist or pessimist?

1 Look at the photos. How might Megan and Tom each describe the glass of water?

2 Write the names (Megan or Tom) next to the descriptions.
   1 A pessimist sees a half empty glass and expects the worst to happen:
      ...............................
   2 An optimist sees a half full glass and looks for the best in everything:
      ...............................

3 Are you an optimist or a pessimist? Work with a partner and do the quiz together to find out.

4 ▶ 084 Listen to a conversation between two friends, Carla and Mike. Answer the questions.
   1 Who is feeling pessimistic? Why?
   2 What four suggestions does Mike make?

### Are you a pessimist or an optimist?

**1** You go to your favourite coffee shop. There is a long queue of people waiting. Do you …?

| a | stay and join the queue. It will move quickly. |
| b | leave the shop immediately. It will take forever. |

**2** You walk past some people you know. They're talking and you hear your name. What do you think?

| a | I'm sure they're saying good things about me. |
| b | Oh no! They probably hate me. |

**3** You have planned a BBQ for the weekend. The weather forecast says it will rain. Do you …?

| a | go ahead and hope the forecast changes. |
| b | cancel. A BBQ in the rain is a really bad idea. |

**4** A friend sends you a text message. They want to talk to you immediately. What do you think?

| a | Great! They obviously have some exciting news. I can't wait to hear it. |
| b | Oh no! They're angry with me. I've done something wrong. |

**5** How do you feel about flying?

| a | I love it. It's fun and relaxing and I love travelling. |
| b | I hate it. I can only relax when we land safely. |

**6** A good friend has lost his/her job. What do you say?

| a | Don't worry. You'll get another job really soon. |
| b | Oh no. I'm sorry to hear that. The job market is very bad at the moment. |

#### Results

***Mostly as:*** You're an optimist. The glass is half full for you and you always look on the bright side of life.
***Mostly bs:*** You're a pessimist. The glass is half empty for you and you expect the worst to happen.

**5** ▶085 Complete six of Carla's sentences with the words in the box. Listen and check.

| out (x2)   up (x2)   for   in |

1 James <u>split</u> .................. <u>with</u> me on Monday.
2 Today I <u>found</u> .................. that I've lost my job.
3 I'll be depressed and miserable if I <u>go</u> ...................
4 I'll just stay in and <u>look</u> .................. a new job online.
5 I can't even <u>move</u> .................. <u>with</u> James now.
6 I don't know why you <u>put</u> .................. <u>with</u> me and all my negativity.

**6** Match the underlined phrasal verbs in exercise 5 to the meanings below.
a try to find something
b end a relationship
c start to share a home
d accept someone/something even when it's difficult to do this
e hear news or discover something
f leave your home to do something

**7** Work with a partner. Complete the phrasal verbs in the advice.

"So, your partner has ¹.................. up with you? And now you need somewhere else to live? Don't feel depressed. Get online and ².................. for your own flat immediately. Don't ³.................. in with family."

"So you've ⁴.................. out that some of your friends are saying bad things about you? Don't ⁵.................. up with it – call them and arrange to ⁶.................. out together so you can talk about what's going on."

**8** ▶084 Listen to Carla and Mike's conversation again. Complete the sentences with the correct verbs.
1 If you <u>come</u> out, you <u>'ll feel</u> much better.
2 I .................. depressed and miserable if I .................. out.
3 If I .................. running, it .................. it worse.
4 If they .................. my CV, they .................. interested in me.
5 What .................. you do if you .................. a job soon?
6 I .................. any money if I .................. something soon.

**9** Complete the grammar box with the words in the box.

| future   won't   Present Simple   will |

**GRAMMAR: First conditional** ▶ PAGE 123
We make first conditional sentences with:
If + subject + ¹.................., subject + ².................. + verb.
The negative of will is ³...................
We use the first conditional to talk about possible ⁴.................. situations and their results: *If I go running, it will make it worse.*
We often use the contraction *'ll* instead of *will*: *If you come out, you'll feel much better.*

**10** Complete the first conditional sentences with the correct form of the verbs in brackets.
1 If she .................. hard, she .................. a successful lawyer in five years. (study, be)
2 What .................. you .................. if it .................. tomorrow? (do, rain)
3 If they .................. a lift from the station, they .................. you. (need, call)
4 If you .................. the piano every day, it .................. easy to improve. (practise, be)
5 He .................. another girlfriend if Katie .................. with him. (not find, split up)
6 If I .................. out tonight, no one .................. to me and I .................. awful as usual. (go, talk, feel)

**11** ▶086 Listen to the conversations and check.

**12** ▶087 Underline the contractions in the sentences. Listen, repeat and practise.
1 She'll be a successful lawyer in five years.
2 They'll call you.
3 It'll be easy to improve.
4 He won't find another girlfriend.
5 I'll feel awful as usual.

**13** Work with a partner. Ask and answer questions in the first conditional about the situations.
- it rains at the weekend
- lose your job/fail your exams
- you feel ill tomorrow
- get a well-paid job

> How will you feel if …?   What will you do if …?

## 11B The grass is always greener?

▶ **Vocabulary:** Adverbs
▶ **Grammar:** Second conditional
▶ **Listening:** If I lived in London, ...

1 Look at the pictures. Where would you prefer to live? Why?

A

B

2 Read Nick Baker's profile. Why do you think he is unhappy?

### NICK BAKER

| | |
|---|---|
| **About you:** | 25 years old and living in a village with parents in Oxfordshire countryside |
| **Studied at:** | Manchester University |
| **Relationship:** | Single |
| **Employment:** | Unemployed |

3 Read Nick's blog post and answer the questions.
   1 Why has Nick moved back in with his parents?
   2 What three things are good about Jack's life?
   3 What do you think Nick should do?

I'm so bored with my life right now! I finished uni 8 months ago, and moved back in with my parents because I haven't got any money! I just can't find a job near here. And there's nothing to do!

My best mate, Jack, has got a really well-paid job in London – he lives in a really cool apartment and he's got a new girlfriend now. We got the same degree from Manchester, so I could easily have the same life. I just need to get out of here!

4 ▶088 Listen to Nick talking to his friend, Amy. Answer the questions.
   1 What negative points to living with his parents does he mention?
   2 Why does Amy think life is easy for Jack?
   3 What does Nick decide to do?

5 ▶088 Listen again and complete the sentences with the correct verbs.
   1 If I _lived_ in the city, I _would be_ closer to my friends.
   2 If you _____ here, you'd definitely have more things to do in the evening.
   3 If I lived in London, I _____ need to drive everywhere.
   4 If I _____ my own apartment, I wouldn't have to tell my parents what I was doing all the time!
   5 If you won the lottery, you _____ able to have an apartment like Jack's.
   6 I think it would be easier if I _____ actually in London.

6 Look at the sentences in exercise 5 again. Then choose the correct words to complete the grammar box.

### GRAMMAR: Second conditional ▶ PAGE 124

We make second conditional sentences with:

If + subject + ¹*Past Continuous / Past Simple*, subject + ²*would / had* + verb.

Note that we can use *were* instead of *was*: *I think it would be easier if I **were** actually in London.*

We use the second conditional to talk about ³*imagined / real*, unlikely or impossible situations and their results: *If I lived in the city, I'd be closer to my friends.*

We use the second conditional, not the first conditional, when we are ⁴*less / more* certain about a future situation.

98

**7** Work with a partner. Choose the correct words to make second conditional sentences. Do you agree with sentences 2–6?
1 What would you do if you suddenly *became / become* rich?
2 If I *am / were* fitter, I'd run a marathon.
3 If I lived in the countryside, *I / I'd* possibly get some chickens and sheep.
4 I would probably be a lot more stressed if I *lived / would live* in the city.
5 *I'd / I'll* travel the world if I won the lottery.
6 If I had a dog, I definitely wouldn't *lived / live* in an apartment.

**8** Find and underline these adverbs in exercise 7: *possibly*, *probably*, *definitely*. Answer the questions.
1 Which adverb shows the speaker is …
   a 30% certain? ......................
   b 70% certain? ......................
   c 100% certain? ......................
2 Where does the adverb go in positive and negative second conditional sentences?

**9** Complete the second conditional questions. How likely are these situations?
1 What .................. you .................. if you .................. a lot of money? (do, win)
2 What kind of home .................. you .................. if you .................. a celebrity? (buy, be)
3 If you .................. president of your country, what changes .................. you ..................? (be, make)

**10** Work with a partner. Ask and answer the questions in exercise 9. Use adverbs from exercise 8 in your answers.

**11** Work with a partner. Discuss things you would like to change in your life. How could things be different?

> *If I had a less stressful job, I would definitely have more time for my hobbies.*

**12** What do you think happened to Nick when he went to London? Read Amy's article and check your ideas.

**13** Work with a partner and discuss the questions.
1 Are you surprised about what happened to Nick? Why? / Why not?
2 Do you think comparing is always a bad thing? Why? / Why not?
3 Do you think the grass is ever greener on the other side?

## The grass isn't always greener on the other side!

Comparing ourselves to other people – we all do it, but experts say it's an illness and we should stop doing it. This is because comparing any two things means that we decide that one is good and the other is bad. But this isn't always the reality and it's not a healthy way to think.

Look at my friend Nick, for example. He compared his life to his friend Jack's. He kept saying … if I lived in London, like Jack … if I had a well-paid job, like Jack … if I had a nice apartment, like Jack. Well – do you know what happened? He moved to London, found a job and hated it. The job was stressful, he could only afford to live in a shared house, and he hated the noise and pollution. He ended up setting up his own online business and moving back to his parents' village … in his own house this time! He even met his new girlfriend in the village pub! I think Nick just found out that the grass is greener where you water it!

# 11C Thinking negatively

▶ Reading: *The power of pessimism*
▶ Vocabulary: *Collocations*

1 Work in groups. Do you think it is healthier to be an optimist or a pessimist? Why?

2 Look at the pictures and read the introduction to the article. What three examples of positivity does it talk about? In what ways do you think being a pessimist might be better for us?

# The power of pessimism

**Is there too much positivity around us? When we turn on the TV, we see reality shows where positive people sing to achieve their life goals. We 'Like' posts on social media. We hear politicians talk about 'great' futures. But is it good for us to be optimistic all the time? Or could being pessimistic be better for us?**

## Success

We've all heard of those self-help books that tell you to think positively. But can we really achieve our goals just because we believe that we will? Optimists would say that we can, but some scientists now think that being pessimistic can have some advantages.

Let's look at a job interview, for example. A positive-thinking optimist believes they will get the job and they feel confident. However, a pessimist worries about all the things that can go wrong in the interview. A particular type of pessimist — a 'defensive pessimist' — will use these worries to help them prepare. They will have a plan for how to deal with the problems they have imagined. The pessimist will be more prepared than the optimist when they walk into that interview room, and so they are more likely to succeed.

## Health

How does pessimism affect someone's health? A lot of studies suggest that being pessimistic is bad for you and that optimists get better quicker. And it's certainly true that pessimists are more likely to be depressed. However, if we think of those 'defensive pessimists' again — the pessimists that plan and take action to stop bad things happening — then the answer is different. These pessimists expect to be ill, so they do things to make the situation less serious. They take care of themselves by eating healthily, not smoking, doing exercise, and seeing the doctor. They are also more likely to wash their hands if flu is going round, so they are often actually healthier than optimists.

## Enjoying life

When things go wrong, optimists don't usually think it's their own fault, so they forget about it quite quickly. Pessimists, however, often blame themselves or decide that the situation is typical for them because things always go wrong. They can't <u>move forward</u> – they think it will happen again because of who they are or because of their bad luck. This can make it harder to enjoy life.

But what about humour? Have you ever met an optimistic comedian? If you are always positive and think that everything is great, what is there to laugh about? Most comedians like to look at the bad things that can happen to us, and make a joke of it – pessimists are funnier! And laughing helps you both de-stress and fight illnesses, which can only be a good thing.

## The best kind of pessimism

So, is it really better to see the glass as half full? It depends on how you deal with your pessimism. If you expect the worst and do nothing about that, then your life will be really difficult and depressing. However, the best kind of pessimism is the one that allows you to see problems and take action or <u>make changes</u>, so you will <u>handle</u> <u>situations</u> better than an optimist … and, when good things happen, you will be both happy and surprised!

**3** Read the whole article and answer the questions.
1. What do most self-help books tell us to do?
2. What would a pessimist do if they had a job interview? Why?
3. What health problem are pessimists more likely to have?
4. What do 'defensive pessimists' do to stop themselves becoming ill?
5. How do optimists react when things go wrong?
6. Why can life be harder to enjoy for some pessimists?
7. What kind of people are most comedians?
8. What is the 'best kind of pessimism'?

**4** Work with a partner. Look at the underlined collocations in the text. Try to work out what they mean.

**5** Complete the sentences with the correct form of the words in the box.

| move | deal | achieve | take care of |
|------|------|---------|--------------|
| make | handle | take | |

1. I ............... myself – I eat healthily, I exercise three times a week and I sleep more than seven hours each night.
2. If you ignore problems and don't ............... with them, they usually go away.
3. I have a friend who runs away when things get hard. He doesn't ............... difficult situations very well.
4. If you just ............... some small changes to your life, you'd feel much better.
5. People who work hard always ............... their goals.
6. If you want to feel happier, you have to forget the past and ............... forward with your life.
7. If you fail an exam, don't give up! You just need to ............... action so that it doesn't happen again!

**6** Work with a partner. Which of the sentences in exercise 5 are true for you? Which do you agree with? Why?

**7** Work in small groups and discuss the questions.
1. Do you agree that it is good to be a pessimist? Why? / Why not?
2. Why might too much positivity be bad for a person or a society?
3. Are you a pessimist or an optimist? Are you happy about this?
4. Do you think people can change from being a pessimist to an optimist and the other way? Why? / Why not?
5. Do you agree with this quote? Why? / Why not?

> "The man who is a pessimist before 48 knows too much; if he is an optimist after it, he knows too little."
> — Mark Twain

# 11D Making a complaint

- **Speaking:** Making and dealing with complaints
- **Pronunciation:** Apologizing
- **Writing:** An email of complaint; Key language for emails

## Speaking

1 Work with a partner. Look at the photos. What could go wrong in each situation?

2 ▶090 Listen to three conversations. Match them to the photos in exercise 1 and complete the information in the table.

| | Photo | Problem | Solution |
|---|---|---|---|
| 1 | B | | new room |
| 2 | | wrong size trousers | |
| 3 | | | free drink |

3 ▶090 Complete the phrases in the *Key Language* box with the words in the box. Then listen again and check.

> afraid  apologies  apology  available  complaint  exchange  give
> hear  house  Let me  ordered  overcooked  refund  terribly sorry  wrong

### KEY LANGUAGE Making and dealing with complaints

1 I'm in room 207 and I have a _____ . Is the manager _____ ?
2 I'm _____ she's busy at the moment.
3 I'm _____ about that, Mr Wallace.
4 _____ see if I can find a different room for you.
5 I _____ a pair of trousers from you and they're the _____ size.
6 Could you _____ me your customer number?
7 I'd like to _____ it for a size 12.
8 I'll _____ your money to your credit card right away.
9 I'm sorry to _____ that. What was the problem?
10 My steak was _____ .
11 Please accept my _____ for that.
12 Would you like some drinks on the _____ as an _____ ?

4 Match the sentences in the *Key Language* box to the functions below.
  a making a complaint
  b finding out information
  c giving bad news
  d saying sorry
  e finding/suggesting a solution

5 ▶091 Listen to the phrases for apologizing and giving bad news. What do you notice about the intonation?

6 ▶091 Listen again, repeat and practise.

### YOUR TURN

7 Work with a partner. Student A turn to page 127. Student B turn to page 129.

8 Work with a partner. Tell your partner about a time when you made a complaint. Then take turns to roleplay each student's situation.

  1 Where were you?
  2 What was the problem?
  3 What was the solution?

# Writing

**1** Look at the advert. Would you like to stay in this cottage? Why? / Why not?

- Beautiful cottage in quiet village.
- 3 bedrooms, 2 bathrooms
- Hot tub, WiFi, Free parking.

**2** Read the email Jason wrote to the owner of the cottage after he stayed in it. Answer the questions.
1. Which sentence gives his reason for writing?
2. What three problems does he write about?
3. What words does he use to introduce each problem?
4. What solution does Jason suggest?

**Subject:** Problems with the cottage

Dear Sir/Madam

I'm emailing to complain about the cottage where we stayed at the weekend.

Firstly, your advert said there was free parking. However, when we arrived there was no parking near the cottage. We had to park ten minutes away!

Secondly, we had problems with the WiFi. It only worked for about two hours in total!

And finally, the noise! Your advert says the cottage is in a 'quiet village', but it doesn't describe the noisy building work going on next door!

I would be grateful if you could refund some of the money that we paid for this holiday.

I look forward to hearing from you.

Yours faithfully,
Jason Dawson

**3** Read the reply. What solution does Don offer?

Dear Mr Dawson,

Thank you for your email. I'm really sorry to hear about the problems you had in our cottage.

Please accept a refund of £200 with our apologies. We have also corrected the advert so that it no longer says 'Free parking'.

Please accept our apologies once again.

Yours sincerely,
Don Woods

**4** Work with a partner. Complete the *Key Language* box with phrases from both emails.

### KEY LANGUAGE Emails

**Starting an email**
Dear Sir/Madam ¹..............

**Complaining & suggesting solutions**
I'm ².............................. about …
Firstly/Secondly/Finally, your advert said …, but …
I would be grateful if you could …

**Apologising & offering**
I'm really ³.............................. about …
Please accept a refund of X with our apologies.

**Closing an email**
⁴..............................
Please accept our apologies once again.

**Signing off**
Yours faithfully
⁵..............................

**5** Order the words to make sentences.
1. your / accept / the / our / with / Please / order / mistakes / apologies / for
2. full / if / grateful / I / cost / be / immediately / you / refund / would / could / the
3. complain / weekend / hotel / I'm / to / your / emailing / in / our / about
4. forward / to / I / you / from / hearing / look

## YOUR TURN

**6** Write an email complaining about a holiday, an order, or a restaurant.
- Give the reason for writing.
- Give details of the complaint.
- Suggest a solution.

**7** Swap emails with a partner and write a reply.

103

# 12 Technology

- **Vocabulary:** *Word families*
- **Grammar:** *Passives*
- **Reading:** *Bicycles then and now*

## 12A New designs, old ideas

1. What things can you think of that are made of wood? Make a list with a partner.

2. Read the fact file about wood. Does it mention any of the things you listed?

### Wonderful wood

Humans have used wood for thousands of years. Look around you! You'll find something that is made using wood in almost every direction.

**HOME:** Many houses are built using wood, and wood is used to make lots of different items of furniture – both traditional and modern.

**FUN:** Many musical instruments, such as violins and pianos, are made of wood. In the past, wood was used to make toys for children, and even now wooden toys are loved by children all over the world. And of course there's the paper in our books.

**TRANSPORT:** Traditional ships were built with wood, as were horse-drawn carriages. And in fact, the first bicycle was made in 1817 by Baron von Drais using wood.

3. Look at the sentences and answer the questions.
   A: The first bicycle was made in 1817 by Baron von Drais using wood.
   B: Baron Karl von Drais made the first bicycle using wood in 1817.
   1. Do the sentences have the same meaning?
   2. Which sentence focuses on the idea of 'the first bicycle'?
   3. Which sentence focuses on the person, Baron Karl von Drais?
   4. Which sentence uses a passive verb form? Which uses an active verb form?

4. Read the grammar box, then find more examples of passive forms in the fact file.

> **GRAMMAR: Passives** ▶ PAGE 125
>
> We make Present Simple Passive sentences with *am/is/are* + past participle: *Many house are built using wood*.
>
> We make Past Simple Passive sentences with *was/were* + past participle: *Wood was used to make toys for children*.
>
> We use the passive when we <u>don't know</u> who did or does the action of a verb, or when it's <u>not important</u> who did the action: *My house was built in 1968*.

5. Complete the sentences with the Present Simple Passive or the Past Simple Passive.
   1. Most modern bicycles ................ of metal. (make)
   2. The first kind of paper ................ by the Chinese in around 100BC! (invent)
   3. A lot of the UK's food ................ from Europe. (import)
   4. No – you're wrong! *Oliver Twist* ................ by Shakespeare! (not write)
   5. Plastic ................ in too many products these days. (use)
   6. We parked our bikes outside the station yesterday and they ................! (steal)

6. Look at the pictures of the two bicycles. When do you think they were made? What do you think they are made of?

Technology

**7** ▶093 Read the article and choose the correct verb forms to complete it. Listen and check. Were your ideas in exercise 6 correct?

**8** ▶094 Complete the questions with the correct passive form of the verb in brackets. Then write the answers to the questions in full sentences. Listen and check.

1. What _was_ Baron Von Drais' invention _called_? (call)
   It was called the 'laufmaschine' or 'running machine'.
2. What ............ it ............ of? (make)
3. Why ............ no pedals ............ in the design? (use)
4. How ............ Woodster bikes ............? (design)
5. ............ Woodster bikes ............ in a factory? (produce)
6. When ............ a new tree ............? (plant)

**9** ▶095 Find the words in the article to complete the table. Practise saying the words, then listen and check.

| | NOUN | VERB |
|---|---|---|
| 1 | invention | .............. |
| 2 | .............. | create |
| 3 | .............. | design |
| 4 | production | .............. |

**10** Work with a partner and discuss the questions.
1. Drais' running machine wasn't as successful as later designs. Why do you think this was?
2. Would you like to buy a Woodster bike? Why? / Why not?
3. Do you know any more modern products that are made using traditional materials?

**11** Make notes about some of your favourite things. Think about (or find out) who wrote/ designed/invented/produced each thing.

| My favourite things | |
|---|---|
| book .............. | invention .............. |
| piece of clothing .............. | work of art/painting .............. |
| piece of furniture .............. | tech item .............. |
| song .............. | |

**12** Work with a partner. Talk about your favourite things using passive verb forms.

> My favourite tech item is my mobile. It was produced by Apple.

> It was given to me for my birthday.

## BICYCLES then and now

### The father of the bicycle

In June 1817, lots of people watched Baron Karl von Drais ride his new invention down a road in Mannheim, Germany. His invention ¹*was called / were called* the 'laufmaschine' or 'running machine' and it was the first bicycle! It ²*wasn't made / weren't made* of metal – it was made of wood. And it ³*was designed / designed* before pedals ⁴*were invented / are invented*, so the rider had to use his or her feet to move along the road. Drais is often called 'the father of the bicycle'.

### The bike that goes back to its roots

Over the next 200 years, production techniques ⁵*are changed / changed* and most modern bikes ⁶*are made / aren't made* of wood. However, some companies are now looking to the past for their new creations! The Slovenian company, Woodster ⁷*is used / uses* beautiful Slovenian wood to create modern bikes. Woodster bikes ⁸*are designed / designed* using 3D computer technology, but they ⁹*aren't produced / weren't produced* in factories. They're made in small workshops and each bike ¹⁰*are finished / is finished* by hand. The design results in bikes that are beautiful, comfortable, and most importantly – they can get wet! The company also respects the environment – the plan is that every time a bike ¹¹*is ordered / is order*, a new tree ¹²*plants / is planted*!

*Matej Kolakovic / Woodster*

## 12B Tech free

> **Vocabulary:** Verb + noun collocations
> **Grammar:** Reported speech
> **Listening:** A digital detox

1 Work with a partner and discuss the questions.
  1 What technology do you use every day? What do you use it for?
  2 Have you ever tried to live without technology for a day? If so, what was it like? If not, would you like to try it?

2 Read Maddie's blog post. Complete the underlined verb + noun collocations in the blog with the words in the box.

> emails   film   friends   music   the news
> photos   research   social media

3 Work with a partner and discuss the questions.
  1 How similar is Maddie's use of technology to yours? What is the same? What is different?
  2 What do you think she will find difficult about her 'digital detox'? Why?

4 ▶096 Listen to the phone call between Maddie and her dad, Joe. What effect is her digital detox having on these things?
  1 social life: ..........
  2 studying: ..........
  3 music: ..........
  4 sleep: ..........
  5 cooking: ..........

5 ▶096 Listen again and match the sentence halves.
  1 I feel like
  2 I don't know what's
  3 It's so much more difficult to
  4 I've really missed
  5 I'm sleeping better because
  6 I'll try to spend

  a listening to music.
  b less time on social media.
  c a bit of an outsider.
  d do research for my history essay.
  e I can't check my newsfeed in bed.
  f happening at the weekend.

6 ▶097 Now listen to a conversation between Joe and Maddie's mum, Kay. How does Joe report what Maddie said? Complete the sentences.
  1 She told me that she .......... like a bit of an outsider.
  2 She said she .......... what was happening at the weekend.
  3 She said it .......... so much more difficult to do research for her history essay.
  4 She told me that she .......... really .......... listening to music.
  5 She told me she .......... better because she .......... check her newsfeed in bed.
  6 She said she .......... try to spend less time on social media.

## A DIGITAL detox

Technology is central to my life. I love my phone – I use it to ¹message my .........., and I ²go on .......... to chat to my friends and catch up with what they're doing. I ³check my .......... two or three times a day to see if there's anything I need to answer, and I ⁴stream .......... to listen to. I ⁵take .......... of myself and my friends and I ⁶read .......... once a day, so I know what's happening in the world. So I use it for pretty much everything, really. And I have a laptop which I use for my studies – I ⁷do online .......... to find the information that I need to write my essays and presentations ... and when I've finished studying, I can ⁸download a .......... to watch.

But is this a healthy way to live? Around 63% of British school kids wish social media didn't exist – and more and more young people are now trying a digital detox! So I've decided to see if I can do it. I'm going to live without technology for a weekend!

*Wish me luck!*

**7** Work with a partner. Look at the direct speech in exercise 5 and the reported speech in exercise 6. What differences can you see?

**8** Complete the rules in the grammar box with the correct tenses and verb forms.

> **GRAMMAR: Reported speech** ▶ PAGE 125
>
> We use reported speech to report what another person said. The verb in the reporting sentence usually moves one tense back in time: *'I **feel** like an outsider.'* She said she **felt** like an outsider.
>
> Present Simple → ¹ <u>Past Simple</u>
> Present Continuous → ² ................ ,
> Present Perfect → ³ ................ ,
> Past Simple → ⁴ <u>Past perfect</u>
> can → ⁵ ................ ,
> will → would.
>
> Notice the difference between *said* and *told*:
> She **said** (that) it was more difficult to do research.
> She **told me** (that) she was sleeping better.

**9** Complete the reported speech sentences.

1 "I hate people who always look at their phone during dinner."
   She said that ................................................. .
2 "I've just downloaded a new fitness App."
   He told me that ................................................. .
3 "I'm living with my grandparents and there's no WiFi!"
   Lucy said that she ................ and ................ .
4 "We can easily live without social media."
   They told me ................................................. .
5 "I'll send you a WhatsApp message about the party."
   Patrice said he ................................................. .
6 "I don't know how to use Google maps."
   Jana told us that she ................................................. .
7 "I broke the screen on my iPhone!"
   Ron told me he ................................................. .

**10** Work with a partner. Look at the Instagram posts. Which is the most interesting? Which is the most annoying? Why?

**1** I did two hours in the gym! I'm getting stronger every day!

**2** I've used JM Shampoo on my hair for three weeks. I can't believe the amazing results!

**3** I am so in love with Hana – she is amazing!

**4** I made a delicious breakfast with no carbs! I won't be hungry again till 1pm!

**11** Take turns to report the Instagram posts to your partner. Then think of a recent social media post you read. What did he/she say?
   *He said that he'd done two hours in the gym ...*

**12** Now take turns to tell each other three things about your life at the moment.
   1 Make notes on what your partner says.
   2 Use reported speech to tell a new partner what you heard.

107

## 12C Social media

▶ **Reading:** *Social media – do you love it or hate it?*
▶ **Vocabulary:** *Compound nouns*

1 Work in groups. Do you agree with the quote? Why? / Why not?
  "What you see on social media isn't real."

2 Maria is a big fan of social media, but Simon doesn't like it. Work with a partner. Look at the four headings in the article. What pros and cons do you think they might talk about?

Maria            Simon

3 Work in two groups. Group A: read *Friends and family* and *Work*. Group B: read *Photo Evidence* and *Health*. Then read the sentences for your group. Are they True or False? Correct the false sentences.

   **Group A**
   1 Maria uses Skype to keep in touch with a friend who is travelling in Spain.
   2 She has made a lot of new friends through online groups.
   3 Simon feels happy when he looks at posts from his friends.
   4 LinkedIn has helped Maria find a lot of work.
   5 Her Facebook adverts are not very successful.
   6 Simon thinks that most employers will look at our social media profiles.

   **Group B**
   7 Maria never prints out her photos.
   8 Simon kept all his photos from the 1990s.
   9 He thinks that people should video everything.
   10 Maria uses fitness apps and follows fitness experts on Instagram.
   11 Simon thinks that comparing ourselves to other people motivates us.
   12 He thinks we spend too much time on our phones.

4 Work with a partner from the other group. Tell your partner about what you read.

# SOCIAL media
– do you love it or hate it?

## FRIENDS AND FAMILY

**MARIA:** 👍 Technology is great for keeping in touch with friends and family around the world. Instagram and Facebook allow me to see what my cousins in Spain are doing. And Skype means that I can speak to my friend who is travelling in India at the moment.

But it's not only about people you already know. It's also great for meeting new people. I've joined several Facebook groups where I can chat online with like-minded people. I've also met some of these new friends in real life – at events or just at the pub.

**SIMON:** 👎 I know it's designed to help you connect with other people, but I think social media disconnects you. When I look at posts from my friends, I always compare myself with them. I start to think … they look better than me, they've got more friends, they're more successful, etc. It makes me feel different and alone. And what about cyberbullying, where a group of people send horrible messages to someone they don't like? That happens a lot these days, especially to teenagers.

## Technology

### WORK

**MARIA:** 👍 I have my own business, and I've got so much work through LinkedIn. It's great – people can look at my profile, and if they like what they see, they can send me a message.

I'm also a member of a community group on Facebook that allows adverts on the first day of every month. I always post something about my business – usually a special offer for new customers – and it always works. I get so many emails on the 1st and 2nd of every month!

**SIMON:** 👎 I know that people use social media to get work and advertise their businesses, but I don't think it helps everyone's careers. Did you know that 93% of employers look at our social media profiles? They want to know if you're sociable, if you have certain political views, if you're generally happy, etc. Watch out if you like to party – they might think you're not serious. But the worst thing you can do is have bad spelling or grammar in your posts – they really don't like that.

### PHOTO EVIDENCE

**MARIA:** 👍 I take so many photos and I never print them … but I know I'll never lose them, because I put them on Instagram and Facebook. I love it when I get a Facebook memory with a photo from years before. And WhatsApp is great for photos too, because I can keep the pictures that my friends have taken … with me in them!

**SIMON:** 👎 I was a teenager in the 1990s – and I'm very happy about that. We didn't take many photos, and I threw away photos of me doing stupid things – and they can never be seen again! It's not like that for teenagers today – people take photos all the time and you can't control what they do with them! And I think people also live their lives through their phones – I noticed this at a <u>music festival</u> recently. Everyone around me was videoing the band, but I was watching them with my own eyes and really enjoying the moment.

### HEALTH

**MARIA:** 👍 I know some people think using social media is bad for you, but it's not like that for me. I've got an app that tracks my bike rides and runs – and I can post what I did on social media. All the likes and comments on these posts really motivate me. I also follow a lot of fitness experts on Instagram. They post recipes and suggest exercises, which is really useful.

**SIMON:** 👎 I think technology is bad for our health in so many ways. Comparing ourselves to other people all the time makes us depressed. I also find that I when I look at my phone, it's <u>information overload</u> – messages, updates, photos, news articles … it's too much and my brain hurts! And then there's the <u>time-wasting</u>! Think about all the face-to-face conversations, exercise or healthy cooking you could be doing, instead of looking at a screen. And we know that too much <u>screen time</u> means that we get less sleep. The best thing you can do for your health is put your phone down!

▶ 098

---

**5** Complete the sentences with the underlined compound nouns in the article.

1. My phone shows messages, news, status updates. It's ........................!
2. We saw some amazing bands at the ........................ .
3. I try to limit my ........................ to two hours a day.
4. ........................ is a real problem. If kids are having a bad time at school, it continues at home through social media!
5. How can you be friends if you've never met in ........................ .
6. I have a real problem with ........................ – I need to stop reading stuff online and do something useful instead.

**6** Discuss the questions in groups.

1. Do you agree or disagree with these statements:
   - If you aren't on social media, you'll lose friends.
   - You shouldn't share your political opinions on social media.
   - When you post a photo online, it's there for the world to see, forever.
2. Are you more like Maria or Simon? Why?

# 12D What did you hear?

▶ **Speaking:** *Talking about and reacting to the news*
▶ **Pronunciation:** *Emphasizing your feelings*
▶ **Writing:** *A summary; Note-taking*

## Speaking

1 Work in small groups. Discuss the questions.
   1 Where do you usually find out about the news?
   2 Who do you talk to about the news?
   3 Which news topics are you interested in at the moment? Why?

2 ▶ 099 Listen to four conversations about news. Complete the opening questions. Then match the photos to the conversations.
   1 *Do you know* what the weather is going to be like today? *B*
   2 _____ about Robin Edwards? _____
   3 _____ the headlines this morning? _____
   4 _____ the X Factor last night? _____

3 ▶ 099 Complete the phrases in the *Key Language* box with the words in the box. Then listen again and check.

> annoying   awful   great news   disappointing
> pleased   rubbish   surprise   typical

### KEY LANGUAGE  Reacting to the news

1 Really? That's so _____. I need to cycle to the station this morning …
2 I don't believe it! That's _____. He's so rich!
3 … and he always does a lot of work for charity. It's really _____.
4 That's _____! He's only sorry we found out, but he's not sorry he did it.
5 That's no _____. People just aren't spending money at the moment.
6 That's _____! She's lying.
7 Wow! That's _____! I love him.
8 How lovely! I'm so _____. I'll definitely download his album.

4 Which phrases in the *Key Language* box show a positive reaction to the news? Which show a negative reaction?

5 ▶ 100 Listen to the sentences in the *Key Language* box and notice the intonation the people use to emphasize their feelings.

6 ▶ 100 Listen again, repeat and practise.

7 ▶ 101 Read and listen to the quotes from people involved in the four news stories.
   1 "Rain clouds are moving towards the UK and the wind is increasing."
   2 "I've seen the news headlines. I'm very sorry. I have sent a message to all my fans on Twitter."
   3 "I am certain that we will see improvements in the economy very soon."
   4 "I can't believe that I won the X Factor! I love singing and it's a perfect ending to my journey!"

8 Work with a partner. Report what each person said in exercise 7, using reported speech.
   1 She said that _____ and the wind _____.
   2 He said that he _____, he _____ and that he _____ to all his fans on Twitter.
   3 She said she _____ that we _____.
   4 He said he _____, he _____ and it _____ to his journey.

### YOUR TURN

9 Work with a partner. Student A turn to page 127. Student B turn to page 129.

10 Think of a news story you have seen recently. Then work with a partner. Talk about your story.
   • Introduce the story.
   • Report what happened and what people said.
   • Listen to your partner's new story and react to it. Use intonation to emphasize your feelings.

# Technology

## Writing

**1** Work with a partner. Look at the photos and answer the questions.
1. Which person is more comfortable with technology? Why do you think this is?
2. Do you know anyone who is not comfortable with technology? What problems do they have?

**A**

**B**

**2** ▶102 Listen to a short talk. Which person from exercise 1 is a 'digital native'?

**3** ▶102 Listen again. Complete the notes with the words in the box.

| equal | newspapers | natural |
| social media | after | multitask |

**DIGITAL NATIVES**
born ¹.................... 1980s
tech = completely ².................... – grew up with it
check ³.................... before TV for news
no ⁴....................
find info quickly, ⁵.................... easily
think everyone = ⁶.................... – share opinions BUT want to be best

**4** Read the summary below that was written from the notes in exercise 3. Then answer the questions.
1. What kind of words are missing from the notes in exercise 3, e.g. nouns, verbs, pronouns, articles?
2. What abbreviations (short forms) can you see in the notes?
3. What symbols are used in the notes? What do they mean?

**Digital natives**
Digital natives are people who were born after the 1980s. Technology is completely natural to them because they grew up with it.
They check social media before the TV for news and they don't buy newspapers. They can find information quickly and can multitask easily.
Digital natives think that everyone is equal because it's normal for them to share their opinions with everyone.

**5** Read the *Key Language* box. Then make notes from the sentences below. Miss out some words and use abbreviations and symbols.
1. Older people often look for information in books and newspapers. They don't use modern technology.
2. Digital natives often compare themselves to other people on social media and this often can lead to depression.
3. Social media has led to a number of new problems, for example, cyberbullying and fake news.
4. The biggest time-waster in most people's lives is social media. Spending too much time on social media leads to a fall in economic productivity at work.

### KEY LANGUAGE  Note-taking

**Abbreviations**
  info *(information)*
  probs *(problems)*
  tech *(technology)*
**Symbols**
  = *(is or means)*

+/& *(and)*
⟶ *(leads to)*
↑ *(rise/increase)*
↓ *(fall/decrease)*
e.g. *(for example)*
@ *(at)*

## YOUR TURN

**6** ▶103 Listen to a talk about 'digital immigrants'. Make notes.

born ....................
3 types:
avoiders ....................
half-adopters ....................
complete adopters ....................

**7** ▶103 Listen again and check.

**8** Write a summary using your notes. Then swap notes and summaries with a partner and compare them.

**9** Discuss the questions in groups.
1. Who in your family is a digital immigrant? What type are they?
2. Is it fair to expect digital immigrants to shop and bank online? Why? / Why not?

# Video 6: Are you addicted?

## 6 Are you addicted?

**1** Look at the infographic and tick the sentences that you think are true for you. Compare your ideas with a partner. Who uses their phone the most?

- Two thirds of people show signs of being addicted to their phone.
- We unlock our phones 150 times a day.
- Many people spend nearly three hours a day on their phone.
- Nearly everyone checks their phone within one hour of waking up.
- Over 70% of people sleep next to their phone.
- 40% of people check their phone in the middle of the night.

**2** Read the article and answer the questions.
1. How often do we check our phones?
2. What two things cause more arguments between parents and teenagers than phones?
3. What causes teenagers to feel stressed?
4. How soon do teenagers check their phones after they wake up in the morning?
5. What can poor sleep lead to?
6. What do people in their twenties frequently do at work?
7. How much of our life might we spend on our phone?

## PHONE addiction

Mobile phones are taking over our lives. Looking at our phone is often the last thing we do before going to bed and the first thing we do when we wake up. Most of us check our phones several times an hour. This is starting to affect our personalities and our relationships with other people.

For parents and teenagers, it's the third most common cause of conflict, only behind housework and when to go to bed. And teenagers are starting to feel the pressure of other people being able to contact them at any time, day or night. Two thirds feel the pressure to answer messages immediately, and nearly half feel they get too many messages. Teenagers are often only out of bed for five minutes before they check their phone.

So how is this addiction affecting people? Heavy social media users are much more likely to suffer from depression. One cause of this may be that people are sleeping less due to their technology use, and poor-quality sleep can be linked to depression. We are also interacting less with those around us. Most people use their phones while they are talking to friends or family and many people now sit in silence with friends while checking their phones.

Smartphone use is also affecting people's ability to do their jobs because most people check their phone while they are at work. Furthermore, a third of people in their twenties spend two hours a day on their phone for personal reasons at work. These constant interruptions can make it difficult for people to pay attention to their work.

Currently, people are likely to spend nearly nine years of their life on a mobile phone and just three years of quality, technology-free time with their friends. Smartphones have taken over our lives and it's time to change this.

3 ▶ Watch the video. Put the topics in the order they are mentioned.
a  how smartphones affect your mind
b  phantom phone ringing
c  the number of mobile phone users  1
d  why we use social media more
e  addiction to new things
f  chemicals that make you feel good about yourself

4 ▶ Watch the video again. Complete the sentences with one or two words.
1  Of the nearly eight billion people in the world, ............... have a smartphone.
2  In the past, people worried about addiction to ............... and ................
3  People now find it harder to make ................
4  People think they are good at ..............., but this is not true.
5  We check our phones every ..............., but often there hasn't been a message or call.
6  You release more dopamine when you talk about ................
7  We like people we meet online more than when we then meet them ................
8  People who meet online might have a ............... future.

5 Work with a partner and discuss the questions.
1  Do you worry about how much you use your phone? Why? / Why not?
2  Do you think smartphones have a positive or negative effect on our lives? Why?
3  How do you feel about the idea that you might spend nine years of your life on your phone? Why?

# Review

**LESSON 11A** — Which of these words can we use with *up* to form phrasal verbs? *find, split, put?*

**LESSON 11A** — Answer this question with a first conditional: *How will you feel if you wake up early tomorrow?*

**LESSON 11B** — Write 3 second conditional sentences about unlikely things you would like to happen.

**LESSON 11B** — Which adverbs show 30%, 70% and 100% certainty?

**LESSON 11C** — Write 3 sentences about your life now using: *deal with, handle* and *take care of.*

**LESSON 11D** — List 3 things you might make complaints about.

**LESSON 11D** — List 3 phrases to apologize and offer solutions after a complaint.

**LESSON 12A** — Use passives to describe how something in your house is made.

**LESSON 12A** — What are the nouns from *invent, create, design* and *produce*?

**LESSON 12B** — List 5 verb and noun collocations to describe how you use technology.

**LESSON 12B** — In reported speech, what do these tenses change to: Present Simple, Present Perfect, Past Simple?

**LESSON 12C** — Write a sentence giving your opinion about whether screen time is a waste of time or not.

**LESSON 12D** — Write 3 phrases for reacting to news.

**LESSON 12D** — What abbreviations for *information, problems* and *technology* might you use when you are making notes?

113

# Grammar Reference

## Unit 1

### 1A Questions

#### Questions with *be*

In questions with *be* we put the verb *be* before the subject.

| Question word | be | Subject | |
|---|---|---|---|
| Where | is | the post office? | |
| How | was | your holiday? | |
| | Are | you | busy? |

#### Questions with other verbs

We add an auxiliary verb to questions with other main verbs. We put the auxiliary before the subject.

| Question word | Auxiliary verb | Subject | Main verb | |
|---|---|---|---|---|
| Where | do | you | work? | |
| Who | do | you | live | with? |
| | Do | they | live | in New York? |
| | Does | she | like | her new flat? |

#### Yes / No questions

We do not use a question word in *yes / no* questions.

**Are** we late?   **No**, we **aren't**. / **Yes**, we **are**.
**Do** you speak French?   **No**, I **don't**. / **Yes**, I **do**.

#### Word order with *what, which* and *whose*

1 We can follow *what*, *which* and *whose* with a noun.
   **Whose pen** is this?
   **Which flat** is yours?
   **What restaurant** did you book?
2 We often follow *how* with an adjective, adverb or *much / many*.
   **How old** is your car?
   **How quickly** can you finish the report?
   **How much** is this?
   **How many** people are on your course?

### 1B Present Simple and Continuous

#### Present Simple – Form

| | I / you / we / they | he / she / it |
|---|---|---|
| + | I **live** on Kings Road. | He **lives** on Kings Road. |
| - | I **don't watch** a lot of TV. | She **doesn't watch** a lot of TV. |
| ? | Where **do** they **live**? | Where **does** he **live**? |

#### Use

1 We use the Present Simple to talk about:
   • habits and routines
   I **drink** a lot of coffee.
   • things that are generally true
   We **live** in France.
   • states (state verbs) and feelings
   I **don't like** tea.
   Do you **know** Paul Hughes?
2 We use the Present Simple with adverbs of frequency (*often*, *never*, *sometimes*, etc.)
We put the adverb of frequency **before** the main verb but **after** the verb *be*.
I **always eat** breakfast at work.
He **is never** on time.

#### Present Continuous – Form

| | I | he / she / it | you / we / they |
|---|---|---|---|
| + | I **am cooking** dinner | Mark **is helping** me. | We're **working** a lot. |
| - | I'm not **working** today. | It **isn't working**. | They **aren't helping** us. |
| ? | | **Is** he **meeting** us later? | **Are** you **enjoying** the show? |

#### Use

1 We use the Present Continuous to talk about:
   • actions happening right now
   They **are watching** TV at the moment.
   • actions happening around now
   I'm **staying** with my parents this week.
   • changing situations
   She **is working** a lot more in the evenings now.

114

2 We often use time expressions with the Present Continuous. For example, *right now*, *at the moment*, *today*, *this winter*.

I'm **working** at home **today**.
She**'s driving** to work **right now**.

### Spelling rules for -ing forms

| Infinitive | -ing form | Spelling rule |
|---|---|---|
| sleep | sleeping | Most verbs add -ing |
| cook | cooking | It **isn't working**. |
| live | living | Verbs ending in -e. Drop the -e and add -ing |
| have | having | |
| stop | stopping | Stressed vowel + one consonant. Double the final consonant. |
| get | getting | |

# Unit 2

## 2A Past Simple and Past Continuous

### Past Simple – Form – Regular verbs

To form the Past Simple of regular verbs, add -ed to the base form (infinitive without *to*). The Past Simple form is the same for all persons (*I, you, he/she/it, we, they*).

I **cooked** pasta for dinner yesterday.
Jane **walked** to work on Monday.
We **watched** TV last night.
! Be careful with spelling.

| Regular verb | Past simple ending |
|---|---|
| Most verbs: **work**, **play**, **watch** | Add -ed: **worked**, **played**, **watched** |
| Verbs ending in -e: **like**, **phone**, **live** | Add -d: **liked**, **phoned**, **lived** |
| Verbs ending in stressed vowel + consonant: **stop**, **plan** | Double the consonant, add -ed: **stopped**, **planned** |
| Verbs ending in consonant + -y: **try**, **marry** | Change the *y* to *i*, add -ed: **tried**, **married** |

### Form – Irregular verbs

Many common verbs are irregular, so the -ed rule cannot be used. You will need to learn the past simple form of these verbs. See the Irregular verb table on p157.

We **went** to Australia last Christmas.
We **saw** the Sydney Opera House.
I **was** sad when we **left**.

### Questions and negatives

1 To form questions in the past simple, use *did* + the base form (infinitive without *to*) of the verb. To form the negative, use *didn't*.

**Did** you **go** to school yesterday?    No, I **didn't**.
Who **did** you **see** on Tuesday?    I **saw** Dan, but I **didn't see** Jess.

2 Questions with be don't use did.

**Were** you busy yesterday?
Where **were** they on Tuesday?

### Use

We use the Past Simple to talk about completed past actions or situations.

I **lived** in Paris when I was a child.
The weather **was** amazing yesterday.

### Past Continuous – Form

To form the Past Continuous, use *was/were* + base form of the verb + *-ing*.

It **was raining** all day.
We **were playing** football yesterday afternoon.

| | I | he / she / it | you / we / they |
|---|---|---|---|
| + | I **was** working. | She **was** working. | They **were** working. |
| - | I **wasn't** working. | He **wasn't** working. | We **weren't** working. |
| ? | **Was** I working? | **Was** he working? | **Were** they working? |

### Use

We use the Past Continuous to talk about actions in progress in the past.

He **was waiting** at the bus stop at 8.30 a.m.
We **were watching** the football match at that time.

### Past Continuous with Past Simple

1 We use the Past Continuous with the Past Simple when we want to talk about a shorter action and a longer action together.

I **was having** a bath when the phone **rang**.
(*Long action* = **was having** a bath
*Short action* = the phone **rang**)

2 We also use the Past Continuous in stories, to describe the background or set the scene. We then use the Past Simple to describe the actions.

The rain **was falling** to the ground and it **was splashing** everywhere. I **was getting** cold and wet, so I **went** into the nearest café.

## 2B Present Perfect Simple + *yet, already, just, ever* and *never*

### Form

To form the Present Perfect Simple, we use *have/has* + Past Participle.

| Positive and negative | | |
|---|---|---|
| I/You/We/They | have | booked a holiday. |
| He/She/It | has | booked a holiday. |

| Question | | |
|---|---|---|
| Have | I/you/we/they | finished yet? |
| Has | he/she/it | finished yet? |

! We often use contracted forms of *has/have*, but NOT in short answers.

I**'ve** never **been** to Italy.
He**'s** just **passed** his driving text.
'**Have** you **seen** Dan?' 'Yes, I **have**.' ~~'Yes, I've.'~~

### Use

1 We use the Present Perfect Simple to talk about recent actions with present effects.

I**'ve finished** my homework, so now I can watch TV!

We often use *already, just,* and *yet* with the Present Perfect. Notice the position of each word, and note that *yet* is only used in questions and negatives.

Jess **has** just **had** some great news!
I**'ve** already **seen** this film.
**Have** you **finished** your dinner yet?

2 We also use the Present Perfect to talk about experiences in your life up till now.

We**'ve met** a lot of interesting people over the years.
We often use *ever* and *never* with this use.

She**'s been** to Spain, but she**'s never** been to South America.
**Have** you **ever run** a marathon?

# Unit 3

## 3A Quantity: *much, many, some, any, a few, a lot of,* etc.

| | Countable | Uncountable |
|---|---|---|
| Large quantity | There are **a lot of** cups. | There isn't **much** coffee left. |
| No specific amount | There are **some** apples. | I'd like **some** water, please. |
| Small quantity | There aren't **many** tickets left. | There isn't **much** time left. |
| Zero quantity | There are **no** pens. | There's **no** time. |
| | There aren't **any** shops open. | There isn't **any** juice. |
| Questions | Are there **any** tickets? | Is there **any** cheese? |
| | **How many** people are here? | **How much** milk is there? |

### *Some* and *any*

1 We use *some* in positive sentences and questions that are offers and requests.

Would you like **some** coffee?
I'd like **some** milk, please.

2 We use *any* in negatives and questions.

There isn't **any** sugar.
Are there **any** apples?

### *Much* and *many*

We use *much/many* in negative sentences and questions, and *a lot of* in positive sentences.

There isn't **much** milk.
How **many** apples do you need?
I have **a lot of** work to do!

### Too

1 We use *too* with adjectives and adverbs when something is more than necessary.

It's **too** hot in here!

We use *too much* with uncountable nouns and *too many* with countable nouns.

I have **too much** work to do!
I have **too many** clothes.

### Enough / not enough

1 We use *enough* with nouns when something is the correct amount.

I think I have **enough** time to finish this.

2 We use *not enough* with nouns when the amount is less than necessary.

There are **not enough** hours in the day.

## 3B Something / anything / nothing, etc.

### Form

| | | | |
|---|---|---|---|
| **People** | somebody / someone | anybody / anyone | nobody / no one |
| **Things** | something | anything | nothing |
| **Places** | somewhere | anywhere | anything |

### Use

1 We use *somebody, someone, something, somewhere* in positive sentences and in offers and requests.

There's **somebody** at the door.
Would you like **something** to drink?

2 We use *anybody, anyone anything, anywhere* in negative sentences and questions.

I can't find my phone **anywhere**.
Is there **anyone** we forgot to invite?

3 We use *nobody, no one, nothing, nowhere* with a positive verb.

It's too late. There's **nowhere** open for dinner.

4 We use *nobody, no one, nothing, nowhere* in short answers.

Is anything wrong?   No, **nothing**.

# Unit 4

## 4A *Used to*

### Form

To form sentences with *used to*, use *used to* + base form (infinitive without *to*) of the verb. The form is the same for all persons.

I **used to live** in Portugal.
She **used to drive** to work.
We **used to have** an outside toilet.

### Negatives

Form negatives with *didn't* + *use to* + base form of the verb.

He **didn't use to have** a TV.
They **didn't use to eat** chocolate.

### Questions

Form questions with *did* + subject + *use to* + base form of the verb.

**Did you use to live** in London?
Yes, I **did**. / No, I **didn't**.

### Use

1 We use *used to* to talk about past situations or habits that have now changed.

I **used to smoke.** *(I don't anymore.)*
Most people **didn't use to own** a car. *(Most people own a car now.)*

2 We can use the Past Simple instead of or as well as *used to* to talk about past situations and habits.

I **smoked** when I was in my 20s.
Most people **didn't use to own** a car, so they **cycled** or **walked** to work.

## 4B Modals of obligation and permission: can, have to, must

### Form

Can, must, and have to are followed by the base form of the verb.

#### Can

|   | I / you / he / she / it / we / they | | |
|---|---|---|---|
| + | I **can wear** jeans to school. | She **can stay** at our house. | We **can park** here. |
| - | I **can't wear** jeans to school. | She **can't stay** at our house. | We **can't park** here. |
| ? | **Can** I **have** a biscuit? | **Can** she **stay** at our house? | **Can** we **park** here? |
|   | No, you **can't**. | Yes, she **can**. | No, you **can't**. |

The past of can is could.

> I **could wear** earrings at school when I was a child. *(was allowed)*
> We **couldn't eat** in the playground at my school. *(wasn't allowed)*s

#### Must

1 We don't often make questions with must.

|   | I / you / he / she / it / we / they | | |
|---|---|---|---|
| + | You **must speak** to Dan. | She **must stay** inside. | They **must park** here. |
| - | You **mustn't speak** to Dan. | She **mustn't stay** inside. | They **mustn't park** here. |

2 We don't use must or mustn't in the past. We use had to or wasn't/weren't allowed to. We can also use couldn't as a past form of mustn't.

> You **must** stay inside. / We **had to** stay inside.
> You **mustn't** go out. / We **couldn't/weren't allowed to** go out.

#### Have to

1 Use the auxiliary verb do/don't to make negatives and questions with have to.

|   | I / you / we / they | he / she / it |
|---|---|---|
| + | I **have to eat** healthy snacks. | She **has to walk** to work. |
| - | We **don't have to eat** healthy snacks. | He **doesn't have to walk** to work. |
| ? | **Do** they **have to wear** school uniform? | **Does** he **have to** get up early? |
|   | No, they **don't**. | Yes, he **does**. |

2 The past of have to/has to is had to.

> She **had to** take the bus to work.
> We **had to stay** at school until we were 16.

### Use

#### Can

Can is a modal of permission. We use can and can't to say that something is allowed or not allowed.

> You **can leave** your bag at the reception desk. *(allowed)*
> You **can't eat** in here. *(not allowed)*
> **Can** I **park** here? *(asking if something is allowed)*

#### Have to and must

1 Have to and must are modals of obligation. In positive sentences, the meanings of have to and must are very similar. We use them for rules and to talk about what is necessary.

> You **must arrive** by 7a.m.
> You **have to arrive** by 7 a.m.

2 Must can be a little stronger than have to, and is often used in written rules.

> All visitors **must show** ID.
> Do you **have to get up** early every day?

3 Mustn't and don't have to have different meanings. We use mustn't to say something is not allowed – it is stronger than can't.

> You **mustn't smoke** in this building.

4 We use don't have to to say that something is not necessary. It can also be used in the past.

> 'Do I **have to pay** for the ticket?'   'No, you don't.'
> You **don't have to bring** a packed lunch, but you can if you want to.
> I **didn't have to learn** French at my school.

# Unit 5

## 5A *Will* for decisions, offers and promises

### Form

*Will* is followed by the base form (infinitive without *to*) of the verb. The form is the same for all persons. The contraction is *'ll*.

> I **will help** you with your project.
> She **will give** you a lift to the station.
> They**'ll look after** your cat for you.

The negative of *will* is *won't* (or *will not*). Again, the form is the same for all persons.

> I **won't forget** my homework.
> He **won't be** late.
> We **won't tell** anyone about the surprise party.

### Use

We use *will* to talk about the future. It can be used in many different ways. We can use it for:

- spontaneous decisions (decisions we make at the time of speaking, NOT before).

> I don't know what to order … I know, I**'ll have** the fish pie.
> 'I'm training for a 10k run – join me.' 'Erm … OK, I**'ll do** it!'

- offers

> I**'ll help** you with your homework.
> We**'ll take** you to the airport tomorrow.

- promises

> I promise I**'ll come** home before midnight.
> We**'ll work** really hard this term, Mr Smith.

## 5B Future forms: *will*, *be going to*, Present Continuous

### Form

**Will**
See 5A for the form of *will*.

**Be going to**
We form *be going to* with subject + *am/is/are* + *going to* + verb.

|   | I | He / She / It | You / We / They |
|---|---|---|---|
| + | I'm going to leave. | He's going to leave. | You're going to leave. |
| - | I'm not going to leave. | She's not going to leave. | We're not going to leave. |
| ? | Am I going to leave? | Is he going to leave? | Are they going to leave? |
|   | No, I'm not. | Yes, he is. | No, they aren't. |

**Present Continuous**
See 1B for the form of the Present Continuous.

### Use

*Will* **for predictions**

We can use *will* to make predictions about the future.

> I think we**'ll produce** a lot more electric cars over the next few years.
> I'm sure the government **will increase** taxes next year.

Look back to 5A for other uses of *will*.

*Be going to* **for predictions**

When we have more evidence for our prediction, we use *be going to*, not *will*. Sometime the speaker describes the evidence, but sometimes the speaker doesn't talk about the evidence directly.

> Look out! That book i**s going to fall** off the table! (evidence = the speaker can see the book on the edge of the table)
> If you look at the research, it's clear that temperatures **are going to go up**. (evidence = the research)

*Be going to* **for future plans and intentions**

We also use *be going to* to talk about future plans and intentions.

> When I finish this project, I**'m going to have** a long break.
> We**'re going to get married** in the summer.

**Present Continuous for the future**

Even though it is usually used as a present tense, we also use the Present Continuous to talk about the future – for fixed arrangements and appointments.

> I**'m seeing** my doctor tomorrow at 10 a.m.
> They**'re having** a party at their house next Saturday.

# Unit 6

## 6A Comparatives

### Form

| Adjective | Comparative | Rule |
|---|---|---|
| rich | **richer** | one syllable: add -er |
| big | **bigger** | one vowel + one consonant: double the final consonant |
| hot | **hotter** | |
| easy | **easier** | ending in -y: drop the y and add -ier |
| busy | **busier** | |
| interesting | **more interesting** | more + adjective |
| boring | **more boring** | |

| Irregular adjectives | | |
|---|---|---|
| good > **better** | bad > **worse** | far > **further** |
| tired > **more tired** | stressed > **more stressed** | |

### Use

1 We use a comparative adjective, usually with *than*, to compare two things or people.

This job is **more interesting** than my last one.
Your phone is **newer** than mine.

2 We use *less* as the opposite of *more*.

This job is **less interesting** than my last one.

3 We use *as … as* to show that two things are equal. We use *not as … as* to show that they are not equal.

James is **as tall as** Daniel.
This film was**n't as good as** his last one.

## 6B Superlatives

### Form

| Adjective | Superlative | Rule |
|---|---|---|
| short | **shortest** | one syllable: add -est |
| fat | **fattest** | one vowel + one consonant: double the final consonant |
| wet | **wettest** | Are they going to leave? |
| pretty | **prettiest** | ending in -y: drop the y and add -iest |
| friendly | **friendliest** | |
| beautiful | **most beautiful** | most + adjective |
| relaxed | **most relaxed** | |

| Irregular adjectives | | |
|---|---|---|
| good > **best** | bad > **worst** | far > **furthest** |
| tired > **most tired** | stressed > **most stressed** | |

### Use

1 We use *the* + superlative adjective to talk about extremes.

This is **the oldest** building in the town.
I feel **the most relaxed** when I'm on holiday.

2 We use the Present Perfect with *ever* with superlatives.

This is **the best** book I have **ever read**.
She's **the kindest** person I've **ever met**.

# Unit 7

## 7A Tense review

| Tense | Example | Use |
|---|---|---|
| Present Simple | I **live** in America. She **doesn't play** any sports. | things that happen always or usually |
| Present Continuous | They **are moving** house. | things happening right now or in the near future |
|  | I**'m meeting** Paul on Sunday. | future arrangements |
| Past Simple | We **didn't go** anywhere yesterday. Our team won the match last weekend. | finished actions in the past |
| Past Continuous | I **was playing** tennis. | actions in progress at a time in the past |
|  | I **was working** in Moscow when I met my wife. | interrupted past |
| be going to + infinitive | We**'re going** to the cinema this weekend. | Future plans and intentions |
|  | Look at the clouds! It**'s going to rain**. | Predictions based on evidence |
| will + infinitive | You**'ll love** that restaurant! | predictions |
|  | I**'ll have** the burger. | decisions |
|  | I**'ll cook** tonight. | offers |
|  | Don't worry. We**'ll finish** it by the end of the day. | promises |
| present perfect | I**'ve** just **spoken** to Tom. | recent actions |
|  | **Have** you ever **been** to Japan? | past experiences |

## 7B Present perfect: *for* and *since*

### Form
See 2B for form.

### Use

1. We use the Present Perfect with *for* and *since* to talk about actions or states that started in the past and are still true now.

   I**'ve worked** here **for** five years.
   I**'ve worked** here **since** 2020.

2. We use *How long…?* to ask about the duration of an activity.

   A: **How long have** you worked here?
   B: I**'ve worked** here **for** six years.

3. We also use the present perfect to talk about experiences in your life up till now.

   We've met a lot of interesting people over the years.

4. We use *for* with periods of time. We use *since* to show when the period of time started.

| For | Since |
|---|---|
| two weeks, ten years, a long time | Monday, the weekend, the summer, 1980 |
| three months, ages, a couple of hours etc | 10 o'clock, lunchtime |

# Unit 8

## 8A Past Perfect

### Form
To form the Past Perfect we use *had* + past participle.

|  | I / you / he / she / it / we / they | |
|---|---|---|
| + | I h**ad eaten** all the chocolates. | They **had fallen** in love. |
| - | She **hadn't seen** his car. | They **hadn't worked** very hard. |
| ? | **Had** you **done** your homework? | **Had** they **watched** the match? |
|  | No, I **hadn't**. | Yes, they **had**. |

## Use

1. We use the Past Perfect to show that a past action happened before another past action.

> When I arrived at the restaurant, everyone **had** already **ordered** their food.

2. We use the Past Simple with the Past Perfect to show the order of past events. Actions in the Past Perfect happened before actions in the Past Simple.

> The man **shouted** at the woman because she **had damaged** his car. (First action = woman damaged the car; Second action = man shouted)

3. When we use the Past Perfect and Past Simple together, we often join the two parts of the sentence with *when*, *because* or *so*.

> When they **arrived** at the station, the train **had left**.
> She **was** happy because she **had passed** her exams.
> The match **had finished**, so we **went** home.

## 8B Narrative tenses

The Past Simple, Past Continuous and Past Perfect are sometimes called narrative tenses. This is because we use them when we tell stories or describe past events.

### Form

See 2A for the form of the Past Simple and the Past Continuous.

See 8A for the form of the Past Perfect.

### Use

**Past Simple**

We use the Past Simple to say what actions happened.

> He **stole** the money and **ran** fast down through the busy streets until he **reached** his home.

**Past Continuous**

1. We use the Past Continuous to talk about actions that were in progress in the past.

> They **were painting** their living room on Wednesday.

2. We can use it with the Past Simple to show when a longer action was interrupted by a short action.

> I **was watching** TV when the pizza **arrived**.
> (*Long action* = watching TV; *Short action* = pizza arrived)

3. We often use the Past Continuous to start a story and/or give background details.

> The waves **were crashing** onto the sand and the wind **was blowing** hard when Joe saw the boat far out at sea.

**Past Perfect**

We use the Past Perfect to talk about the past in the past, i.e. to show that a past action happened before another past action. We often use it with the Past Simple.

> I **had seen** the film before.
> He **called** the police because he **had seen** a man take some money from an old lady.
> (*First action* = see the man take some money; *Second action* = call the police)

**Using all the narrative tenses**

We use the three tenses together to show the order and duration of past actions.

> The sun **was shining** and it was a lovely afternoon. The boys **were playing** football when the bus **crashed** into the tree. The driver had seen a cat in the road and he **couldn't** stop in time.
>
> *Background to the story* = the sun was shining
> *Longer past action* = the boys were playing football
> *Short past action (interrupting the longer action)* = the bus crashed into the tree
> *Past action* = the driver couldn't stop in time
> *Past in the past (happened before the driver couldn't stop)* = the driver had seen a cat in the road

# Unit 9

## 9A Infinitive with *to*

1. We use the infinitive with *to*
   - after some verbs, e.g. *would like, want, decide,* etc.

> They **decided to book** the local Italian restaurant.
> I **would like to go** for a walk later.

   - after adjectives.

> Is it **possible to speak** to the manager?
> It's **hard to stop** smoking.

   - to give a reason for doing something

> He bought a card **to give** to his friend.
> He turned on the TV **to watch** the news.

   - It can also be used in the negative.

> She **promised not to tell** anyone.

## Unit 9B Gerunds

### Form

We form the gerund with the base form of the verb + -ing: *eating, reading, buying*, etc.

My sister gets quite nervous about **flying**.
**Shopping** is one of my favourite hobbies.
I love **meeting** new people.

### Use

We use the gerund:
- after some verbs such as *like, hate* etc.

I **hate driving** in the rain.
I **enjoy hanging** out with friends.

- after a preposition

She's not very good **at speaking** in public.
I'm worried **about passing** my driving test.

- as the subject of a sentence

**Flying** makes me nervous.
**Phoning** someone during dinner is rude.

- It can be positive or negative.

I really **enjoy doing** exercise.
I really **enjoy not having** any work to do.

# Unit 10

## 10A Modals of advice

1. We use *should/shouldn't* + the infinitive without *to* to give advice or suggest the right or wrong thing to do. *Should* and *shouldn't* are the same for all persons.

He **should eat** more fruit.
You **shouldn't go** to bed so late.

2. We can also use *ought to/ought not to* + the infinitive without *to* instead of *should/shouldn't*. It has the same meaning as *should/shouldn't*.

We **ought to leave** now.
You **ought not to park** your car here. You'll get a fine.

3. We often use both with the phrase *I think you …*

**I think you should leave** now.
**I think we should wait** another five minutes.
**I think you ought to phone** your grandma.

4. We can use *could* to give advice or make a suggestion that is less certain.

You **could try** phoning instead of texting.

## 10B *Will, may, might*

### Use

1. We use *will* and *won't* to make predictions about the future. They are followed by the infinitive without *to*. This type of prediction is usually based more on opinion than fact or something we know. See 5B for more information.

I don't think we **will win** the World Cup.
We **won't have** driverless cars in the near future.

2. We can use *may* and *might* to make predictions that are less certain. We use these to talk about future possibilities.

I **might see** you at the weekend.
We **may need** a lift to the station.
We could have a barbeque. It **might not** rain.
Susie **may not** get the job.

3. We often ask questions about future possibilities with *Do you think you will …?*

**Do you think** you'll pass the test?
I'm not sure. I **might** do.

# Unit 11

## 11A First Conditional

### Form

1. We form the First Conditional with *if* + subject + Present Simple + subject + *will* + base form (infinitive without *to*).

**If** you **work** hard, you **will pass** your exams.

2. There are two clauses in a First Conditional sentence – the *if* clause and the main clause. The *if* clause can go before the main clause OR after it. We need a comma between the clauses when the *if* clause comes first.

**If** I **have** time, I**'ll go** to the shops.
I**'ll go** to the shops **if** I **have** time.

### Use

We use the First Conditional to talk about a possible future situation and the result of that situation. The *if* clause talks about the possible future situation and the main clause talks about the result.

**If** the company **closes**, I **will look** for a new job straight away.
(Possible future situation = the company closes
Result of that situation = look for a new job straight away)
They **will buy** a house if they **save** enough money.
(Possible future situation = they save enough money
Result of that situation = they will buy a house)

### Negatives

The verb in either, or both clauses can be negative.

If they **don't stop** talking, the teacher **will be** angry.
If you **don't study**, you**'ll fail** the exams.
If I **lose** my phone, I **won't get** another one.
If she **isn't** sociable, she **won't find** any new friends.
We **won't be** successful if we **don't get** some money from the bank.

### Questions

Questions can start with the main clause OR the *if* clause.

What **will** you **do if** you **fail** your driving test?
**If** they **don't pay** the restaurant bill, what **will happen**?
'**If** you **lose** your job, **will** you move to another town?'
'Yes, I **will**.'
'**Will** he **break up** with his girlfriend **if** he **gets** a place at university?' 'No, he **won't**.'

## 11B Second Conditional

### Form

1 We form the Second Conditional with *if* + subject + Past Simple + subject + *would* + base form (infinitive without *to*).

If I **lived** in London, I**'d have** a more interesting social life.

2 As with the First Conditional, there are two clauses in a Second Conditional sentence – the *if* clause and the main clause. The clauses can come in either order.

If I **started** running chocolate, I**'d get** fit.
I**'d get** fit if I **started** running.

### Use

1 We use the Second Conditional to talk about imagined/unreal/impossible situations and their results. The *if* clause talks about the imagined situation and the main clause talks about the result.

**If** I **lived** near the beach, I**'d swim** in the sea every day.
(Imagined situation = living near the beach
Result = swim in the sea everyday)
He**'d feel** much healthier **if** he **stopped** smoking.
(Imagined situation = he stops smoking
Result = he feels much healthier)
**If** I **won** the lottery, I**'d buy** a castle in Scotland.
(winning the lottery is highly unlikely to happen)
**If** we **were** younger, we**'d move** to Australia.
(being younger than they are now is impossible)

2 We use the Second Conditional, not the First Conditional, when we are less certain about a future situation. Compare the following sentences. The choice of tense depends on how the speaker feels about the situation.

**If I see** Jacky, **I'll ask** her why she quit her job.
(I think it's likely I will see Jacky.)
**If I saw** Jacky, **I'd ask** her why she quit her job.
(I don't think it's likely I will see Jacky.)

3 Note that when *be* is the verb in the *if* clause, we can use *were* instead of *was* for *I*, *he*, *she* and *it*.

**If** I **were** you, I**'d look** for a new job.
**If** she **were** rich, she**'d buy** a holiday home in Barbados.
**If** it **were** possible, we**'d retire** tomorrow.

### Negatives

The verb in either, or both clauses can be negative.

If she **didn't criticize** other people so much, she **would have** more friends.
If you **cooked** more often, you **wouldn't find** it so difficult.
There **would be** more people at the barbecue, if the weather **wasn't** so awful.
We **wouldn't learn** so much if we **didn't have** such a good teacher.
You**'d find** a better job if you **weren't** so lazy.

### Questions

Questions can start with either the main clause OR the *if* clause.

What **would** you **do if** you **lost** your job?
If we **didn't pay** our rent, what **would happen**?
'If you **broke up** with your boyfriend, **would** you **go** travelling?' 'Yes, I **would**.'
'**Would** she **be** angry if you **borrowed** her iPad?' 'No, she **wouldn't**.'

# Unit 12

## 12A Passives

### Form

1  We form the Present Simple Passive with *be* (*am/is/are*) + past participle.

My bed **is made** of metal.
These chocolates **are sold** in many different supermarkets.

2  We form the Past Simple Passive with the Past Simple of *be* (*was/were*) + past participle.

This T-shirt **was made** in India.
These chairs **were left** outside in the rain.

|   | Present Simple Passive | Past Simple Passive |
|---|---|---|
| + | This programme **is produced** by the BBC. | The song **was produced** in America. |
| – | These cars **aren't sold** in Europe. | These toys **weren't made** in China. |
| ? | **Is** this cake **made** with butter? No, it **isn't**. | **Was** the movie **filmed** in Spain? Yes, it **was**. |

### Use

1  We use the passive when we <u>don't</u> <u>know</u> who did the action or when it's <u>not</u> <u>important</u> who did the action.

My phone **was stolen** yesterday! (*We don't know who stole it.*)
This bike **was made** in 1981. (*It's not important who made it – the date is more important.*)
These toys **are produced** in China. (*It's not important who produces the toys – the place they are produced is more important.*)

2  Note that we can often use a passive or active sentence to say the same thing. The tense we choose to use depends on what we are interested in.

<u>Passive</u>: Facebook **was invented** in 2004. (*We are more interested in Facebook.*)
<u>Active</u>: Mark Zuckerberg **invented** Facebook in 2004. (*We are more interested in who invented Facebook.*)

3  We can use *by* in passive sentences if we want to say who/what did the action.

The Harry Potter books **were written by** JK Rowling.
This school **was opened** in 1984 **by** Princess Diana.

## 12B Reported speech

### Form

We form reported speech by using a reporting verb (e.g. *said* or *told*), and then moving the tense in the reported words back one tense.

'I **love** football.' (Present Simple)
He **said** he **loved** football. (Past Simple)

| Direct speech | Reported speech |
|---|---|
| Present Simple: 'I **work** for BMW.' | Change to Past Simple: He **told** me he **worked** for BMW. |
| Present Continuous: 'Joe **is writing** a book.' | Change to Past Continuous: She **said** that Joe **was writing** a book. |
| Present Perfect: 'We**'ve never seen** the Northern lights.' | Change to Past Perfect: They **told** me they**'d never seen** the Northern lights. |
| *Can*: 'Julie **can play** the piano.' 'I **can't drive**.' | Change to *could*: He said that Julie **could play** the piano. She said she **couldn't** drive. |
| *Will*: 'I**'ll take** you to the station.' 'Ben **won't pass** his exams.' | Change to *would*: She told me she **would take** me to the station. He said that Ben **wouldn't pass** his exams. |

### Use

We use reported speech to report what somebody said.
'I live with my parents,' Gina said.
Gina **said she lived** with her parents.

### Reporting verbs

1  The most common reporting verbs are *say* and *tell*. After these verbs, we can add the word *that*.

They **said (that)** they were tired.
He **told me (that)** he'd seen the film already.

2  Note that the reporting verb *tell* needs an object e.g. a pronoun or person.

He **told me** that he **wanted** to move house.
NOT He **told** that he **wanted** to move house.

### Pronouns

Pronouns often need to change in reported speech.

'I love **you**.'          She said that she loved **me**.
'**My** dad can't drive.'   He said **his** dad couldn't drive.

# Communication Bank

## 2D Speaking, Exercise 6

### Student A

1 You are a hotel guest. Student B is the receptionist at Hotel Sophia. Prepare for and have three conversations.

1
- Your name is Richard Sutton. Your email address is richard_sutton@yazoo.co.uk.
- You want a hotel room for 2 nights, from Tuesday 2 February till Thursday 4 February.
- Call Hotel Sophia and ask to book a room.
- Ask about the price.

2
- You arrive at Hotel Sophia. Tell the receptionist about your reservation.
- Ask about breakfast and WiFi.

3
- Call reception from your room. Tell them about two problems: you have no hot water, the TV isn't working.
- Ask for a 7.00 a.m. alarm call tomorrow.

---

2 You are the receptionist at Hotel York. Student B is a guest. Prepare for and have three conversations. Look at audioscript 018 on page 136 to help you prepare.

1
- Answer the phone and speak to the guest.
- Double rooms = £180 per night. Single rooms = £130 per night.
- Make the booking – ask for a name and email address.

2
- You are working at reception.
- Check in the guest.
- Breakfast is not included. It costs £15 per person and is served from 7 a.m. till 9 a.m. WiFi is free.

3
- Answer a call at reception. Deal with the problems and the request.

## 4D Speaking, Exercise 7

### Student A

1 You have a problem. When you left university, you didn't have any money so you moved back in with your parents. But your parents still think of you as a young child:
- Dinner is at a set time.
- They worry when you come home late.
- They have an opinion on everything you do.
- You want to get your own place, but you can't really afford to at the moment.

Explain your problem to Student B. Then listen to and respond to the advice.

2 Listen to Student B. Give some advice.

## 5D Speaking, Exercise 8

### Student A

1 You are a patient. Student B is the doctor.
- You don't feel very well. These are your symptoms: stomach ache, fever, you can't stop being sick.
- Go to the doctor and describe how you feel. Answer his/her questions.

2 You are a doctor. Student B is a patient.
- Ask questions and find out what's wrong.
- Ask more questions. Tell the patient what you think the problem is.
- Give some advice about how to get better.

## 8D Speaking, Exercise 8

### Student A

1 Follow the instructions a–h. When it is your turn to show your feelings, use your face and body. Don't speak to your partner.
   a Show that you are worried.
   b Watch your partner and guess how they are feeling.
   c Show that you are shocked.
   d Watch your partner and guess how they are feeling.
   e Show that you are excited.
   f Watch your partner and guess how they are feeling.
   g Show that you are nervous.
   h Watch your partner and guess how they are feeling.

2 Discuss situations where you might have these feelings.

## 11D Speaking, Exercise 7

### Student A

1 You are the customer in a restaurant. Student B is the waiter/waitress.
   - Your meal wasn't very nice. The soup was cold and there was a hair in your fish pie.
   - Complain to the waiter/waitress.

2 You are the receptionist in a hotel. Student B is a guest.
   - Answer the phone.
   - Listen to the guest's complaint.
   - Say sorry and find a solution.

3 You are a customer with an online delivery company. Student B works for the company.
   - You ordered some chocolate chip cookies. They have arrived, but they are all broken.
   - Call the company to complain.
   - Ask them to exchange the cookies or give you a refund.

## 12D Speaking, Exercise 9

### Student A

1 You have read a news story about pollution in your city. Tell your partner about it.
   - Read the facts and the quote.
   - Introduce the story.
   - Tell your partner about the story and report what the local politician said.

   > LOCAL POLITICIAN:
   > "I am very worried about this situation. I will do whatever I can to improve the air in our city."

   FACT: Air pollution in the city is at dangerous levels.

2 Your partner will tell you about a news story.
   - Listen to your partner's story.
   - You haven't heard or read about this story.
   - React to the facts and Lily Mason's quote.

## 6D Speaking, Exercise 5

### Student A

1 Look at the map and ask Student B for directions to:

   Cinema    Art gallery
   Bus station    Greyhound Restaurant

2 Look at the map and give Student B directions.

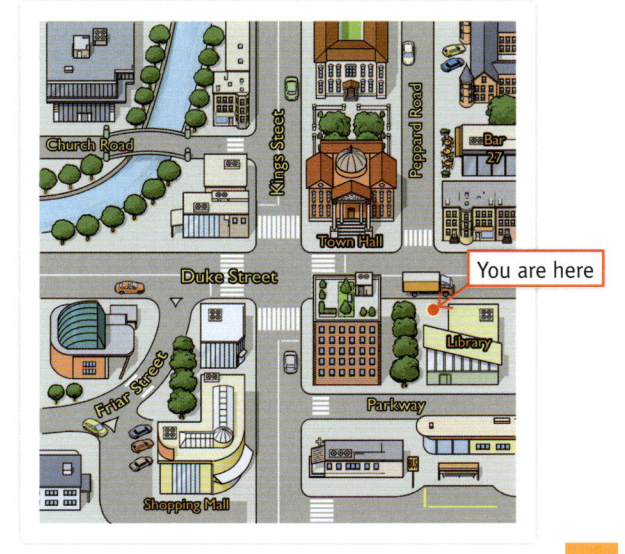

## 2D Speaking, Exercise 6

### Student B

1 You are the receptionist at Hotel Sophia. Student A is a guest. Prepare for and have three conversations. Look at audioscript 018 on page 136 to help you prepare.

1
- Answer the phone and speak to the guest.
- Double rooms = £90 per night. Single rooms = £80 per night.
- Make the booking – ask for a name and email address.

2
- You are working at reception. Check in the guest.
- Breakfast is included and is served from 6.30 a.m. till 9.30 a.m. WiFi is free.

3
- Answer a call at reception. Deal with the problems and the request.

2 You are a hotel guest. Student A is the receptionist at Hotel York. Prepare for and have three conversations.

1
- Your name is Amy Lomas. Your email address is amy_lomas22@boogle.com.
- You want a hotel room for 3 nights, from Friday 15 April till Sunday 17 April.
- Call Hotel York. Ask to book a room.
- Ask about the price.

2
1 You arrive at Hotel York. Tell the receptionist about your reservation.
2 Ask about breakfast and WiFi.

3
1 Call reception from your room. Tell them about two problems: the bedsheets are dirty, the air conditioning isn't working.
2 Ask for an 8.30 a.m. alarm call tomorrow.

## 4D Speaking, Exercise 7

### Student B

1 Listen to Student A. Give some advice.

2 You have a problem. You love your partner and a few months ago you decided to move in together. Living together has made the relationship much harder:
- Your partner is very untidy and really lazy.
- They never do any cleaning and they buy a takeaway for every meal.
- Most evenings your partner just plays computer games or falls asleep.
- You feel like you are living with a teenager not an adult.

Explain your problem to Student A. Then listen to and respond to the advice.

## 5D Speaking, Exercise 8

### Student B

1 You are a doctor. Student A is a patient.
- Ask questions and find out what's wrong.
- Ask more questions. Tell the patient what you think the problem is.
- Give some advice about how to get better.

2 You are a patient. Student A is the doctor.
- You don't feel very well. These are your symptoms: a fever, a headache, you keep coughing and sneezing.
- Go to the doctor and describe how you feel. Answer his/her questions.

## 8D Speaking, Exercise 8

### Student B

1 Follow the instructions a–h. When it is your turn to show your feelings, use your face and body. Don't speak to your partner.
   a  Watch your partner and guess how they are feeling.
   b  Show that you are bored.
   c  Watch your partner and guess how they are feeling.
   d  Show that you are upset.
   e  Watch your partner and guess how they are feeling.
   f  Show that you are frightened.
   g  Watch your partner and guess how they are feeling.
   h  Show that you are delighted.

2 Discuss situations where you might have these feelings.

## 11D Speaking, Exercise 7

### Student B

1 You are the waiter/waitress in a restaurant. Student A is a customer.
   - Ask a customer if they enjoyed their meal.
   - Listen to the customer's complaint.
   - Say sorry and find a solution.

2 You are a guest in a hotel. Student A is the receptionist.
   - Call reception from your room.
   - Your room is too hot and you can't sleep.
   - Complain to the receptionist.

3 You work for an online delivery company. Student A is a customer.
   - Answer the phone.
   - Listen to the customer's complaint.
   - Say sorry and find a solution.

## 12D Speaking, Exercise 9

### Student B

1 Your partner will tell you about a news story.
   - Listen to your partner's story.
   - You haven't heard or read about this story.
   - React to the facts and the politician's quote.

2 You have read a news story about a famous actress. Tell your partner about it.
   - Read the facts and the quote.
   - Introduce the story.
   - Tell your partner about it and report what Lilly Mason said.

   > LILLY MASON: "I'm very sorry. I was driving dangerously. I won't drive again for a year and I have learnt an important lesson."

FACT: Police stopped actress Lilly Mason on the motorway. She was driving at 160kms per hour.

## 6D Speaking, Exercise 5

### Student B

1 Look at the map and give Student B directions.

2 Look at the map and ask Student B for directions to:

   Town Hall   Shopping mall
   Library     Bar 27

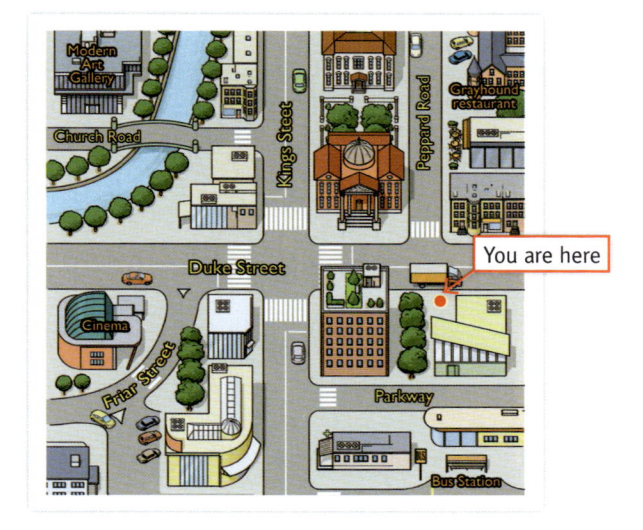

# 8C Reading, Exercise 5

When Holmes and Watson arrived at Thor Place, they went to see Sergeant Coventry and asked him to find some string. The three men then went to Thor Bridge. Holmes found a large, heavy stone. He tied some string around it and then attached the string to Watson's gun. Holmes then stood on the bridge, where Maria's body had been found. The heavy stone was hanging over the side of the bridge, above the water. Holmes held the gun to his head, and then let go of it. The stone pulled the gun to the side of the bridge – it hit the wall – and then fell into the water below.

Coventry then found Watson's gun in the water, attached to the stone … and he also found another gun in the same place, which was also attached to a stone! Holmes had solved the mystery. Maria Gibson had killed herself, but had put the other gun from the pair in Miss Dunbar's wardrobe. She had also asked Miss Dunbar to write her a note, so that it seemed as if Miss Dunbar had killed her. Miss Dunbar was innocent!

▶ 065

# Irregular verbs

The following irregular verbs are used very often in English. It's really important to learn them. Write in a translation of the infinitives to help you remember what each verb means.

| Infinitive (without to) | Translation | Past Simple | Past Participle | Infinitive (without to) | Translation | Past Simple | Past Participle |
|---|---|---|---|---|---|---|---|
| be | | was/were | been | leave | | left | left |
| become | | became | became | lose | | lost | lost |
| begin | | began | begun | make | | made | made |
| break | | broke | broken | meet | | met | met |
| bring | | brought | brought | pay | | paid | paid |
| build | | built | built | put | | put | put |
| buy | | bought | bought | read /riːd/ | | read /red/ | read /red/ |
| catch | | caught | caught | ride | | rode | ridden |
| choose | | chose | chosen | run | | ran | run |
| come | | came | come | say | | said | said |
| cost | | cost | cost | see | | saw | seen |
| cut | | cut | cut | sell | | sold | sold |
| do | | did | done | send | | sent | sent |
| drink | | drank | drunk | shut | | shut | shut |
| eat | | ate | eaten | sing | | sang | sung |
| fall | | fell | fallen | sit | | sat | sat |
| feel | | felt | felt | sleep | | slept | slept |
| fight | | fought | fought | speak | | spoke | spoken |
| find | | found | found | spend | | spent | spent |
| fly | | flew | flown | stand | | stood | stood |
| forget | | forgot | forgotten | steal | | stole | stolen |
| get | | got | got | swim | | swam | swum |
| give | | gave | given | take | | took | taken |
| go | | went | gone/been | tell | | told | told |
| grow | | grew | grown | think | | thought | thought |
| have | | had | had | understand | | understood | understood |
| hear | | heard | heard | wake | | woke | woken |
| hit | | hit | hit | wear | | wore | worn |
| keep | | kept | kept | win | | won | won |
| know | | knew | known | write | | wrote | written |
| learn | | learnt/ learned | learnt/ learned | | | | |

# Audio Scripts

## Unit 1
### Track 001

**1**
A: Is this seat taken?
B: No, it's free.
A: So, are you enjoying the conference?
B: I am. It's been really good so far.
A: What do you do?
B: I'm an accountant, but it's more of a management role really. How about you?
A: I work in advertising.
B: Oh right. Who do you work for?
A: I work for New Wave advertising.
B: You must know Martin. Martin Joyce.
A: I do. I know him well.

**2**
A: Hi, it's Mark, isn't it?
B: That's right. How did you know?
A: I think you live in the same student flats as Ana.
B: Oh, I know Ana. We went to a party in her flat last weekend.
A: Sounds good! What do you like doing at the weekend?
B: Just hanging out with friends really. Going to the cinema, a party, a bar. You know the usual student stuff! What do you do in your free time?
A: Mainly spend time with friends, but I'm also trying to get fit. I joined the student gym yesterday.
B: I probably need to do the same! Where are you from? I can't quite tell by your accent.
A: Oh, I've lived in loads of places so it's really hard to tell. My family are originally from Northern Ireland but I don't really have an Irish accent.
B: Do you have any brothers or sisters?
A: Yes, I do.
B: Do they have Irish accents?
A: My brother does, but he was 14 when we left Northern Ireland.

**3**
A: You look tanned!
B: I was on holiday in Greece last week.
A: Did you have a good time?
B: It was amazing! It was my first time there. We spent the week going from island to island on boats.
A: Sounds great! Where do you usually go on holiday?
B: I often go to France or Spain so we decided to try Greece for a change. What about you? Do you have any holiday plans this summer?
A: Actually, I'm going to Greece! Any tips on where to go?

### Track 002

**1**
A: What do you do?
B: I'm an accountant, but it's more of a management role really. How about you?

**2**
B: Who do you work for?
A: I work for New Wave advertising.

**3**
A: What do you like doing at the weekend?
B: Just hanging out with friends really. Going to the cinema, a party, a bar. You know the usual student stuff!

**4**
B: What do you do in your free time?
A: Mainly spend time with friends, but I'm also trying to get fit. I joined the student gym yesterday.

**5**
B: Where are you from? I can't quite tell by your accent.
A: Oh, I've lived in loads of places so it's really hard to tell. My family are originally from Northern Ireland but I don't really have an Irish accent.

**6**
B: Do you have any brothers or sisters?
A: Yes, I do.

**7**
A: Where do you usually go on holiday?
B: I often go to France or Spain so we decided to try Greece for a change.

**8**
B: Do you have any holiday plans this summer?
A: Actually, I'm going to Greece! Any tips on where to go?

### Track 003

1 Do you have any hobbies?
2 What did you do last weekend?
3 Where did you go on holiday last summer?
4 Do you like going on city breaks?

### Track 004

1 Mark is very reliable. If he promises to do something, he will do it.
2 Their daughter is so curious. She's always exploring everything.
3 Harry is always really careless with his work. It's full of mistakes!
4 Thank you for the flowers! It was very thoughtful of you.

| | |
|---|---|
| 5 | Lisa is so confident. She never seems nervous or shy. |
| 6 | Tom really loves himself. I don't think I know anyone else so arrogant. |
| 7 | Lucas is a really sociable guy. Whenever there's a party, he's there. |
| 8 | Ahmed is really efficient. He finishes everything really quickly and never wastes time. |

## Track 005

**1**

| | |
|---|---|
| Hayley: | Right, Matt. Shall we divide the bill or pay for our own meals? |
| Matt: | Let's pay for our own meals. |
| Hayley: | Typical! How much do I owe? |
| Matt: | You owe £32.50. |
| Hayley: | Here's my card. |

**2**

| | |
|---|---|
| Hayley: | So, Mia…Shall we go to The Lime Bar again tonight? |
| Mia: | We always go there! Let's go to this new restaurant I've found – The night room. |
| Hayley: | Um, okay. What's it like? |
| Mia: | You eat your dinner in complete darkness. It sounds so cool. |
| Hayley: | Really? Not sure I like the sound of that. |
| Mia: | Come on! It will be fun. |

**3**

| | |
|---|---|
| Hayley: | Hi Mohammed. What are you doing? |
| Mohammed: | I'm buying flowers for Sam. |
| Hayley: | Is it her birthday? |
| Mohammed: | Yes, have you forgotten again? |
| Hayley: | Yes! Can you get a bigger bunch of flowers and make it from both of us? |
| Mohammed: | Fine! |

**4**

| | |
|---|---|
| Hayley: | Hi, Nicki. |
| Nicki: | You sound depressed. |
| Hayley: | I am. I feel terrible. |
| Nicki: | What's the matter? |
| Hayley: | I think I'm breaking up with Dave. |
| Nicki: | Oh no! Why? |
| Hayley: | We're spending less and less time together and he never calls. |
| Nicki: | Shall I come around? |

**5**

| | |
|---|---|
| Hayley: | I want to go somewhere different for holiday this year. |
| Emma: | Where are you going to go? |
| Hayley: | Maybe Uganda. On a safari. Everyone says Uganda's really beautiful. |
| Emma: | I went to Uganda when I was a teenager. You'll love it! |
| Hayley: | You always say that! |
| Emma: | What? |
| Hayley: | Any new idea I have, you have done it! |

## Track 007

**1**

| | |
|---|---|
| Paulo: | Hi, I'm Paulo. |
| Maria: | Hi, Paulo. Nice to meet you. I'm Maria. So, do you know many people here? |
| Paulo: | No, not really. Do you? |
| Maria: | No, hardly anyone! Can I get you a drink? |
| Paulo: | That would be great. I'd love a cola. What did you think of the dinner? |
| Maria: | Not, great. I'm vegetarian and it's often pretty bad at these types of events. |
| Paulo: | How long have you been vegetarian? |
| Maria: | Fifteen years now. |

**2**

| | |
|---|---|
| Daphne: | Hi, do I know you from somewhere? |
| Frank: | Um, I'm not sure. |
| Daphne: | Your face is definitely familiar. Where do you live? |
| Frank: | In Clapham. |
| Daphne: | That's probably where I recognize you from. I live there as well. Are you enjoying the party? |
| Frank: | Kind of. I don't really like the music, though. It's not my kind of thing. |
| Daphne: | What kind of music do you like? |
| Frank: | I like a lot of nineties music. Grunge and Britpop. That kind of thing. |
| Daphne: | Me too! Did you go to the festival in Tooting the other week? |
| Frank: | I did. It was amazing! |

**3**

**Ana:** Hi, Mark. This is my friend Tara.
**Mark:** Hi Ana. Nice to meet you, Tara.
**Ana:** Sorry, one moment. I've just seen Michael.
**Mark:** Um, OK. So, Tara, where are you from?
**Tara:** Manchester.
**Mark:** Is this your first time in London?
**Tara:** Um, no.
**Mark:** Right, sorry silly question. So, what do you think about the Conservatives winning the election again?
**Tara:** I don't really like talking about politics to be honest. Well, it was great to meet you.
**Mark:** Um, yeah. Ok.

**4**

**Mia:** Would you like a drink?
**Harry:** Sure. Thank you. So, did you have a good weekend?
**Mia:** It was a bit tiring actually. I got back from holiday late on Friday so I spent the weekend unpacking and doing washing. Nothing exciting.
**Harry:** How was your holiday?
**Mia:** Brilliant, but too short. I want to be back there now. It's so hard starting work again.
**Harry:** I can imagine. What do you do, by the way?
**Mia:** I work in children's TV.
**Harry:** Ah. You do look familiar. I think I saw you on TV. My kids watch your show.
**Mia:** Oh right. Will you excuse me one moment? I'll be right back.

## Track 008

1. Did you have a good weekend?
2. This is my friend Tara.
3. Would you like a drink?
4. I'd love a cola!
5. How was your holiday?
6. It was amazing!

# Unit 2
## Track 010

| | |
|---|---|
| was replace with / were | became |
| climbed | decided |
| drove | felt |
| knew | realised |
| saw | started |
| stayed | stopped |
| took | told |
| travelled | visited |

## Track 011

I was on holiday in Zambia with my wife and we were having a great time. First, we visited Victoria Falls – the largest waterfall in the world. It was absolutely amazing and we took hundreds of photos! After that, we travelled to one of the National Parks, where we stayed in a small lodge in a bushcamp. Our guide told us that evenings are the best times to see the animals, so one night, we decided to go on a 'dusk' safari. We climbed into the jeep. As we were driving along, we saw a large group of elephants – it was an amazing sight. We drove closer and suddenly realised that it was a group of mothers with their babies. They started to cross the road in front of us, but then they stopped. One of the babies was left on the wrong side of the road. Now we knew we were in danger! One elephant became very angry and started to run towards our jeep. Our guide drove faster and faster, but the elephant was still following us, even though we were driving at 30km/h. I was terrified – the elephant's angry face was so close to ours. It was like being in Jurassic Park! Luckily, after a few minutes, the elephant became tired and stopped and we drove back to camp. We all felt lucky to be alive!

## Track 012

I was with my boyfriend, Neil, and we were flying to Las Vegas for a two-week holiday. We were looking forward to a break, because we both had really stressful jobs at the time. The plane took off from Heathrow and we relaxed. But everything changed after about three hours. I was reading my book and Neil was watching a film, when suddenly the plane dropped dramatically. All of the doors on the overhead lockers opened and the air stewards who weren't in their seats were lying on the floor in the aisle of the plane! Then the pilot spoke to us. He told us to stay calm and put our seatbelts on. We were in a clear air pocket and it wasn't dangerous, but there would be turbulence for a while.  He wasn't kidding! The next three hours were the most frightening of my life. The plane bumped up and down and most of the passengers were feeling really sick. I was panicking, but Neil stayed calm. Finally, we landed in Las Vegas! We had a good holiday, but I was really worried about the flight back. Luckily it was fine … and in the end, it was actually the best holiday of my life – as we were having dinner on our last night, Neil asked me to marry him!

## Track 013

| 1 | I was walking to work when my phone rang. |
|---|---|
| 2 | Did you have a nice weekend? |
| 3 | It started to rain while the children were playing football. |
| 4 | |
| A: | Did you see the sun go down – it was so fast! |
| B: | Sorry, I wasn't watching! |
| 5 | I ran the London marathon in 2017. |
| 6 | He was cooking the dinner, when suddenly he had an amazing idea! |

## Track 014

| 1 | She's playing tennis. |
|---|---|
| 2 | She was playing tennis. |
| 3 | We were meeting our friends for dinner. |
| 4 | We are meeting our friends for dinner. |

## Track 015

**1**
- **A:** I really want to **book a holiday** to Florida for next summer!
- **B:** You definitely should! I went there two years ago – it was amazing!

**2**
- **A:** What time does your train **arrive in** London?
- **B:** It gets in at 10.53.

**3**
- **A:** We stayed with a local family in Jamaica and it was a chance to really **experience the culture**!
- **B:** Sounds great … and much more interesting than staying in a hotel.

**4**
- **A:** We like to plan every detail before we go. We **book restaurants, trips, tickets** – everything we want to do!
- **B:** Really? I don't like to plan … I prefer to make decisions when we get there.

**5**
- **A:** She wants to **get a job** in Chile for a year so that she can learn Spanish.
- **B:** Really? Won't that be difficult if she can't speak Spanish yet? What kind of job is she looking for?

**6**
- **A:** My brother wants to **go travelling** in India next year.
- **B:** Oh, I love India! It's such an amazing country – he'll love it!

**7**
- **A:** I don't think it's possible to **fall in love** with someone you meet on holiday.
- **B:** Why not? My neighbour met her husband in Greece when they were both 21. They're still in love!

**8**
- **A:** We want to **get married** in Norway in winter so we can see the northern lights!
- **B:** That sounds amazing! It will be freezing cold though!

## Track 016

**Presenter:** Today we're talking about falling in love on holiday and I have Will Hayward on the line to tell us about what happened to him. So, Will, tell us your story.

**Will:** Well, after university I wanted an adventure, and I was really interested in Asia … so I got a job teaching English in Japan. The plan was to stay there for a year, experience the culture and learn some Japanese. So, erm, I arrived in Tokyo five years ago and I'm still here – and it's all because of Yuki!

**Presenter:** OK! So, I guess you weren't expecting that! And how did you meet Yuki?

**Will:** Well, she's a receptionist in the Language School where I work and she was really helpful when I first arrived … we chatted every day. And after a few months, I realized I was in love with her … so I told her! Fortunately, she felt the same!

**Presenter:** So, what happened next?

**Will:** Well, we got married 4 years ago, and we've just had a son, Nori – he's 2 months old!

**Presenter:** And do you want to stay in Japan or will you go back to Scotland?

**Will:** We've decided to live here and not in Scotland, but it hasn't always been easy.

**Presenter:** Really? So, what difficulties have you had?

**Will:** Well, I've tried to learn Japanese, but it's really hard and I still can't speak it very well! And I've never liked fish, so a lot of the food is a problem for me!

**Presenter:** Oh, yes. I guess with all that sushi, it must be difficult! So, when was the last time you were in Scotland?

**Will:** It was over a year ago, but we've just booked a holiday to see my parents, so I'm really looking forward to that. And Yuki hasn't met my granny yet, so we've also arranged a trip to Manchester, where she lives. And we've already booked tickets to see a Manchester United game! I can't wait!

**Presenter:** Ah, that'll be great – I hope you have an amazing time. Well, thanks for talking to us, Will. Now on to our next caller …. [fade]

## Track 018

**1**

**Receptionist:** Crown hotel, how can I help you?

**Guest:** Hello. I'd like to book a room for three nights, from Monday the 7th October till Thursday the 10th of October. Do you have any rooms free for those nights?

**Receptionist:** Let me have look on our system. Er, yes, we do have rooms available. Would you like a single or a double?

**Guest:** A double, please. Could you tell me the price for that room?

**Receptionist:** Yes, it's £109 per night. Is that OK for you?

**Guest:** Yes, that's fine. Can I go ahead and book it, then?

**Receptionist:** Of course. So, I just need your details. What's your full name?

**Guest:** It's Esther King, that's E-S-T-H-E-R … K-I-N-G.

**Receptionist:** Thank you. And what's your email address?

**Guest:** It's ester underscore king at t mail dot com.

**Receptionist:** Great. We'll send confirmation of the reservation to your email address in the next few minutes.

**Guest:** Thanks very much.

**Receptionist:** No problem. We look forward to seeing you in October.

**2**

**Receptionist:** Good afternoon.

**Guest:** Hi. I have a room reserved in the name of King.

**Receptionist:** OK. Let me have a look. Ah, yes. You're in room 301 on the third floor. Could you just fill this form in for me, please?

**Guest:** Of course. Erm, is breakfast included?

**Receptionist:** Yes, it is. We serve breakfast from 7.00 a.m. until 10.00 a.m.

**Guest:** Great. And do you have free WiFi?

**Receptionist:** Yes, we do. The login details are in your room. Do you need help with your luggage?

**Guest:** No, thanks. Is there a lift?

**Receptionist:** Yes, it's just over there on the right.

**3**

**Receptionist:** Reception. How can I help?

**Guest:** Oh, hi. I'm in room 301 and there's a problem with the WiFi – it won't accept the password.

**Receptionist:** OK. Did you try using zero instead of Oh?

**Guest:** Oh, no – OK that might be why it's not working! I'll try zero … yes, it's working now. Thank you. Oh, and the hairdryer in my room isn't working.

**Receptionist:** Oh, I'm really sorry about that. I'll send someone up to have a look.

**Guest:** Thanks. And would it be possible to have an alarm call tomorrow?

**Receptionist:** Of course. What time?

**Guest:** 6.30, please.

**Receptionist:** Certainly.

## Track 019

**1**
**Guest:** Do you have any rooms free for those nights?

**2**
**Guest:** Could you tell me the price for that room?

**3**
**Guest:** Can I go ahead and book it, then?

**4**
**Guest:** Would it be possible to have an alarm call tomorrow?

# Unit 3
## Track 022

| | |
|---|---|
| **Bethany:** | Hi David. How's the new job? |
| **David:** | It's interesting, but I have a lot of work to do! Actually, I only have a bit of time before I have to go back to the office. |
| **Bethany:** | Really? Already! |
| **David:** | Yes. I start work at 7:30 and I don't finish until 6. I'm under too much pressure really. |
| **Bethany:** | Wow! Why do you work so many hours? |
| **David:** | It's mainly because I'm responsible for too many projects. They're all really interesting, I'm in charge of four different projects and it's too much work for one person. |
| **Bethany:** | What are your colleagues like? |
| **David:** | They're nice! A few of my colleagues are really friendly, and we go out for drinks together every Thursday. |
| **Bethany:** | What about the salary? Are you paid enough for all the responsibility? |
| **David:** | No, I don't think so. I'm not paid enough money for the number of hours I work. |
| **Bethany:** | That's often the situation. What about other things? You know holidays, pensions, bonuses. How much holiday do you get? |
| **David:** | We don't get many weeks paid holiday. We just get four. But I don't think I could take more time off anyway. I'm too busy! |
| **Bethany:** | So, do you think you will stay there? |
| **David:** | Oh, yes. I love the work I do every day. There are just too many things to do! |

## Track 023

1. I have a lot of work to do!
2. I only have a bit of time before I have to go back.
3. I'm responsible for too many projects.
4. It's too much work for one person.
5. A few of my colleagues are really friendly.
6. I'm not paid enough money for the number of hours I work.
7. How much holiday do you get?
8. We don't get many weeks paid holiday.
9. I'm too busy!

## Track 024

**1**

| | |
|---|---|
| **Interviewer:** | So, I see from your CV, you studied at Birmingham University? |
| **Candidate:** | Yes, I studied marketing. |
| **Interviewer:** | So, which module has been most useful in your work so far? |
| **Candidate:** | Um, all of them really. It's hard to pick one. |
| **Interviewer:** | Ok, well I'm interested in your final year project. We'd like to do something similar here. Could you tell me a bit about what you found out? |
| **Candidate:** | Um, well it was a long time ago. |
| **Interviewer:** | Really? Um. It was four years ago. |

**2**

| | |
|---|---|
| **Interviewer:** | We've just got a new account in Germany so it's great that you can speak German. |
| **Candidate:** | Yes, um well, quite well. |
| **Interviewer:** | But it says here you're fluent in German. |
| **Candidate:** | Um, yes. |
| **Interviewer:** | OK. Lass uns diesen Teil des Interviews auf Deutsch machen. |
| **Candidate:** | Sorry? |

**3**

| | |
|---|---|
| **Interviewer:** | So, I'd like to find out more about how much of your last job was managing people. You say you managed a team? |
| **Candidate:** | Yes. It was a team of eight people. |
| **Interviewer:** | And you were in charge of them in all aspects of their role? |
| **Candidate:** | Yes, from start to finish. |
| **Interviewer:** | Sorry, what do you mean 'from start to finish'. |
| **Candidate:** | Well from the launch of the project to the end. |
| **Interviewer:** | Oh, so you managed a project? |
| **Candidate:** | Yes. |
| **Interviewer:** | Not a team. |
| **Candidate:** | Well a team for that project. |
| **Interviewer:** | Right. |

## Track 026

| Narrator: | Nick |
|---|---|
| Nick: | I absolutely love performing in front of people. It's the best part about my work. I also like writing songs although I'm not the main writer for our group. The one thing I can't stand is all the travelling. I feel like I live in hotels and only ever have a few clothes in a suitcase! |
| Narrator: | Tanya |
| Tanya: | I'm passionate about sport and living a healthy life. Exercise just makes me feel so much more positive about everything. The one thing I'm not very keen on is the early starts and late finishes. Anybody I work with nearly always wants to do training before or after work. |
| Narrator: | Jake |
| Jake: | To be honest, I hate my job. I only started it because it was the first job I found after school. At first it was quite interesting but now I don't like working with cars. I've started going to night college. I want to work as a chef. I'm keen on working in something more creative and being a chef will let me do that. |

# Unit 4
## Track 028

| Narrator: | Pat |
|---|---|
| Pat: | Well actually our kitchen had electricity, so we had an electric oven and we used to toast our bread in a plug-in toaster! We didn't use to have an electric kettle – we still had to heat water on the hob. We also had a basic washing machine – my mum used to fill the machine with water from the sink. But it wasn't like modern washing machines – you had to stand next to it the whole time! A milkman used to deliver milk to our house every day and my mum used to go food shopping several times a week. We used to keep all our meat, milk, and cheese in our fridge so that it stayed fresh. |
| Narrator: | Brian |
| Brian: | We didn't use to have electricity. We got hot water from a kettle or pan which was heated on the gas hob. And we had no electric lights – we used to light candles in the bedrooms and we had gas lamps downstairs. My mother used to wash all the clothes on a Monday – it was a very complicated job – not like today with modern washing machines. She washed some of the clothes by hand in the sink and the rest in a huge pan of boiling water and soap.<br><br>We didn't use to own a fridge. People used to buy food most days of the week so we didn't really throw much food away. |

## Track 029

1
| Pat: | We didn't use to have an electric kettle. |
|---|---|

2
| Pat: | A milkman used to deliver milk to our house every day. |
|---|---|

3
| Pat: | We used to keep all our meat, milk, and cheese in our fridge. |
|---|---|

4
| Brian: | We used to light candles in the bedrooms. |
|---|---|

5
| Brian: | My mother used to wash all the clothes on a Monday. |
|---|---|

6
| Brian: | We didn't use to own a fridge. |
|---|---|

## Track 030

1
| Adam: | My eyes used to hurt! |
|---|---|

2
| Clare: | It used to be freezing cold in winter. |
|---|---|

3
| Roy: | We didn't use to have a TV. |
|---|---|

4
| Lisa: | We didn't use to have a remote control. |
|---|---|

## Track 031

| A: | Rosie's a good girl. She always does her homework. She follows all the school rules and she passes every exam!" |
|---|---|
| B: | I'm your form teacher for the year. Remember, I make the rules! I also like to give you a lot of homework – but that's only because I don't want any of you to fail the end-of-year exams! |
| C: | My school is really strict. We get a lot of homework and we have to take exams every month! And anyone who breaks the rules will be sent home! |

## Track 032

1
**A:** They really don't have to be so strict.
2
**B:** You have to walk or drive to school.
3
**C:** You have to eat a carrot or apple as a snack.

## Track 033

**Katie:** Have you seen this article about this strict school in Birmingham?

**John:** Yes, I have. What do you think about it?

**Katie:** Well, what I want to know is, can they take mobile phones into class? I think this is the biggest problem for kids these days – mobile phones do not belong in classrooms!

**John:** Yes – that's a good point. It doesn't actually say anything about mobile phones, even though they seem to have loads of rules!

**Katie:** Well I think all of those rules are pretty stupid. The students there have no freedom to say what they feel or think. And they'll never be independent if all they do is follow rules. And if the teachers send them home all the time, what will happen to their education – I'm not surprised the parents are angry.

**John:** Really? I completely disagree. This school just wants the kids to have a good education. When kids follow rules, it's easier for all of them to study. I think the parents are stupid to be angry about this.

**Katie:** I'm not sure about …

## Track 035

**Presenter:** So, how do we know that UK kids are unhappy?

**Expert:** Well, some years ago, UNICEF published a list comparing the general happiness of children in 21 developed countries – and the UK came bottom … 21st, just after the United States! The Netherlands, Sweden and Denmark were at the top. The study found that UK parents didn't spend as much time 'just talking' to their kids, compared with other countries. And then, more recently, the Children's Society found that one in 11 UK children between the ages of 8 and 15, had a low sense of wellbeing – so basically, one in 11 aren't happy and are possibly even depressed – that's really not great!

**Presenter:** Mmm – that does sound bad. So, what are the reasons for this?

**Expert:** That's a good question. Some experts believe the UK has put too much importance on work and money. Parents are working long hours and there just isn't enough time in the day for the parents to connect with their kids, and so they're left with their iPad screens!

There's also a lot of pressure on UK parents to buy their kids the latest technology and fashion – so, again, they feel they need to work more and earn more money.

**Presenter:** And what about schools? Is there something about UK schools that's causing problems?

**Expert:** Well, some educational experts think that UK children have to take too many tests. Others think it's more to do with nature and the outdoors – kids are spending too much time indoors and this affects how they feel. Basically, we need to look at all of these factors so that we can make changes to improve the happiness of UK children.

## Track 036

| | |
|---|---|
| Narrator: | 1 Emma |
| Emma: | Hi. |
| Callum: | Hi, Emma. You look exhausted! |
| Emma: | Thanks! To be honest, I'm not sleeping very well at the moment. |
| Callum: | Are you stressed? I often don't sleep well when I'm stressed at work. |
| Emma: | No, not really. |
| Callum: | What do you do in the evenings? |
| Emma: | Well, I usually just watch TV, mess about on my phone or go online. |
| Callum: | If I were you, I would turn off all screens an hour or two before bed. |
| Emma: | Really? I'm not sure about that. What would I do without my phone? |
| Callum: | Try reading a book. Also, what do you eat and drink before bed? |
| Emma: | A lot of junk food! Crisps, chocolate, fizzy drinks. |
| Callum: | It's probably worth eating something healthier! |
| Emma: | I guess you're right. It's just not as fun to eat a banana or drink a glass of water! |
| Narrator: | 2 Simon |
| Simon: | Hi, Mum. |
| Mum: | Oh, hi Simon. How's the new flat? |
| Simon: | Great! Really good and I love the new job. |
| Mum: | Oh, that's good. Did you do anything interesting at the weekend? |
| Simon: | No, not really. I don't know anyone in the city yet. I went for drinks with some colleagues last week, but it wasn't that much fun. |
| Mum: | It's much better to try to meet people with similar interests to you. Have you joined any clubs yet? |
| Simon: | No, I haven't. That's a great idea! I'll take a look online. |
| Mum: | Also, Simon, it's about time you got a girlfriend. |
| Simon: | Seriously? I don't think so. I just want some mates to hang out with - not a relationship! |
| Mum: | Simon, you're not getting any younger you know! I think you should start using one of those dating apps. You could meet a girl and then lots of friends of hers to hang out with. |
| Simon: | It's not happening mum! Anyway, how's dad? |
| Narrator: | 3 Robert |
| Louise: | Hi, Robert. How are you? |
| Robert: | I'm good but I'm so busy. I never have time for anything! |
| Louise: | Hmm. Is it work? |
| Robert: | Yep. I have a huge project on and I never have any free time. I can't remember the last time I did any exercise. I used to love playing tennis and football but I'm just too busy! |
| Louise: | Why don't you go for a run? It only takes 20 to 25 minutes to run 5 kilometres. |
| Robert: | Perhaps, but I don't really enjoy running. Also, the weather is awful at the moment! |
| Louise: | Well, how about doing some weights at home then? Just 15 minutes a day would make a huge difference. |
| Robert: | That's so true! I could fit that in easily. |
| Louise: | Go for it! Then when you have more time, we can go for a run together. |
| Robert: | Hmm. Maybe. |

## Track 037

| | |
|---|---|
| 1 | |
| Callum: | If I were you, I would turn off all screens an hour or two before bed. |
| Emma: | Really? I'm not sure about that. |
| 2 | |
| Callum: | It's probably worth eating something healthier! |
| Emma: | I guess you're right. |
| 3 | |
| Mum: | Have you joined any clubs yet? |
| Simon: | No, I haven't. That's a great idea! |
| 4 | |
| Mum: | Also, Simon, it's about time you got a girlfriend. |
| Simon: | Seriously? I don't think so. |
| 5 | |
| Louise: | Why don't you go for a run? It only takes 20 to 25 minutes to run 5 kilometres. |
| Robert: | Perhaps, but I don't really enjoy running. |
| 6 | |
| Louise: | Just 15 minutes a day would make a huge difference. |
| Robert: | That's so true! I could fit that in easily. |

# Unit 5
## Track 039

| | |
|---|---|
| Thomas: | Mmm, this burger is really good! |
| Larissa: | I know. I love this restaurant! |
| Thomas: | Me too. But don't you think we eat out a bit too much? I've been feeling really tired and unhealthy recently. |
| Larissa: | Yeah, I guess we aren't really that healthy, are we? I'm running a half marathon in three months, so I really should cut down on junk food! |
| Thomas: | Why don't we try to get healthy together? |
| Larissa: | Good idea. In fact, I've just read an article about three different plans to improve your health. I think you should try one of them. |
| Thomas: | Really? So, what are they? |
| Larissa: | Well, there's going vegan … so many people are doing it nowadays and there's a new vegan restaurant in town that has really good food. |
| Thomas: | No way! That's not for me. I'll never give up meat – I love burgers too much. |
| Larissa: | But you can have a vegan burger. I'll cook for you – I can do chickpea burgers or vegetable curry … and you love curry! |
| Thomas: | No, sorry but it won't work for me. What are the other options? |
| Larissa: | Well, there's clean eating. |
| Thomas: | What's that? |
| Larissa: | Hang on, I'll show you this article on my phone … so look – it's basically eating natural food and cutting out all the junk. |
| Thomas: | OK, but what about meat? |
| Larissa: | You can still eat meat, but probably not burgers, because they're processed and might have too much salt and added sugar in them. |
| Thomas: | That sounds alright. I'm quite a good cook so I'm sure I can make natural food taste really good. I think I'll try it. So, what was the third plan? |
| Larissa: | Oh, it was the 16:8 plan – you know, when you only eat during an eight-hour window. |
| Thomas: | That sounds hard – I always have dinner at eight in the evening, so that would mean no breakfast the next day! |
| Larissa: | Well, I'm never hungry in the morning … so actually, I think I'll follow that plan! |
| Thomas: | And what about exercise? We need to get active, and you've got that half marathon coming up. |
| Larissa: | My plan is to go running three times a week and swimming twice a week. Why don't you join me? |
| Thomas: | I won't go swimming with you – I hate swimming, but I'll go running with you – I'm a bit slow, though! |
| Larissa: | Great. Let's start tomorrow. I'll come to your house at 7 a.m. and we can run along the river and I promise I'll run slowly at first! |
| Thomas: | Alright – it's a deal. And I'll cancel our table at Pizza Express for tomorrow, shall I? |

## Track 040

**1**
Female: Dad, you have to do something about your health!
Male: Look, I'll stop smoking in the New Year, I promise.

**2**
Male: I booked a taxi to the station but it's still not here!
Female: Don't worry, I'll give you a lift.

**3**
Female: Emma never comes out with us, does she?
Female: No, never! I won't ask her again. There's no point!

**4**
Male: What would you like to order?
Female: Oh, I really don't know! Erm, OK, I'll have the chicken burger.

**5**
Female: You want me to run ten kilometres? Oh, It's impossible!
Male: I'm a fitness trainer - this is my job! I'll help you get fit and then it'll be easy!

**6**
Male: We're going out for drinks later. Would you like to come?
Male: Er … look, thanks for the offer, but I won't come this time. I'm trying to save money.

## Track 041

| | |
|---|---|
| improve | improvement |
| populate | population |
| grow | growth |
| produce | production |
| research [verb] | research [noun] |
| increase [verb] | increase [noun] |
| create | creation |
| act | action |

## Track 042

| | |
|---|---|
| **Narrator:** | Prisha |
| **Prisha:** | Look at the statistics on world population – it's going to be impossible to feed everyone. That's why I'm going to become a vegan – so no meat, fish, milk, cheese, eggs, etc. Farm animals need so much more water, land and energy than plants. |
| **Narrator:** | Rob |
| **Rob:** | We have to stop climate change and I want to help with that! I'm going to buy solar panels for our roof. In fact, a salesman is coming to my house next week to arrange it. |
| **Narrator:** | Jürgen |
| **Jurgen:** | I'm going to stop flying. We're driving to our holiday home in Italy this summer – no planes this time … just seven hours in the car! |
| **Narrator:** | Nicole |
| **Nicole:** | We're going to grow fruit and vegetables in our garden so we won't need to buy so much food shipped from other countries. We often end up throwing food away when it goes bad, but if it's fresh from our garden, this won't happen. So, we'll probably save money as well, because we'll have less waste and we also know food prices are going to go up. In fact, I think I'll go to the garden centre right now to buy some seeds. |
| **Narrator:** | Ed |
| **Ed:** | I'm not going to do anything. I don't think all these small decisions will help. It's governments, not ordinary people, who should make changes. |

## Track 044

| | |
|---|---|
| **Narrator: 1** | |
| **Doctor:** | Come in. So, how can I help you today? |
| **Patient 1:** | Erm, well, I don't feel very well. I've got a sore throat, a cough and I can't stop sneezing. |
| **Doctor:** | OK. And can you still do what you normally do? |
| **Patient 1:** | Er, yes. I'm going to work after this. |
| **Doctor:** | OK, you've got a bad cold, so take some paracetamol and drink lots of water. |
| **Narrator: 2** | |
| **Doctor:** | Hello. How can I help you? |
| **Patient 2:** | Ugh! I've got a really bad stomach ache and diarrhoea … and I keep being sick. |
| **Doctor:** | Is anyone else ill in your family? |
| **Patient 2:** | No, but I ate a takeaway yesterday and it didn't taste good. |
| **Doctor:** | Right, well it sounds likes food poisoning. Drink lots of water and try a small banana for energy. |
| **Narrator: 3** | |
| **Doctor:** | Come in. What seems to be the problem? |
| **Patient 3:** | I feel terrible! I've got a fever, a headache and I feel a bit sick. |
| **Doctor:** | OK. Hmm. Yes, you are very hot. Do you have much energy? |
| **Patient 3:** | No, not at all. It was really hard to get here to see you today – I just want to stay in bed. |
| **Doctor:** | Right, then I think you've got flu. |
| **Narrator: 4** | |
| **Doctor:** | Come in. So, how can I help? |
| **Patient:** | Well, I've got a rash on my arms. It's really itchy. |
| **Doctor:** | Ah yes, I can see that. Have you been gardening? |
| **Patient:** | Yes, I have – in fact I was gardening all day yesterday. |
| **Doctor:** | You've got an allergy. It's probably one of the plants in your garden. Take this medicine and it should get better. |

## Track 045

| | |
|---|---|
| cough | diarrhoea |
| stomach | fever |
| temperature | headache |

# Unit 6
## Track 047

**Paul:** How was your trip to Suffolk, Amy?
**Amy:** Really nice. It's such a relaxing and peaceful place.
**Paul:** How is Tom getting on there?
**Amy:** He loves it! There's a great little community of artists and he's made loads of new friends. I couldn't live there though.
**Paul:** Oh, why?
**Amy:** I think I'd be bored. It isn't as convenient as living in a big city. I mean, there is a shop, a café, a couple of pubs, but there really isn't much else to do.
**Paul:** What did you do in the evening?
**Amy:** We went to a pub a couple of times. It's a really charming old English pub near a beautiful village green, but well, there are only two pubs. I'd much rather live somewhere livelier with loads of stuff going on.
**Paul:** What about walking in the countryside and along the beach?
**Amy:** Oh, that was enjoyable. There are more relaxing beaches to go to though.
**Paul:** How can the beach not be relaxing?
**Amy:** There's a huge nuclear power station right next to it! It's a bit worrying!
**Paul:** ha-ha. That doesn't sound great!

## Track 048

**Lucy:** Hi, Tom. Did you have a good weekend away in Bristol?
**Tom:** It was great to see Amy, but it's definitely not the place for me.
**Lucy:** Really? I thought Bristol was an amazing city?
**Tom:** Well, everything is nearby and really convenient but the weekend wasn't as relaxing as I wanted. It was really tiring actually!
**Lucy:** Why was it so tiring?
**Tom:** Well, we were always going somewhere or doing something. It's fun, but after a while I just wanted to sit down and relax.
**Lucy:** You sound like an old man, not someone who left university two years ago!
**Tom:** I know. I did enjoy the nightlife and the arts scene, though. The best thing was on Saturday afternoon walking around the city and looking at Banksy's street art.
**Lucy:** I loved that when I was there as well. It's like being in an outside gallery.
**Tom:** I just prefer somewhere calmer with a simpler way of life like Walberswick.
**Lucy:** Some of the ancient buildings and cultural sites in Bristol are amazing though.
**Tom:** Perhaps, but it's ruined by how many tourists and visitors there are!
**Lucy:** Wow! You really are a grumpy old man!

## Track 049

1. It isn't as convenient as living in a big city.
2. I'd much rather live somewhere livelier, with loads of stuff going on.
3. It wasn't as relaxing as I wanted.
4. I just prefer somewhere calmer with a simpler way of life.

## Track 051

**1**
**Narrator:** One. Maria.
**Maria:** Could you tell me, is there a good restaurant near here?
**Receptionist:** There are lots of good restaurants on Via Roma. Take a look at this map. We're here in the Hotel Metropolis. If you go out of the hotel and turn left, and go straight on for about five minutes until the crossroads and then turn right. In front of you, you'll see a bridge. Cross the bridge and the road directly in front of you is via Roma.
**Maria:** Great. Thank you! Can I keep this map?
**Receptionist:** Of course! Try the restaurant Pepe Sale. It's really good!

**2**
**Narrator:** Two. Leon
**Leon:** Excuse me, can you help me? I'm looking for the Piazza San Marco. Is this the right way to get there?
**Woman:** No, I think you've got a bit lost! Via Roma goes out of town. Turn back and go the way you came. Take the third left turning. In front of you you'll see a park. Go through the park. The other side of the park is Piazza San Marco.
**Leon:** Is it far?
**Woman:** Don't worry the park is small. It's a ten-minute walk from here.
**Leon:** Great, thank you!

**3**

**Narrator:** Three. Diana
**Diana:** Hi, Sorry to bother you, but how do I get to Hotel Tre Fontana?
**Man:** Um I'm not sure. Um Lucia. Do you know where the hotel Tre Fontana is?
**Woman:** Um let me think. I'll just check on my phone.
**Diana:** Thank you! My phone has run out of battery!
**Woman:** Ah, here it is. Right. Keep going until you reach the end of the road. At the traffic lights turn left. Walk along via Milano and then take the second left. The hotel is just past the corner on your right.
**Diana:** That's brilliant! Thank you so much!

# Unit 7
## Track 053

**Presenter:** So, continuing with our topic of happiness I have professor Jackson here with us in the studio today. Welcome Professor Jackson.
**Professor:** Thank you for inviting me on the show.
**Presenter:** So, professor – how does time affect our happiness?
**Professor:** Well, many of use tend to focus too much on the past, present or future. For example, some people always focus on how good things used to be. Traditions such as national holidays are very important to some people and they celebrate them every year. Often because they connect these with positive memories of childhood. They enjoyed these holidays and they were happy times for them. So, they try to have the experiences again and again.
**Presenter:** I have a friend like that. He's a good friend from childhood actually.
**Professor:** These people often keep friends from childhood. They also love collecting photos or things that remind them of the past.

## Track 054

**Presenter:** But for some people the past isn't so positive, is it?
**Professor:** No, it isn't. Some often think about how their life might be different now. They think about decisions in their past that they want to change. For example, they think about the boyfriend they were going out with when they were at university. They imagine still being with that person and what their life together would be like.
**Presenter:** I know I have done that before but surely, that can't be good for our happiness?
**Professor:** It's fine. It's good to have regrets but just don't spend too much time thinking about it. It's also important to live in the moment. What we are doing now and who we are doing it with. People can live too much in the past or the future and forget how important now is.
**Presenter:** I try to do that and not worry about the future too much.
**Professor:** Not worrying about the future is fine, but you still need to think about the future. We need targets such as I'm going to buy a flat next year. We can use these plans to predict things about our future. For example, we'll be happier in a bigger flat. Just don't have so many goals that we forget to enjoy now.
**Presenter:** True. What about fate? Do we have any control over our lives or is it just decided by fate?
**Professor:** Some people do believe in fate. They think it doesn't matter what they do they have no control anyway. Personally, I don't believe in fate. It's important to remember that we have a lot of control. We aren't usually in our current situation by chance. We are there because of decisions we made. We don't go on a date by chance. We go on a date because we thought, 'I like him. I'll go on a date with him'.
**Presenter:** So, to be happy, should we live in the past, present or future?
**Professor:** All of them. Living too much in any of them will make us unhappy.
**Presenter:** I definitely live in the moment too much.
**Professor:** You need to plan your future as well.
**Presenter:** Don't worry. I'll do that from now on.

# Track 055

| 1 | What do you usually do at the weekend? |
|---|---|
| 2 | Are you watching any good TV series at the moment? |
| 3 | Where did you go on holiday last year? |
| 4 | What were you doing at 7 o'clock last night? |
| 5 | What are you doing this weekend? |
| 6 | Do you think you will be rich one day? |
| 7 | Have you ever seen Beyoncé in concert? |
| 8 | Did you enjoy traditional holidays when you were a child? |

# Track 057

| Narrator: | 1 |
|---|---|
| Man: | So, my wife had our baby last night! |
| Woman: | I'm so happy for you! Was it a boy or a girl? |
| Man: | A girl! Lily Rose. |
| Woman: | Oh, that's a lovely name. How much did she weigh? |
| Man: | 3.6 kilos. |
| Woman: | How are they both doing? |
| Man: | Great. Rachel is really tired though. |

| Narrator: | 2 |
|---|---|
| Man: | Are you okay? |
| Woman: | No, not really. I've broken up with Jimmy. |
| Man: | Oh, sorry to hear that. What happened? |
| Woman: | We've been arguing a lot lately. It's probably for the best. |
| Man: | Still it must be difficult. |
| Woman: | It's strange being on my own. We got together three years ago so I haven't been single for a long time. |
| Man: | Let's go out for drinks to take your mind off it. |

| Narrator: | 3 |
|---|---|
| Woman 1: | So, big news. |
| Woman 2: | What? |
| Woman 1: | Lee and I have got engaged. |
| Woman 2: | Wow! Congratulations! How did he propose? |
| Woman 1: | He didn't. I did! |
| Woman 2: | Ooh. Were you nervous? |
| Woman 1: | Terrified! But he said yes straight away. |

| Narrator: | 4 |
|---|---|
| Man: | How was the interview? |
| Woman: | I got the job! |
| man: | That's fantastic news! When do you start? |
| Woman: | The 1st of October. |
| Man: | Oh so soon! What did your boss say about it? |
| Woman: | He was fine actually. He knows I've wanted a new job for a while. |

| Narrator: | 5 |
|---|---|
| Man: | How was the meeting? |
| Woman: | Well, I don't have a job any more. |
| Man: | Oh no! What are you going to do? |
| Woman: | I've started to apply for new jobs already. |
| Man: | That's good. If there's anything I can do, just let me know. |
| Woman: | Thanks. I will do. |

| Narrator: | 6 |
|---|---|
| Man: | Hi Chloe. I'm sorry to hear about Max. When did it happen? |
| Woman: | He died last Saturday. |
| Man: | I'm so sorry for your loss. Anytime you need to talk, just call me. |
| Woman: | Thank you. I still feel really sad, but in a few weeks, I might get another dog. I miss having a dog. |
| Man: | What type are you going to get? |
| woman: | I'm not sure yet. I might get another sheep dog. |

# Track 058

| Narrator: | 1 |
|---|---|
| Man: | I passed my driving test! |
| Woman: | Congratulations! Good for you! |

| Narrator: | 2 |
|---|---|
| Woman: | Well I don't have a job any more. |
| Man: A | Oh no! What are you going to do? |

# Unit 8

## Track 060

**Narrator:** 1
**A:** Why is it surprising that Agatha's mother taught her at home?
**B:** Because she had sent Agatha's older sister to school.

**Narrator:** 2
**A:** Why did Agatha Christie set her first novel in Cairo?
**B:** Because she had spent three months there with her mother.

**Narrator:** 3
**A:** Why was it not surprising that her father died?
**B:** Because he had been very ill.

**Narrator:** 4
**A:** Why did Archibald and Agatha get divorced?
**B:** Because Archibald had fallen in love with his secretary.

**Narrator:** 5
**A:** Why was is surprising that Agatha married Max in 1930?
**B:** Because they had only met six months earlier.

## Track 061

**Narrator:** 1
**A:** I gave my copy of *Murder on the Orient Express* to Ben because I'd read it before.
**B:** Oh – who wrote that? Was it any good?
**A:** It's by Agatha Christie. It was great – I thought you'd already read it too?

**Narrator:** 2
**A:** My parents weren't very happy with me because I had failed my exams.
**B:** Oh no! Why did you fail?
**A:** I hadn't studied enough – simple as that really!

**Narrator:** 3
**A:** Most people had left by the time we arrived at the party.
**B:** Really? How come?
**A:** We'd been stuck in traffic and we didn't get there till half eleven!

**Narrator:** 4
**A:** I'd left my books at college, so I didn't do my homework.
**B:** Oh no! Was your teacher angry?
**A:** Yeah – and it's the second time this term I hadn't done it, so she called my parents!

**Narrator:** 5
**A:** We wanted to go to Venice on holiday because we hadn't been there before.
**B:** And did you like it?
**A:** Yes, but we hadn't realized how busy and crowded it is – that was a bit annoying at times.

## Track 062

1  I'd read it before.
2  I hadn't studied enough.
3  We'd been stuck in traffic.
4  We hadn't realized how busy and crowded it is.

## Track 066

**Narrator:** Jill
**Jill:** I can't stop thinking about it. Our cat went missing 3 days ago. I'm really worried! I hope she's OK. I really want her to come home.

**Narrator:** Mark
**Mark:** I remember when my brother and I went on these Go-Karts when we were at my aunt's wedding. We were so excited – and we both still love driving now that we're adults.

**Narrator:** Claire
**Claire:** I often had bad dreams when I was a kid. I thought monsters were trying to get me. I was really frightened when I woke up!

**Narrator:** Jess and Dan
**Dan:** I just can't believe it! They only met two months ago and now they've put their wedding date on Facebook!
**Jess:** I know! I was so shocked when I saw that! I never thought Luke would get married – and I don't really know Amy at all. I hope they know what they're doing!

## Track 067

1  Our cat went missing 3 days ago. I'm really worried!
2  We were so excited – and we both still love driving now that we're adults.
3  I was really frightened when I woke up!
4  I was so shocked when I saw that!

# Unit 9
## Track 069

**Narrator:** Liam
**Liam:** A while ago I was getting bored of speaking to the same people all the time at a party. So, I decided to do something unusual. I decided to only speak to women in green and men in black. Just for a bit of fun, really. It was one of the luckiest things I have ever done. There were only two women in green. One of those women is now my wife.
**Narrator:** Michaela
**Michaela:** I try to walk to work a different way every day. I find if I go the same way too often, it becomes dull and uninteresting. Nothing new ever happens. Perhaps the most exciting thing is finding a nice new café. However, one day as I was walking to work I met our Head of Department. She recognized me and we started talking and getting on really well. I got the chance to tell her some of my ideas for the company. She really liked some of them and so I was put in charge of two new projects. After 6 months I got promoted.
**Narrator:** Sam
**Sam:** I think I was really lucky at the weekend. I was driving to see my parents when I suddenly started to have a bad feeling about the motorway. A couple of people were driving really badly. There are often one or two bad drivers on the road, so it was nothing new. However, I decided to leave the motorway and go a different route. Later, when I got to my parents', they were really panicking. There had been a bad accident on the motorway and they were worried I was involved. The accident happened two kilometers after I left the motorway!

## Track 070

1. Nice to meet you.
2. What are you planning to do this weekend?
3. I hope to finish this by Friday.
4. Just my luck! It has started to rain!
5. I need to email Maria about the meeting.
6. It's important to go out with friends and relax.
7. I've decided to quit my job and find a new one.
8. The trains aren't working this weekend. You'll need to drive to London.
9. My parents have offered to help me buy a new car.
10. I promise not to be late again!

## Track 071

**Narrator:** 1
**Woman 1:** Generally, I enjoy my job but one of the worst things is attending meetings. They often last for two hours and nothing much happens. People spend hours talking about the same things and never do anything about them.
**Narrator:** 2
**Man 1:** I love being outside at the weekends. One of my favourite hobbies is hiking. It's a really calm and relaxing experience. Sitting at the top of a hill or mountain is very satisfying after a day of climbing.
**Narrator:** 3
**Woman 2:** I only work 35 hours a week but I spend 15 hours a week getting to and from work. I don't mind walking at the start and end of the journey but I hate taking the train every day. It's packed and there's never anywhere to sit!
**Narrator:** 4
**Man 2:** I do so many more new and interesting things since I met my girlfriend. I'm not very good at finding new things to do. I just end up doing the same things all the time. I'd never been to the theatre until we got together but now I love it.

## Track 073

**A:** Have you seen Mark's new car?
**B:** No. What's he bought?
**A:** A Porsche!
**B:** Really? But he drives as slowly and carefully as my grandmother!
**A:** He's not the best driver, is he?
**B:** He does seem to have all the luck though.
**A:** I'm not sure about that. He does work really hard.
**B:** Yes, but he has all the right connections. His parents were rich. It's easy for someone like him.
**A:** I'm sorry, but I don't think that's true. Sure, that helps him, but he's really talented at what he does. Money, connections and family can only help so much. You have to have some talent as well.
**B:** That's true. But I think someone from a poorer background and without his connections wouldn't be so successful.
**A:** I'm afraid I don't agree. I think if you have talent and work hard then anyone can be successful.
**B:** Really? I don't think so. His parents gave him lots of money and their connections helped him a lot. The bank of mum and dad can be a real help!
**A:** Definitely! He has had a lot of help. Perhaps he wouldn't be so successful at such a young age without their help, but I still think he would be successful.
**B:** I know. I sound bitter. He's a great guy and I'm just a bit jealous. I'm sure he's just bought a Porsche because he knows it's my dream car! I do think there are a lot of talented people out there and they don't become successful because they haven't got the money or connections.
**A:** Maybe. I guess people from a rich background can take more chances and not worry as much because they have the financial support.
**B:** Exactly! I'd like to see more rich people provide money to support business ideas from people who don't have much money. I think that could really help.
**A:** You're absolutely right. Some people like Bill Gates and other rich people try to do that, but it doesn't happen enough.

## Track 074

1  I'm not sure about that.
2  Yes, but he has all the right connections.
3  I'm sorry, but I don't think that's true.
4  That's true
5  I'm afraid I don't agree
6  Really? I don't think so
7  Definitely!
8  Maybe. I guess people from a rich background can take more chances.
9  Exactly!
10  You're absolutely right!

# Unit 10
## Track 076

| | |
|---|---|
| **Presenter:** | So, following on from our show yesterday called Going Green. We decided to interview some members of the public to find out what changes people are making to become greener. |
| **Presenter:** | So, Bella, what changes have you made to live a greener life? |
| **Bella:** | Well our family decided to quit eating meat. |
| **Presenter:** | And how did that go? |
| **Bella:** | It went well at first, but then my children started to complain when I replaced normal burgers and sausages with vegetarian ones. |
| **Presenter:** | They weren't happy with the vegetarian ones? |
| **Bella:** | No. To be honest the vegetarian ones don't taste anything like the meat ones. In the end we agreed to cut down on the amount of meat we eat. We used to eat meat every day but now we have it just twice a week. |
| **Presenter:** | Erdem, what changes have you made to become greener? |
| **Erdem:** | Umm nothing recently, but a year ago I decided to start cycling more. I used to drive everywhere. I wanted to reduce how often I used my car. |
| **Presenter:** | How has that gone? |
| **Erdem:** | Fine. Apart from the cycle ride to work was a bit far. Especially when it was raining. I now share a car journey to work. It's not perfect, but one car on the road instead of three is better. |
| **Presenter:** | That sounds great. |
| **Erdem:** | Oh, and I also increased the number of holidays I have here in England so that I fly less. |
| **Presenter:** | So, why did you start to try to live a greener life, Mable? |
| **Mable:** | Well, when I was moving flat, I started to throw out so many things. It was such a waste. |
| **Presenter:** | What did you do instead? |
| **Mable:** | Well, I started by giving away things I didn't want, rather than throwing them away. I gave them to charities, so other people can reuse them and then it's not waste. |
| **Presenter:** | Did you throw a lot less away? |
| **Mable:** | Definitely! Also, when I moved, I needed more furniture. I looked online and found lots for free. I repaired a slightly broken table and chairs. All this old furniture makes my flat look really cool. |
| **Presenter:** | Sounds like you're having fun using less. |
| **Mable:** | I am. It's important to do things like recycling paper and plastic, but this is a lot more fun. |

## Track 077

| | |
|---|---|
| **Presenter:** | I'm sure many of our listeners will have heard or read the report today predicting the world will face many difficult environmental challenges. To discuss these, we have Professor Brown in the studio with us today. So, Professor Brown what kind of a world might we have in thirty- or forty-years' time? |
| **Professor:** | Well I think it's important to say that the world will be a lot better in many ways. Technology will advance making much of our lives easier. Especially, robots and artificial intelligence, but it is true to say that we will face many challenges. |
| **Presenter:** | What do you think some of the biggest challenges might be? |
| **Professor:** | Many of these problems already exist. For example, nearly 1 billion people do not have access to clean water. In the future over 2 billion might not have access to clean water. Rivers and lakes are drying up around the world. One third of the world's rivers are going or gone already. We may see more droughts as well. This dry land will lead to more fires which destroy food, wildlife and homes. |
| **Presenter:** | Can anything be done to solve this? |
| **Professor:** | One thing is that changing is our diets. It takes a lot of water to produce meat. You have to grow all the food to feed the animals. In the future people may need to eat more vegetables and a vegetarian diet may become much more normal. |
| **Presenter:** | That's a huge change for society. Most people I know eat a lot of meat! |
| **Professor:** | Yes, and it's not one people are making at the moment. We simply clear more land by cutting down trees. Experts think half the world's rain forests will disappear in the next thirty years. |
| **Presenter:** | Obviously, we need these to produce oxygen. |
| **Professor:** | It's not just that. We get many of our life saving drugs from nature. Drugs like Taxol, which fight cancer, come from rain forests. There are thousands of plants not tested for how they might help humans. There might be plants that we find more lifesaving medicines from. However, they might not be there because we have cut down all of the trees. |
| **Presenter:** | That's interesting. I had never thought about it in that way. Now one of the key points in the report was about rising sea levels. Is that really a problem? My home town is in a very flat part of the country and I remember predictions about rising sea levels then. I think my town should be on the coast by now but it isn't. |

| | |
|---|---|
| **Professor:** | Oh it's definitely happening. It's difficult to predict how much sea levels will rise. But we won't be able to live in some cities without spending a lot of money to protect them. The ice caps are melting as temperatures rise. It may not be possible to live in cities such as Shanghai and Kolkata. In those two cities alone that's about 30 million people who might need to move. Of course money can be spent to protect these cities so that they won't definitely need to move but they might. |
| **Presenter:** | one other key area mentioned by the report was the spread of diseases. Why might that happen? |
| **Professor:** | Well for a number of reasons. Firstly, … |

## Track 078

| | |
|---|---|
| **1** | |
| **Professor:** | In the future over 2 billion might not have access to clean water. |
| **2** | |
| **Professor:** | This dry land will lead to more fires which destroy food, wildlife and homes. |
| **3** | |
| **Professor:** | In the future people may need to eat more vegetables and a vegetarian diet may become much more normal. |
| **4** | |
| **Professor:** | There are thousands of plants not tested for how they might help humans. |
| **5** | |
| **Professor:** | It may not be possible to live in cities such as Shanghai and Kolkata. |
| **6** | |
| **Professor:** | Of course, money can be spent to protect these cities so they won't definitely need to move |

## Track 079

| | |
|---|---|
| **1** | |
| **Harry:** | Temperatures won't go up. Climate change isn't happening. |
| **2** | |
| **Harry:** | We will have enough food. They can just develop better farming methods. |
| **3** | |
| **Harry:** | There won't be fewer flights. Scientists are building solar planes. |
| **4** | |
| **Harry:** | I don't believe in climate change. Anyway, scientists will find solutions to all of our problems. |
| **5** | |
| **Joanna:** | We might have to live on another planet because we have destroyed this one. |
| **6** | |
| **Joanna:** | Countries might fight wars about water in the future. |
| **7** | |
| **Joanna:** | Air pollution might not be such a big problem, but more changes are needed. |
| **8** | |
| **Joanna:** | I'm not sure, but I think people might not travel to other countries by plane in the future because flying is so bad for the environment. |

## Track 081

**Andre:** Hi, I'm Andre and I am the head of facilities management. Today I'm here to talk to you about how our company, Global Finance, can reduce its carbon footprint. Our aim is to reduce our carbon footprint by twenty five percent.

My talk is divided into two parts. Firstly, I will talk about possible changes we can make to the buildings and then I'll look at individual changes you can all start to make. So, possible changes we will make to the buildings include putting solar panels on all the roofs. This will reduce the amount of pollution we create from our electricity needs. Secondly, we will add a roof garden to the top of the main building. Not only will this be a great outdoor space, but it also helps to keep heat in the building. We are also planning to update the lighting because modern energy efficient lights use 80% less energy than our current lights.

Right, let's move on to changes you can make as individuals. Currently, nearly half of staff do not turn their computers off at night. Simply turning off your computer can save £35 per person per year. That's a huge money and energy saving for us. This leads to my next point, which is reducing the heating costs. The company is going to ban electric heaters as these are the most expensive way to heat a room. We would also like you to turn down the temperature on heating in your offices. Just reducing the temperature by one degree in the whole building saves the amount of energy it takes to print 40 million sheets of paper.

To sum up, the company is going to make huge changes to improve the building and we would also appreciate it if you could make some small changes to your way of working. This will help protect the environment and save the company money. Does anyone have any questions?

## Track 082

| | |
|---|---|
| 1 Andre: | Hi, I'm Andre and I am the head of facilities management. |
| 2 Andre: | Today I am here to talk to you about … |
| 3 Andre: | My talk is divided into two parts. |
| 4 Andre: | Firstly, I will talk about … then I'll look at … |
| 5 Andre: | Right, let's move on to … |
| 6 Andre: | This leads to my next point, which is … |
| 7 Andre: | To sum up, … |
| 8 Andre: | Does anyone have any questions? |

# Unit 11

## Track 084

**Mike:** Hi, Carla. I got your text message. Are you OK?
**Carla:** Not really, Mike.
**Mike:** Why? What's wrong?
**Carla:** Well, I've had a really bad week. James split up with me on Monday and today I found out that I've lost my job. They had to cut five jobs, and just my luck – mine was one of them. I just feel really down.
**Mike:** Look, you've got to stay positive. Why don't you come out with me this evening? I'm meeting up with some friends. If you come out, you'll feel much better. And you never know – you might like one of my friends.
**Carla:** I don't think it's a good idea. I'll be depressed and miserable if I go out. And I really don't want to meet anyone new. It's best if I just stay in and watch a film or something.
**Mike:** OK. Well how about going for a run with me on Saturday morning?
**Carla:** Erm – probably not. I've got a bad knee. If I go running, it will make it worse.
**Mike:** Alright, well what about brunch at Bill's Café after my run, at 11?
**Carla:** At Bill's? No way! James will probably be there and then I'll be really upset.
**Mike:** How do you know he'll be there?
**Carla:** Oh – he often goes there and knowing my luck, he'll be there tomorrow. I'll just stay in and look for a new job online … although it's probably pointless.
**Mike:** Don't be silly. It's a really good idea. In fact, I've just remembered – they're looking for a new accounts manager at my company. Why don't you apply?
**Carla:** Er … I haven't got enough experience. If they see my CV, they won't be interested in me.
**Mike:** Of course they will! Put all your languages on your CV – they'll be really impressed. We really need French speakers at the moment. It's worth trying because what will you do, if you don't get a job soon?
**Carla:** Well, basically I won't have any money, if I don't find something soon. And then I won't be able to pay the rent! And I can't even move in with James now because … [starts crying] oh, sorry Mike! I don't know why you put up with me and all my negativity.

## Track 085

**1**
**Carla:** James split up with me on Monday.

**2**
**Carla:** Today I found out that I've lost my job.

**3**
**Carla:** I'll be depressed and miserable if I go out.

**4**
**Carla:** I'll just stay in bed and look for a new job online.

**5**
**Carla:** I can't even move in with James now.

**6**
**Carla:** I don't know why you put up with me and all my negativity.

## Track 086

**1**
**Male:** How's your daughter doing at university?
**Female:** Good, I think. If she studies hard, she'll be a successful lawyer in 5 years.

**2**
**Male:** What will you do if it rains tomorrow?
**Female:** I don't know. We really want to go on a bike ride, but if it rains, I guess we'll go shopping or something.

**3**
**Female:** Chris and Helen are arriving today. I hope they know how to get here! Maybe I should contact them?
**Male:** Don't worry about it. If they need a lift from the station, they'll call you.

**4**
**Child:** I'm so rubbish – I can't even play *Happy Birthday*!
**Female:** Don't worry – you've only just started lessons. If you practise the piano every day, it'll be easy to improve.

**5**
**Male:** He won't find another girlfriend if Katie splits up with him.
**Female:** I know – he's so boring and lazy. I don't know why she puts up with him.

**6**
**Female:** If I go out tonight, no one will talk to me and I'll feel awful as usual.
**Male:** That's not true. I'll talk to you for a start. Come on, it'll be fun!

## Track 087

1 She'll be a successful lawyer in 5 years.
2 They'll call you.
3 It'll be easy to improve.
4 He won't find another girlfriend.
5 I'll feel awful as usual.

## Track 088

**Mia:** Hi Nick. I saw your blog post yesterday. You sound really depressed. Are you OK?

**Nick:** Not really, but it's this place – there's no future for me here and it's so boring. If I lived in the city, I would be closer to my friends.

**Mia:** That's true. Loads of us are in London now. If you moved here, you'd definitely have more things to do in the evening.

**Nick:** Yeah, I really miss going out. And if I lived in London, I wouldn't need to drive everywhere – I could get the tube or a bus. And if I had my own apartment, I wouldn't have to tell my parents what I was doing all the time!

**Mia:** Yeah – that must be so annoying. But, remember – it's really expensive living here. And you said you've got no money.

**Nick:** Yeah, but there are loads of well-paid jobs in London. It'd be much easier to find a job with a good salary, and then I'd be able to live in a cool apartment like Jack.

**Mia:** Yeah, but Jack's parents have got loads of money so life's easy for him. If you won the lottery, you'd be able to have an apartment like Jack's, but that's not going to happen. You need to get a job before you do anything else.

**Nick:** Yeah, I guess, but I think it'd be easier if I were actually in London. I'm just going to ask my parents to lend me some money, so I can move out. Hopefully they'll help. Wish me luck!

**Mia:** Good luck – and let me know how you get on.

## Track 090

**Narrator:** 1

**Receptionist:** How can I help you?

**Guest:** Oh, hi. This is Mr Wallace. I'm in room 207 and I have a complaint. Is the manager available?

**Receptionist:** I'm afraid she's busy at the moment. Can I help?

**Guest:** Well. Maybe. Basically I've just got into my room and it hasn't been cleaned. There's toothpaste in the bathroom sink and there are no clean towels.

**Receptionist:** Oh, I'm terribly sorry about that, Mr Wallace. Let me see if I can find a different room for you.

**Guest:** Thank you.

**Narrator:** 2

**Customer services:** Customer services. How can I help you?

**Customer:** Hi there. Yes, I ordered a pair of trousers from you - they arrived today and they're the wrong size.

**Customer services:** OK. Erm – let's have a look on the system. Could you give me your customer number?

**Customer:** Yes, it's 1197208.

**Customer services:** Right … er … Mrs Morris.

**Customer:** That's right.

**Customer services:** OK – well it says that you ordered a size 12 and that it was delivered this morning at 10am.

**Customer:** Yes, it did arrive this morning, but it's a size 14 – it's huge. I'd like to exchange it for a size 12.

**Customer services:** Of course. Let me arrange that. … Oh, I'm afraid we don't have any size 12s in that design.

**Customer:** You're kidding! Right, well I'd like a refund, please.

**Customer services:** Certainly, madam. I'll refund your money to your credit card right away.

**Customer:** Thanks.

| | |
|---|---|
| **Narrator:** | 3 |
| **Waiter:** | Let me take those plates. I hope you enjoyed your meal. |
| **Customer 1:** | Erm, well, no actually, we didn't. |
| **Waiter:** | Oh, I'm sorry to hear that. What was the problem? |
| **Customer 1:** | Well, my steak was overcooked – it was really dry, and I asked for it to be medium. |
| **Waiter:** | Oh dear. |
| **Customer 2:** | Yes, and my mushroom risotto was cold and there were hardly any mushrooms in it! It really wasn't very nice. |
| **Waiter:** | Please accept my apologies for that. I'll give your feedback to the chef. Would you like some drinks on the house as an apology? |
| **Customer 1:** | Yes, OK. That would be nice. Thank you. |

## Track 091

| | |
|---|---|
| **Receptionist:** | I'm terribly sorry about that. |
| **Waiter:** | I'm sorry to hear that. |
| **Waiter:** | Please accept my apologies for that. |
| **Receptionist:** | I'm afraid she's busy at the moment. |

# Unit 12
## Track 094

| | |
|---|---|
| **Narrator: 1** | |
| **A:** | What was Baron Von Drais' invention called? |
| **B:** | It was called the 'laufmaschine' or 'running machine.' |
| **Narrator: 2** | |
| **A:** | What was it made of? |
| **B:** | It was made of wood. |
| **Narrator: 3** | |
| **A:** | Why were no pedals used in the design? |
| **B:** | Because it was designed before pedals were invented. |
| **Narrator: 4** | |
| **A:** | How are Woodster bikes designed? |
| **B:** | They are designed using 3D computer technology |
| **Narrator: 5** | |
| **A:** | Are Woodster bikes produced in a factory? |
| **B:** | No. They're made in small workshops. |
| **Narrator: 6** | |
| **A:** | When is a new tree planted? |
| **B:** | Every time a bike is ordered. |

## Track 095

| | |
|---|---|
| invention, invent | creation, create |
| design, design | production, produce |

## Track 096

| | |
|---|---|
| **Joe:** | Hi Maddie, it's dad. |
| **Maddie:** | Oh, hi dad. How are you? |
| **Joe:** | Fine, thanks. But more importantly – how are you? How's the digital detox going? |
| **Maddie:** | Well, it's so much harder than I thought. Do you know what? I feel like a bit of an outsider. |
| **Joe:** | What do you mean? |
| **Maddie:** | Well – I don't know what's happening at the weekend … you know, where all my friends are going, and all that. We usually organise everything through WhatsApp … so I've got absolutely no idea what's going on! |
| **Joe:** | Oh dear! And what about your studies? |
| **Maddie:** | Oh, it's so much more difficult to do research for my history essay. I had to go to the library and actually get some real books out! |
| **Joe:** | Well, that's what I always used to do – it's really not that hard. |
| **Maddie:** | But it's really time-consuming and annoying. And the worst thing is not having any music – I've really missed listening to music. |
| **Joe:** | Well, you could borrow my old record player, if you like? Does that count as something digital? |
| **Maddie:** | I don't know, dad. But I don't really like any of your records anyway! Oh … but there is one good thing about the detox … I'm sleeping better because I can't check my newsfeed in bed! |
| **Joe:** | I told you that was bad for you. |
| **Maddie:** | I know … and I do feel much better. And do you know what? Once this detox is over, I'll try to spend less time on social media. I've realised that I waste so much time on it, when I could be doing other stuff – like exercise, or reading books … or even cooking. |
| **Joe:** | Yes, well I have told you that before. You should be able to cook more meals than just spaghetti Bolognese at your age! |
| **Maddie:** | I know, dad. |

## Track 097

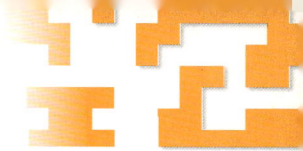

| | |
|---|---|
| Kay: | So how's she doing? Is she OK? I can't imagine her without her phone in her hand. |
| Joe: | Well, she told me that she felt like a bit of an outsider! |
| Kay: | What do you mean? |
| Joe: | Well – she said she didn't know what was happening at the weekend … because all her friends arrange everything last minute on WhatsApp. |
| Kay: | Oh, of course! |
| Joe: | And she said it was so much more difficult to do research for her history essay. She had to go to the library and get some real books out! |
| Kay: | Sounds very difficult! And what about her music – she's always got headphones in her ears. |
| Joe: | Yep – she told me that she had really missed listening to music … But there is a positive! She told me she was sleeping better because she couldn't check her newsfeed in bed. |
| Kay: | Well that is good. She really does need to get more sleep. So, do you think she'll change her habits once she has her phone back? |
| Joe: | Maybe. She said she would try to spend less time on social media. I think she's noticed how much time she wastes on it. She actually wants to spend some time cooking! |
| Kay: | Wow! That is unusual! |

## Track 099

**1**

| | |
|---|---|
| Female: | Do you know what the weather is going to be like today? |
| Male: | Yeah – I saw the forecast on TV. She said that rain clouds were moving towards us and the wind was increasing. |
| Female: | Really? That's so annoying. I need to cycle to the station this morning – I'm going to look terrible when I get to work. Can I borrow your waterproof trousers? |
| Male: | Er, yeah, OK. But why don't I give you a lift instead? Cycling in the wind is really hard. |
| Female: | OK, thanks. |

**2**

| | |
|---|---|
| Male: | Did you hear about Robin Edwards? He was interviewed outside his house last night. |
| Female: | No – what's happened? |
| Male: | He hasn't paid his taxes – a journalist found out and wrote about it. |
| Female: | I don't believe it! That's awful. He's so rich! |
| Male: | I know, and he always does a lot of work for charity. It's really disappointing. |
| Female: | What has he said about it? |
| Male: | He said that he'd seen the headlines, he was sorry, and that he'd sent a message to all his fans on Twitter. |
| Female: | That's typical! He's only sorry we found out, but he's not sorry he did it. I'm not his fan anymore! |

**3**

| | |
|---|---|
| Female: | Have you seen the headlines this morning? The economy is not doing well! |
| Male: | That's no surprise. People just aren't spending money at the moment. Has the government said anything yet? |
| Female: | Well, the business minister was interviewed on TV this morning and she said she was certain that we would see improvements in the economy very soon. |
| Male: | That's rubbish! She's lying. She's just trying to be positive. |
| Female: | Exactly. |

**4**

| | |
|---|---|
| Male: | Did you watch the X Factor last night? |
| Female: | No, I missed it. Who won? |
| Male: | It was that Italian guy – erm – Antonio Mario. |
| Female: | Wow! That's great news! I love him. What did he say when he found out? |
| Male: | He said he couldn't believe he'd won the X Factor, he loved singing, and it was a perfect ending to his journey. |
| Female: | How lovely! I'm so pleased. I'll definitely download his album when it comes out. |

## Track 100

| | |
|---|---|
| 1 | Really? That's so annoying. I need to cycle to the station this morning … |
| 2 | I don't believe it! That's awful. He's so rich! |
| 3 | … and he always does a lot of work for charity. It's really disappointing. |
| 4 | That's typical! He's only sorry we found out, but he's not sorry he did it. |
| 5 | That's no surprise. People just aren't spending money at the moment. |
| 6 | That's rubbish! She's lying. |
| 7 | Wow! That's great news! I love him. |
| 8 | How lovely! I'm so pleased. I'll definitely download his album … |

## Track 101

| 1 | | |
|---|---|---|
| **News reporter:** | | Rain clouds are moving towards the UK and the wind is increasing. |
| **2** | | |
| **Male celebrity:** | | I've seen the news headlines. I'm very sorry. I have sent a message to all my fans on Twitter. |
| **3** | | |
| **Politician:** | | I am certain that we will see improvements in the economy very soon. |
| **4** | | |
| **Singer:** | | I can't believe that I won the XFactor! I love singing and it's a perfect ending to my journey! |

## Track 102

What we call 'Digital natives' are people who were born after the 1980s. Technology is completely natural to them because they grew up with it. A typical digital native checks their social media feeds before the TV if they want news. And you won't ever see them buying a newspaper. They can look through a lot of information quickly and find what they need, and they can multitask easily. On the one hand, digital natives are likely to think that everyone is equal – this is probably because they are used to sharing their opinions with everyone – even with famous people and political leaders. But on the other hand, they also want to be the best – it is normal for digital natives to compare themselves to others.

## Track 103

Digital *immigrants* were born before the 1980s. They didn't grow up in a digital world and this means they are often afraid of using technology. But not all of them have a problem with technology. In fact, there are probably three types of digital immigrants. Type 1 are the 'avoiders' – they prefer to live their lives without technology. They don't have an email account or smartphones, for example. Type 2 are the 'half-adopters' – they use some technology – Google for example, and they have a smart phone, but they don't have a social media account. Type 3 are the 'complete adopters' – they love technology and they are active online, they have social media accounts and they check emails. Technology makes them excited. As time passes, the number of digital immigrants is decreasing and the number of natives is increasing. This means that all digital immigrants need to learn to live with technology.

# Acknowledgements

## Texts

The authors and publishers acknowledge the following sources of copyright material and are greatful for the permissions granted. While every effort has been made, it has not always been possible to identify the sources of all the material used, or to trace all copyright holders. If any omissions are brought to our notice, we will be happy to include the appropriate acknowledgements on reprinting.

**28–29** Used with permission of FastCompany.com Copyright © 2019. All rights reserved.; **36–37** Copyright Guardian News & Media Ltd 2018; **58** blog.parkrun.com; **64–65** © Telegraph Media Group Limited 2011; **78** Richard Wiseman; **90–91** Copyright Guardian News & Media Ltd 2019

## Images

**Cover** Getty Images (Martin Barraud), Munich; **6.1** Shutterstock (Monkey Business Images), New York; **6.2** Shutterstock (nd3000), New York; **6.3** Shutterstock (Anton Gvozdikov), New York; **7.1** Shutterstock (fizkes), New York; **8.1** Shutterstock (Jacob Lund), New York; **9.1** Shutterstock (Lindsay Helms), New York; **9.2** Shutterstock (Max4e Photo), New York; **9.3** Shutterstock (Cookie Studio), New York; **10.1** Shutterstock (2xSamara.com), New York; **10.2** Shutterstock (Basileus), New York; **10.3** Shutterstock (Tirachard Kumtanom), New York; **11.1** Shutterstock (carballo), New York; **11.2** Shutterstock (CGN089), New York; **11.3** Shutterstock (BAHDANOVICH ALENA), New York; **12.1** Shutterstock (Rawpixel.com), New York; **12.2** Shutterstock (Monkey Business Images), New York; **13.1** Shutterstock (GaudiLab), New York; **14.1** Shutterstock (paula french), New York; **14.2** Shutterstock (AJR_photo), New York; **14.3** Shutterstock (sirtravelalot), New York; **14.4** Shutterstock (Przemyslaw Skibinski), New York; **15.1** Shutterstock (Rambleon), New York; **16.1** Shutterstock (Kanuman), New York; **16.2** Shutterstock (dmitry_islentev), New York; **16.3** Shutterstock (shutterupeire), New York; **16.4** Shutterstock (Sven Hansche), New York; **16.5** Shutterstock (lkunl), New York; **16.6** Shutterstock (Santorines), New York; **17.1** Shutterstock (Nfoto), New York; **17.2** Shutterstock (WHYFRAME), New York; **18.1** Nina Mace Photography, Camberley; **18.2** Shutterstock (pavalena), New York; **18.3** Nina Mace Photography, Camberley; **19.1** Nina Mace Photography, Camberley; **19.2** Nina Mace Photography, Camberley; **20.1** Shutterstock (Edvard Nalbantjan), New York; **21.1** Shutterstock (Duncan Andison), New York; **21.2** Getty Images (SolStock), Munich; **22.1** Shutterstock (Nguyen Quang Ngoc Tonkin), New York; **22.2** Shutterstock (Drifta), New York; **23.1** Shutterstock (Tony Duy), New York; **24.1** Shutterstock (Volodymyr Tverdokhlib), New York; **24.2** Shutterstock (metamorworks), New York; **26.1** Shutterstock (muura), New York; **26.2** Shutterstock (Estrada Anton), New York; **27.1** Shutterstock (fizkes), New York; **28.1** Shutterstock (Neyman Kseniya), New York; **28.2** Shutterstock (Roman Kosolapov), New York; **29.1** Shutterstock (Yuliia D), New York; **29.2** Instagram; **29.3** Shutterstock (bernatets photo), New York; **30.1** Shutterstock (Amnaj Khetsamtip), New York; **30.2** Shutterstock (Arthur-studio10), New York; **30.3** Shutterstock (Serge Gorenko), New York; **30.4** Shutterstock (michaeljung), New York; **30.5** Shutterstock (Standret), New York; **30.6** Shutterstock (leungchopan), New York; **30.7** Shutterstock (fizkes), New York; **31.1** Shutterstock (GaudiLab), New York; **32.1** Stephen Barnes/Homes and Interiors / Alamy Stock Foto; **32.2** Getty Images (jlcst), Munich; **32.3** Shutterstock (ben bryant), New York; **32.4** Shutterstock (Krasula), New York; **32.5** Shutterstock (DD Images), New York; **32.6** Shutterstock (Africa Studio), New York; **32.7** Shutterstock (Leszek Glasner), New York; **32.8** Shutterstock (Andrey_Popov), New York; **32.9** Shutterstock (gcafotografia), New York; **32.10** Shutterstock (brizmaker), New York; **32.11** Shutterstock (ILYA AKINSHIN), New York; **32.12** Shutterstock (morkovkapiy), New York; **32.13** Shutterstock (pixelheadphoto digitalskillert), New York; **32.14** Getty Images (AWelshLad), Munich; **33.1** Getty Images (ajr_images), Munich; **33.2** Shutterstock (mimagephotography), New York; **33.3** Getty Images (Anchiy), Munich; **33.4** Shutterstock (Simone van den Berg), New York; **34.1** Shutterstock (Atlaspix), New York; **34.2** Shutterstock (Catherine Murray), New York; **34.3** Getty Images (ajr_images), Munich; **36.1** Alamy (NEIL SPENCE), Abingdon, Oxfordshire; **37.1** Getty Images (PeopleImages), Munich; **37.2** Getty Images (davidf), Munich; **37.3** Alamy (Black Country Images), Abingdon, Oxfordshire; **37.4** Alamy (Hayley Sparks/weestock), Abingdon, Oxfordshire; **38.1** Shutterstock (Maxistock), New York; **38.2** Shutterstock (focal point), New York; **38.3** Shutterstock (Ko Backpacko), New York; **39.1** Shutterstock (RTimages), New York; **40.1** Shutterstock (tomertu), New York; **40.2** Shutterstock (AXpop), New York; **41.1** Shutterstock (Aleutie), New York; **42.1** Getty Images (sturti), Munich; **42.2** Shutterstock (Magdanatka), New York; **42.3** Shutterstock (Lisovskaya Natalia), New York; **42.4** Shutterstock (designelements), New York; **43.1** Shutterstock (zeljkodan), New York; **44.1** Shutterstock (Suzanne Tucker), New York; **44.2** Getty Images (cinoby), Munich; **44.3** Getty Images (JamesBrey), Munich; **45.1** Shutterstock (pathdoc), New York; **45.2** Shutterstock (Dean Drobot), New York; **45.3** Shutterstock (AJR_photo), New York; **45.4** Shutterstock (AJR_photo), New York; **45.5** Shutterstock (UfaBizPhoto), New York; **46.1** Shutterstock (udra11), New York; **46.2** Shutterstock (SeventyFour), New York; **46.3** Getty Images (vgajic), Munich; **47.1** Getty Images (DeanDrobot), Munich; **47.2** Shutterstock (Chinnapong), New York; **47.3** Shutterstock (Rawpixel.com), New York; **48.1** Shutterstock (best_nj), New York; **48.2** Shutterstock (Romariolen), New York; **48.3** Shutterstock (Ermolaev Alexander), New York; **48.4** Shutterstock (g-stockstudio), New York; **48.5** Shutterstock (namtipStudio), New York; **48.6** Shutterstock (Juergen Faelchle), New York; **48.7** Shutterstock (Studio KIWI), New York; **48.8** Getty Images (klebercordeiro), Munich; **49.1** Shutterstock (vesna cvorovic), New York; **49.2** Getty Images (Kemter), Munich; **50.1** Shutterstock (Iakov Kalinin), New York; **50.2** Shutterstock (I Wei Huang), New York; **50.3** Shutterstock (Nick Xiao), New York; **51.1** Shutterstock (Madrugada Verde), New York; **51.2** Shutterstock (Marc Venema), New York; **52.1** Shutterstock (trabantos), New York; **53.1** Shutterstock (canadastock), New York; **54.1** Shutterstock (Donatas Dabravolskas), New York; **55.1** Shutterstock (Lukasz Szwaj), New York; **55.2** Shutterstock (Santiago Cornejo), New York; **57.1** Shutterstock (Valentina Photo), New York; **58.1** Shutterstock (Bravavod161), New York; **58.2** parkrun Global Limited; **59.1** Shutterstock (goodluz), New York; **60.1** Shutterstock (REDPIXEL.PL), New York; **61.1** Shutterstock (Tom Wang), New York; **62.1** Shutterstock (Darren Baker), New York; **63.1** Shutterstock (Monkey Business Images), New York; **63.2** Shutterstock (Prostock-studio), New York; **63.3** Shutterstock (AXL), New York; **64.1** mauritius images / David Cole / Alamy; **64.2** The History Collection / Alamy Stock Foto; **64.3** Shutterstock (Featureflash Photo Agency), New York; **64.4** Shutterstock (s_bukley), New York; **64.5** Shutterstock (Featureflash Photo Agency), New York; **65.1** Shutterstock (Emily Marie Wilson), New York; **66.1** Shutterstock (Artem Tryhub), New York; **66.2** Shutterstock (Antonio Guillem), New York; **67.1** Shutterstock (Galina Tcivina), New York; **67.2** Shutterstock (Studio Romantic), New York; **67.3** Shutterstock (Allies Interactive), New York; **67.4** Shutterstock (Monkey Business Images), New York; **67.5** Shutterstock (Jacob Lund), New York; **68.1** Shutterstock (Bignai), New York; **68.2** Alamy (Granger Historical Picture Archive), Abingdon, Oxfordshire; **68.3** Alamy (Trinity Mirror / Mirrorpix), Abingdon, Oxfordshire; **69.1** Getty Images (bizoo_n), Munich; **70.1** Shutterstock (Migren art), New York; **70.2** Shutterstock (MemoryMan), New York; **70.3** Shutterstock (2p2play), New York; **70.4** Shutterstock (2p2play), New York; **71.1** Shutterstock (marekuliasz), New York; **74.1** Getty Images (AntonioGuillem), Munich; **74.2** Getty Images (GeorgeRudy), Munich; **74.3** Getty Images (RichVintage), Munich; **74.4** Getty Images (PeopleImages), Munich; **74.5** Shutterstock (Andre Luiz Gollo), New York; **75.1** Shutterstock (baranq), New York; **76.1** Shutterstock (Helen Filatova), New York; **76.2** Shutterstock (Attila JANDI), New York; **77.1** Shutterstock (Roelof Nijholt), New York; **78.1** calendar: Shutterstock (Peppermint Joe), New York; **78.1** cat: Shutterstock (Skreidzeleu), New York; **78.1** cloverleaf:

Shutterstock (Kerdkanno), New York; **78.1** horseshoe: Shutterstock (Slaan), New York; **78.1** lucky cat: Shutterstock (Ukki Studio), New York; **78.2** Shutterstock (stickerama), New York; **79.1** Shutterstock (KREUS), New York; **80.1** Shutterstock (TORWAISTUDIO), New York; **80.2** Shutterstock (Claudio Divizia), New York; **80.3** Shutterstock (DGLimages), New York; **80.4** Shutterstock (Daxiao Productions), New York; **80.5** Shutterstock (Joshua Resnick), New York; **80.6** Shutterstock (Taya Ovod), New York; **81.1** Shutterstock (Patryk Kosmider), New York; **81.2** Shutterstock (Roman Voloshyn), New York; **82.1** Shutterstock (sondem), New York; **82.2** Shutterstock (tommaso79), New York; **83.1** Shutterstock (astarot), New York; **84.1** Alamy (Tsuni / USA), Abingdon, Oxfordshire; **84.2** Alamy (Pictorial Press), Abingdon, Oxfordshire; **84.3** Shutterstock (JStone), New York; **84.4** Shutterstock (Jimmie48 Photography), New York; **85.1** Shutterstock (pathdoc), New York; **85.2** Shutterstock (B-D-S Piotr Marcinski), New York; **86.1** Shutterstock (Papakah), New York; **86.2** Shutterstock (kotoffei), New York; **86.3** Shutterstock (Sam';s Studio), New York; **87.1** Shutterstock (9dream studio), New York; **87.2** Shutterstock (Fahroni), New York; **87.3** Shutterstock (KucherAV), New York; **88.1** Shutterstock (ESB Professional), New York; **88.2** Shutterstock (Quick Shot), New York; **88.3** Shutterstock (Jaros), New York; **88.4** Shutterstock (Yevhenii Chulovskyi), New York; **88.5** Shutterstock (Anton Petrus), New York; **88.6** Shutterstock (MrPhotoMania), New York; **89.1** Shutterstock (Tap 10), New York; **89.2** Shutterstock (paintings), New York; **90.1** © Ollie Harrop 2018. Image courtesy of Everyday Plastic; **90.2** Shutterstock (Larina Marina), New York; **91.1** Original Unverpackt, Katja Vogt; **92.1** Shutterstock (ermess), New York; **92.2** Shutterstock (Offcaania), New York; **92.3** Shutterstock (jaroslava V), New York; **94.1** Shutterstock (Sepp photography), New York; **94.2** Shutterstock (Liv Oeian), New York; **96.1** Shutterstock (FGC), New York; **96.2** Shutterstock (marekusz), New York; **96.3** Shutterstock (Pressmaster), New York; **98.1** Getty Images (lleerogers), Munich; **98.2** Shutterstock (Gordon Bell), New York; **98.3** Getty Images (STUDIOGRANDOUEST), Munich; **98.4** Shutterstock (S-F), New York; **99.1** Shutterstock (Alexandra Case), New York; **100.1** Getty Images (paci77), Munich; **100.2** Shutterstock (Photographee.eu), New York; **100.3** Shutterstock (Dejan Stanic Micko), New York; **101.1** Shutterstock (AnnaTamila), New York; **102.1** Getty Images (JohnnyGreig), Munich; **102.2** Shutterstock (Soran Shangapour), New York; **102.3** Getty Images (PeopleImages), Munich; **103.1** Shutterstock (mubus7), New York; **104.1** Shutterstock (mpaniti), New York; **104.2** Shutterstock (Shebeko), New York; **105.1** Alamy (19th era 2), Abingdon, Oxfordshire; **105.2** Matej Kolaković/ Woodster; **106.1** Shutterstock (Elena Kharichkina), New York; **106.2** Shutterstock (Iryna Imago), New York; **107.1** Getty Images (Steppeua), Munich; **107.2** Shutterstock (KimSongsak), New York; **107.3** Getty Images (Andry5), Munich; **107.4** Getty Images (RoBeDeRo), Munich; **107.5** Getty Images (IGphotography), Munich; **108.1** Getty Images (pixelfit), Munich; **108.2** Shutterstock (Filip Warulik), New York; **108.3** Getty Images (AlonzoDesign), Munich; **109.1** Shutterstock (Mr.Thanakorn Kotpootorn), New York; **109.2** Shutterstock (focus_bell), New York; **109.3** Getty Images (DrAfter123), Munich; **110.1** Shutterstock (sirtravelalot), New York; **110.2** Getty Images (MikeCherim), Munich; **110.3** Getty Images (max-kegfire), Munich; **110.4** Getty Images (kupicoo), Munich; **111.1** Shutterstock (Makistock), New York; **111.2** Shutterstock (pathdoc), New York; **112.1** Shutterstock (Julia Tim), New York; **112.2** Shutterstock (Rawpixel.com), New York; **113.1** Shutterstock (SFIO CRACHO), New York

## Illustrations

**56, 72–73, 127, 129, 130** Seb Camagajevac (Beehive Illustration)

**6, 9, 13, 25, 35, 56, 57, 82, 93, 103, 108, 109** Wild Apple Design Ltd.

## Authors' acknowledgements

We would like to thank our editors and all the team at Delta/Klett for believing in our vision and helping us to shape it into coursebooks that we can be truly proud of.

We'd particularly like to thank editors Sheila Dignen, Richard Storton, and Anna Gunn, as well as our excellent Teacher's Book author, Thomas Hadland for their support, advice and professionalism.

Our excellent designers at Wild Apple also deserve special mention. Their creativity, enthusiasm and patience have helped us create beautiful books that bring the words on the page to life.

Special mention also to our audio producer, Jeff Capel. His good humour and fantastic directing skills resulted in clear, yet authentic-sounding audio tracks. And of course, additional thanks to our video producer, James Magrane, who crafted engaging video clips and braved the British weather to film our vox pops.

We'd also like to thank our children, Ruby and Lenny, for their patience with their irritable parents during the intense writing phases of the course!

The publishers would also like to thank the following teachers for their help in developing the course: Sarah Walker, Elaine Hodgson and Sophie Bennet.

# About the authors

**Louis and Cathy Rogers are a husband-and-wife author team. They met back in 2002, whilst teaching at the same language school in Cologne, Germany. Here's some more information about them:**

### Louis Rogers

While studying for a degree in Marketing and English Language Studies, Louis also completed a Trinity Certificate in TESOL and taught in UK language schools for a couple of summers. After graduating, Louis moved immediately to Sicily, in Italy, for his first full-time teaching post. Here he taught general English to teenagers and adults.

In 2001 Louis moved to Cologne, Germany, where he taught business English. His next job was teaching general English in Lisbon, Portugal, followed by a return to Cologne and more business English.

In 2005 he returned to the UK and completed an MA in ELT at Nottingham Trent University, teaching EAP to International students alongside studying. After completing the MA, Louis taught international students for over a decade at the University of Reading. While teaching at the University of Reading, Louis began to write materials for a range of publishers. To date he has authored or co-authored over 50 titles in ELT.

He lives in Reading with his wife, Cathy and their two children, plus the family cat, Rosie. In his spare time he enjoys playing football, coaching kids' football and gardening.

### Cathy Rogers

After graduating from Cardiff University with a degree in English Literature and German, Cathy had a brief career in customer services at a wine company, and then at a pharmaceutical company with customers in both the UK and Germany.

She then took a TEFL course and moved to Cologne, in Germany, where she taught business English and met fellow-teacher, Louis. They then moved to Portugal together and taught general English at a language school in Lisbon. After a year there, an opportunity arose in Cologne, so they returned to Germany and moved back into teaching business English.

They then decided to further their careers by gaining extra qualifications and so both did a masters in ELT at Nottingham Trent University. During this time, they also taught EAP to International students. After completing the MA, Cathy moved into Materials Development and worked in ELT publishing.

She lives in Reading with Louis, their two children and their cat. She now works full time on materials creation, and teaches general English on a voluntary basis through an Oxford-based charity. In her spare time she enjoys running and has recently completed her first half-marathon.